BIOGRAPHY OF WORLD GREAT HISTORIANS

BIOGRAPHY OF WORLD GREAT HISTORIANS

R.N.DHAR

CYBER TECH PUBLICATIONS
4264/3, Ansari Road, Daryaganj, New Delhi-110002 (India)
Ph.: 011-23244078, 011-43559448 Fax: 011-23280028
E-Mail: cyberpublicationsdelhi@yahoo.com
Website: www.cybertechpublications.com

BIOGRAPHY OF WORLD GREAT HISTORIANS

R.N.DHAR

First Edition 2011

Published by :

G.S. Rawat for Cyber Tech Publications
4264/3, Ansari Road, Daryaganj, New Delhi-110002 (India)
Ph.: 011-23244078, 011-43559448 Fax: 011-23280028
E-Mail: cyberpublicationsdelhi@yahoo.com
Website: www.cybertechpublications.com

CONTENTS

Preface

The delights of biography are those of the highest human intercourse, in almost limitless diversity, which no one could hope to enjoy among the living. Even though you were placed so favorably that you became acquainted with many of the most interesting personages of your own time, were it not for this magic art, which makes the past present and the dead to live, you would still be shut out from all acquaintance with your forerunners. But, thanks to biography, you have only to reach out your hand and take down a volume from your shelf in order to converse with Napoleon or Bismarck, Lincoln or Cavour. You need spend no weary hours in antechambers on the chance of snatching a hasty interview. They wait upon your pleasure. No business of state can put you off. They talk and you listen. They disclose to you their inmost secrets. Carlyle may be never so petulant, Luther never so bluff, Swift never so bitter, but they must admit you, and the very defects which might have interposed a screen between each of them living and you are as loopholes through which you look into their hearts. So you may come to know them better than their contemporaries knew them, better than you know your intimates, or, unless you are a master of self-scrutiny, better than you know yourself.

The mixed motives which we seldom dissect in our own acts can usually be disentangled without difficulty in theirs. Through them we discover the true nature of traits, fair or hideous, of which we discern the embryos in ourselves; and however far they rise above us by genius or by fortune, we see that the difference is of degree and not of kind. The human touch makes us all solidaire. Were it not so, the story of their lives would interest us no more than if they were basilisks or griffins, phantasmal creatures having no possible relations with us.

Just now I mentioned at random some of the very great statesmen and leaders in religion and letters, access to whom in the flesh would presumably have been impossible, but with whom the humblest of us find many contacts in their biographies. Often we are surprised by a thought or feeling or experience such as we have had and scarcely heeded, but which at once takes on dignity from being shared with the illustrious man. Still, the touchstone of biography is not merely greatness, but interest and significance; and herein it coincides with its twin art, portraiture.

The finest portraits, assuming equal skill in the technique of their painting, are not of kings and grandees, but those which embody or suggest character. Queen Victoria's face, though a Leonardo had painted it, could never river the world's attention or pique the world's curiosity as Monna Lisa's has done. In ten minutes one has revealed the uncomplex and uninspired nature behind it; while after four hundred years the other still fascinates us by its suggestive and perpetually elusive expression.

So the lives of persons who were inconspicuous, measured on the scale of international or enduring fame, are sometimes packed with the charm of individuality.

—Author

1

Introduction

Biography is the key to the best society the world has ever had. By the best society I do not mean those exclusive circles, based on wealth, privilege, or heredity, which have flourished at all times and in every place. I mean the men and women who, by the richness of their talents or the significance of their careers, or, it may be, by some special deed, have emerged from the throng. One of the strongest instincts planted in us is our aversion to bores Biography, as by a short cut, admits us to the fellowship of the choice spirits of the past four thousand years, among whom we shall find entertainment in endless variety. And not entertainment only; for entertainment is not the end of life, but its sweetener and strengthener. To develop our talents for good, to build up character, to fit ourselves, like the cutwater of a ship, to cleave whatever seas of experience Fate may steer us into, to set ourselves a high, far goal and always consciously, through storm or shine, to seek that goal that is the real concern of life. On this quest biography shows the way by example.

Most of us have intervals of tedium or depression when we try to get out of ourselves. Or it may be some stroke of ill-fortune, some sorrow, some moral lapse, some desperate blunder, locks us up within ourselves as in a dungeon. Then biography comes to our rescue, and we forget ourselves in following the career of other men and women who may have passed through similar ordeals. The loneliness of grief loses some of its poignancy, the agonizing isolation which sin creates round the sinner is broken in upon by the knowledge that others have suffered or failed, and yet found strength to endure and to return.

Evidently, great fiction, whether it be in the form of drama, tragedy, or novel, serves the same purpose of taking us out of ourselves, by teaching us how imaginary persons plan and act, undergo joy or pain, conquer or fall. I do not wish to belittle any fiction which can justify itself by substantial charm or symbolical import; and as I shall discuss later some of the relations between fiction and biography, it will suffice to remark now that the highest praise that can be bestowed on the creations of fiction is that they are true to life. Achilles, sulking in his tent; Othello, maddened by jealousy; visionary Don Quixote, mistaking windmills for giants; Mephistopheles, Becky Sharp, Colonel Newcome, Silas Marner, and all the other immortals in the world of fiction live on by virtue of their life-likeness. But life itself, and not its counterfeit, is the very stuff of biography.

One reason why biography dropped behind in the race for popularity with fiction is that it was taken for granted that the biographer must deal in eulogy only. His subjects were usually marvels—we may almost say monsters—of virtue. Most of us are so conscious of being a composite of good and bad that we are properly sceptical when we read of persons too pure and luminous to cast a shadow. We tolerate the pious fibs carved in an epitaph on a tombstone—the lapidary, as Dr. Johnson remarked, is not under oath; we discount the flattery of the avowed panegyrist, but when the epitaph or the eulogy is puffed out through a volume or two of biography, we balk and decline to read.

Lives of this kind are seldom written nowadays. They are too obviously untrue to deceive any one. Candidates for political or other office may connive at pen portraits of themselves which no more resemble them than Apollo; but these productions, like the caricatures of the day, are soon forgotten. In earlier times, even among English-speaking folk, laudation was the accepted tribute which the lower paid to the higher. Among monarchs, prelates, nobles, generals, poets, artists, or persons of the smallest distinction whatsoever, modesty could not be called a lost art, because it had never been found. And only recently a prime minister, equally cynical and subtly subservient, divulged that even he could not appease his sovereign's appetite for adulation. In general, however, it is now commonly the fashion to assume the virtue of modesty by those who have it not, and the professional flatterer finds fewer opportunities than formerly. Yet we need only glance at the biographies which have come down to us from the ages most addicted to artificial manners and speech in order to see that these, too, bear the stamp of sincerity. There is always the unconscious record, the expression or tone peculiar to the time, to betray them; and then, few writers have ever been cunning enough to dupe more than one generation—their own.

Nobody need forego the inestimable delights of biography from fear of being the dupe of some devious biographer. It requires no long practice to train yourself to sift the genuine from the false—a branch of intellectual detective work which possesses the zest of mystery, abounds in surprises, and can be carried on at your own fireside.

So inevitably does temperament register itself that it cannot be concealed even in autobiography, which some persons unwisely avoid because they suppose that those who write their lives set out with the deliberate purpose of painting themselves as more wise or virtuous, clever or courageous, than they really were. But though any special incident narrated by a Benvenuto Cellini cannot be verified, the sum of his amazing "Life" reveals to us Cellini himself, that perfect product of the Italian Renaissance in its decline—versatile, brilliant, wicked, superstitious, infidel, fascinating, ready to kill himself toiling to perfect a medal, or to kill a neighbor for some passing whim. Even Goethe, who wrote the most artificial of autobiographies, recomposing the events of his childhood and youth so as to give them sequence and emphasis that belong to a work of fiction, even he, Olympian poseur that he was, could not by this device have hidden, if he had wished, his essential self from us.

We may well dismiss, therefore, the suspicion which has sometimes hovered over biography. The best lives are among the most precious possessions we have; even the mediocre, or those less than mediocre, can furnish us much solid amusement; and there are many biographical fragments which reveal to us the very heart of their subject, as surely as a piece of ore-bearing quartz the metal embedded in it.

THE PLEASURE OF BIOGRAPHY

The delights of biography are those of the highest human intercourse, in almost limitless diversity, which no one could hope to enjoy among the living. Even though you were placed so favorably that you became acquainted with many of the most interesting personages of your own time, were it not for this magic art, which makes the past present and the dead to live, you would still be shut out from all acquaintance with your forerunners. But, thanks to biography, you have only to reach out your hand and take down a volume from your shelf in order to converse with Napoleon or Bismarck, Lincoln or Cavour. You need spend no weary hours in antechambers on the chance of snatching a hasty interview. They wait upon your pleasure. No business of state can put you off. They talk and you listen. They disclose to you their inmost secrets. Carlyle may be never so petulant, Luther never so bluff, Swift never so bitter, but they must admit you, and the very defects which might have interposed a screen between each of them living and you are as loopholes through which you look into their hearts. So you may come to know them better than their contemporaries knew them, better than you know your intimates, or, unless you are a master of self-scrutiny, better than you know yourself.

The mixed motives which we seldom dissect in our own acts can usually be disentangled without difficulty in theirs. Through them we discover the true nature of traits, fair or hideous, of which we discern the embryos in ourselves; and however far they rise above us by genius or by fortune, we see that the difference is of degree and not of kind. The human touch makes us all solidaire. Were it not so, the story of their lives would interest us no more than if they were basilisks or griffins, phantasmal creatures having no possible relations with us.

Just now I mentioned at random some of the very great statesmen and leaders in religion and letters, access to whom in the flesh would presumably have been impossible, but with whom the humblest of us find many contacts in their biographies. Often we are surprised by a thought or feeling or experience such as we have had and scarcely heeded, but which at once takes on dignity from being shared with the illustrious man. Still, the touchstone of biography is not merely greatness, but interest and significance; and herein it coincides with its twin art, portraiture. The finest portraits, assuming equal skill in the technique of their painting, are not of kings and grandees, but those which embody or suggest character. Queen Victoria's face, though a Leonardo had painted it, could never river the world's attention or pique the world's curiosity as Monna Lisa's has done. In ten minutes one has revealed the uncomplex and uninspired nature behind it; while after four hundred years the other still fascinates us by its suggestive and perpetually elusive expression.

So the lives of persons who were inconspicuous, measured on the scale of international or enduring fame, are sometimes packed with the charm of individuality. Such, for instance, is "The Story of My Heart," by Richard Jeffries. You may not like it—one friend to whom I recommended it told me he found it so exasperating that he threw it into the fire—but you cannot deny, if you are reasonably sympathetic, that it is the genuine utterance of a genuine man. Solomon Maimon's biography is another of this sort, in which we see an unusual personality shackled by the cruelty of caste. John Sterling had talent, but he died too young to achieve any work of lasting note; and yet, thanks to Carlyle's exuberantly vital memoir of him—which reminds me of one of Rembrandt's portraits—Sterling will live on for years.

THE DIFFICULTY OF BIOGRAPHICAL WRITING

These examples will suffice to prove that a great biography does not require a great man for its original; but it does require a great biographer. For biography is an art, a very high art; and, if we judge by the comparatively small number of its masterpieces, we must conclude that the consummate biographer is rarer than the poet, the novelist, or the historian of similar worth.

The belief that anybody can write a life is one of the widespread fallacies. As if anybody could paint a portrait or compose a sonata! When some notable person dies, it is ten to one that his wife or sister, son or daughter, sets to work to compile his memoir. The result, at its best, must present a partial, family point of view, hardly more to be trusted than the official biographies of kings and queens.

It was the public relations of the gentleman that warranted writing about him at all; but from his wife—doting, perhaps—or from his child—spoiled, possibly—we shall hear of him chiefly in his rôle as husband or as father.

Personal affection, devotion even, may be and usually is a handicap, which the family biographer cannot overcome. The wise surgeon does not trust himself to perform an operation on his dearest; neither should a biographer.

Knowledge, sympathy, and imagination the biographer must possess; these, and that detachment of the artist which is partly intuition and partly a sort of conscience, against which personal considerations plead in vain. Thus, although Boswell, the master biographer among all those who have written in English, felt toward Johnson admiration little short of idolatry, yet, when he came to write, he was the artist striving to make a perfect picture, and not the worshiper hiding his idol in clouds of incense. Sir George Trevelyan was Macaulay's nephew, and therefore likely to be hampered by family reserves; but in him the quality of biographer so far surpassed the accident of nephew that he, too, was able to produce a biography which portrays Macaulay as adequately as Boswell's portrays Johnson.

Such exceptions simply prove the rule: detachment—which ensures fairness—and knowledge, sympathy, and imagination—uniting in a faculty which we may call divination—are indispensable.

CULTIVATING THE TASTE FOR BIOGRAPHY

The taste for biography, if it be not born in you, is quickly acquired. Many and many a person has had it first aroused in boyhood by Franklin's "Autobiography," that astonishing book, which enchants you when you are young by its simplicity and its teeming incidents, and holds you when you are old by its shrewdness, its tonic optimism, its candor, its wisdom, its humor. Franklin has done for himself what Defoe did for the fictitious Robinson Crusoe; but his sphere was as wide as Crusoe's was confined. Follow his fortunes and you will soon be swept into the main currents of history, not in Philadelphia or the Colonies only, but in Europe. And after you have digested the information which

Franklin provides so naturally, you will recall again and again the human touches in which his book abounds: his remarks on his marriage: his confession that, when he began to take an account of stock of his moral condition he found himself much fuller of faults than he imagined; his admission that he acquired the appearance of humility though he lacked the reality; the irony of his report of Braddock's conversation;—but to mention its characteristic passages would be to epitomize the book. Each reader will have his favorites and when he reaches the end of the fragment, with its unfinished sentence, he will regret to part from such a mellow companion. What a treat the world missed because Franklin died before he had narrated his experiences between 1775 and 1785, that decade when, we may truly say that, if Washington was the Father, Franklin was the Godfather of his country.

Perhaps, however, you were led into biography through other channels. The life of Napoleon or of Cæsar, of some painter, poet, man of letters, inventor, or explorer, may have been the first to attract you; but the outcome will be the same. You will feel that you have gained a new companion, as real as your flesh-and-blood intimates, but wittier, wiser, or more picturesque than they; a friend whose latchstring is always out for you to pull; a crony who will gossip when you desire, who will never desert you nor grow cold nor yawn at your dulness, nor resent your indifference. For the relation between you is wholly one-sided. His spirit is distilled in a book, like some rare cordial in a flask, to be enjoyed or not according to your mood. He bestows his all—himself: but only on condition that you supply the perfect sympathy requisite for understanding him.

This relationship between the reader and the dead and gone who have perpetuated themselves in literature is absolutely unique. In all other affairs there must be reciprocity, the interplay of temperaments, the stress of moral obligation; but in this transaction the author gives all, and the reader takes all (if he can) without thought of making returns, and without incurring the imputation of being a sponge or a parasite. If you are a free man, no intermediary stands between you and the author who draws you or repels you according to the subtle laws of affinity. Rarely, rarely among the living is that condition for ideal companionship realized.

THE VARIETY OF BIOGRAPHY

Because of the unique terms which exist between author and reader, we associate with sinners not less than with saints, and are unburdened by a sense of responsibility for their acts. In daily life few of us, happily, come face to face with perverts and criminals; but through biography we can, if we will, measure the limits of human nature on its dark side in the careers of such colossal reprobates as Cæsar Borgia and his father; or monsters of cruelty like Ezzelino and Alva; or traitors, spies, and informers, from Judas to Benedict Arnold and Azeff; or of swindlers and more common scoundrels, George Law and Cagliostro and latter-day "promoters," and that peculiarly offensive brood—the pious impostors.

In the long run, however, we make our lasting friends among those who are normal but not commonplace, who seem to carry our own better traits to a degree of perfection which we have not attained, or who have qualities which we lack but envy. Unlikeness also is often a potent element of charm. I recall a frail little old lady, the embodiment of peace, so gentle that she could not bear to have a fly harmed, who devoured every book about Napoleon and seemed almost to gloat over the details of his campaigns. Conversely, more than one great captain has concentrated his reading in one or two books of religion.

Having entered the realm inhabited by those who live through the magic of biography, we cannot dwell there long without meeting friends for whom we have sought in vain among our actual associates. In finding them we often find our best selves. They comfort us in our distress, they clarify our doubts, they give fresh impetus and straight aim to our hopes, they whisper to us the mystic word which unfolds the meaning of life; above all—they teach us by example how to live. Then we feel that our gratitude is barren and unworthy unless it spurs us to emulation. Unenviable indeed is he whose heart never ran o'er

> With silent worship of the great of old!
>
> The dead but sceptered sovereigns, who still rule
>
> Our spirits from their urns.

No matter what his creed may be, no man is so self-sufficient and original as not to be under the sway, whether he acknowledges it or not, of dead but sceptered kings; and biography brings them nearer to us and humanizes them, and thereby adds to the pertinence of their teaching. These are the supreme benefits conferred by biography; but as no healthy soul lives continuously in a state of ecstasy, so there are many moods in which we turn to other companions than the prophets. We require relaxation. Our intellect not less than our spirit craves its repast. Honest amusement is its own justification. Biography offers the widest possible choice for any fancy.

DR. JOHNSON AND HIS CIRCLE

One of the surest ways to secure unfailing pleasure is to naturalize yourself as a member of some significant group. Take, for instance, Dr. Johnson and his circle. Having disclosed to you the imperishable Doctor, Boswell will whet your curiosity as to the scores of persons, great and small, who figure in the biography. You will go in pursuit of Sir Joshua Reynolds and of Garrick, of Goldsmith and of Burke: and you will soon discover that a mere bowing acquaintance with any of these will not satisfy you. When Gibbon enters the scene, you will be drawn to his autobiography. Chatham and Fox, North and Sheridan, must all be investigated. You will wonder why the other members of the Club unite in declaring Beauclerk the peer of the best of them in wit; and after much digging, you will conclude that, for lack of other evidence, you must accept Beauclerk on the strength of their commendation. As your circle widens, it will take in Fanny Burney—whose memoirs are so much more readable now than her "Evelina"; Mrs. Thrale—that type of the eternal feminine, whose mission it is to cheer Genius by appreciating the man in whom it dwells; Mrs. Montague, the autocratic blue-stocking, who made and unmade literary reputations; and many others, from Paoli the vanquished patriot of Corsica to Oglethorpe the colonizer of Georgia.

The material for knowing Johnson's group is extraordinarily rich. It consists not only of formal biographies and histories, but of letters, recollections, diaries, anecdotes, and table talk which are often the very marrow of both history and biography. You cannot exhaust it in many seasons. Horace Walpole alone will outlast any fashion. Little by little you will come to know the chief personages in youth and in age, from every point of view. You can watch them develop, or trace the interactions of one upon the other. The minor folk also will become real to you—Lovett, the trusty servant, and the old ladies with whom the Doctor drank tea, the chance frequenters of the coffeehouses where he thundered his verdicts on books and politics, the pathetic derelicts whose old age he solaced with a pension. You will experience the pleasure of filling gaps in the dramatis personæ and the stage setting, or in discovering a missing link of evidence. And so at last you can mix with that company at will. No matter what the cares and torments of your day, at evening you can enter their magic city, forget your present, and follow in imagination those careers which closed in time so long ago, but live on with undimmed luster in the timeless domain of the imagination. And during all this delightful exploration, you have been learning more and more about human nature, the mysterious primal element in which you yourself have your being.

Instead of the province over which Dr. Johnson rules, you can choose from among many others. Take up the Lake School of poets—Byron, Shelley, and Keats—the mid-Victorian statesmen and men of letters—the founders of our Republic—Emerson and his contemporaries—and by the same method you will find your interest wonderfully enhanced. It is not the surface of life, but its depth and height that it behooves us to know; and we can get this knowledge vicariously from those who have soared highest or dropped their plummet farthest into the unfathomable deeps.

THE VALUE OF AUTOBIOGRAPHY

Autobiography is an important and often very precious product of biography. The common prejudice, that because it is egotistical it must be tedious, does not hold water. The impulse toward self-expression exceeds all others save the instinct of self-preservation. The artist blessed with great talent expresses himself through that talent, whether it be painting or sculpture, literature or eloquence. Let him strive never so hard to be impersonal, the tinge of his mind will color it; the work is his work. Men of pure science discover abstract laws by experimenting with material sterilized as far as possible from any taint due to a personal equation; but this does not lessen our interest in them as human beings. Far from it. We are all the more curious to learn how men, subject to our passions, contradictions and disabilities, have succeeded in exploring the passionless vastitudes of astronomy and the incomputably minute worlds of atoms and electrons.

We rejoice to find Darwin worthy of being the prophet of a new dispensation—Darwin, the strong, quiet, modest man, harassed hourly by a depressing ailment, but patient under suffering, and preferring truth to the triumph of his own opinions or to any other reward.

If self-conceit, or egotism, be rather too obtrusive in some autobiographies, you will learn to bear it if you regard it as a secretion apparently as necessary to the growth of certain talents as is the secretion which produces the pearl in the oyster. If a pearl results, the pearl compensates. And, after all, such conceit, like the make-believe of little children, is too patent to deceive us. It is the thought that they are trying to humbug us into supposing them greater than we know them to be that irritates us in the conceit of little men. But since conceited men have been great, even very great, although this blemish in them offends us, it ought not to blind us to their other positive accomplishments! And how much harmless amusement we owe to such unconscious humorists! When Victor Hugo grandly announces: "France is the head of civilization; Paris is the head of France; I am the brains of Paris," are we seized with a desire to refute him? Hardly. We smile an inward smile, too deeply permeating and satisfactory for outward laughter. So Ruskin's inordinate vanity in "Præterita" cannot detract from the iridescent beauties of that marvelous book; it seems rather to be the guarantee of truthfulness.

Whatever may be your prepossessions, you cannot travel far in the field of biography without recognizing the value, even if you do not feel the fascination, of autobiographies, of which in English we have a particularly rich collection. I have spoken of Franklin's, to which Gibbon's may serve as a pendant. It discloses the eighteenth-century cosmopolite, placid, rational, industrious, a consummate genius in one direction, but of tepid emotion; who immortalized in a single line his betrothal which he docilely broke at his father's bidding: "I sighed as a lover," he writes, "but I obeyed as a son."

Halfway between the man of pure intellect, like Franklin and Gibbon, and the man of sentiment, comes John Stuart Mill, 3 in whom the precocious development of a very remarkable mind did not succeed in crushing out the religious craving or the life of the feelings. Newman's "Apologia," largely occupied in the vain endeavor to transfuse the warm blood of the emotions into the hardened arteries of theological dogmas, stands at the other extreme in this class of confessions.

Contrast with it John Woolman's "Journal," the austerely sincere record of a soul that does not spend its time in casuistical interpretations of the quibbles propounded by mediæval theologians, but dwells consciously in the immediate presence of the living God. Our only quarrel with Woolman is that, owing to his complete other-worldiness, he disdains to tell us facts about himself and about his time that we would gladly hear.

In other fields there is equal abundance. Many soldiers have written memoirs; enough to cite General Grant's, to parallel which we must go back to Cæsar's "Commentaries." Authors, poets, men of affairs, the obscure and the conspicuous, have voluntarily opened a window for us. From Queen Victoria's "Leaves from a Journal," to Booker T. Washington's "Up from Slavery," what contrasts, what richness, what range!

And in other lands also many of the pithiest examples of human faculty are to be sought in autobiographies. To Benvenuto Cellini's life I have already referred. Alfieri, Pellico, Massimo d'Azeglio, Mazzini, Garibaldi are other Italians whose self-revelations endure. The French, each of whom seems to be more conscious than men of other races that he is an actor in a drama, have produced a libraryful of autobiographies. At their head stands Rousseau's "Confessions," in style a masterpiece, in substance absorbing, by one of the most despicable of men.

THE RELATION OF BIOGRAPHY TO HISTORY

In the larger classification of literature, biography comes midway between history and fiction. One school of historians, indeed, unwilling to cramp their imaginations into so mean a space as a generation or a century, reckon by millenniums and lose sight of mere individuals. They are intent on discovering and formulating general laws of cosmic progress; on tracing the collective action of multitudes through long periods of time; on watching institutions evolve. In their eyes, even Napoleon is a "negligible quantity."

I would not for a moment disparage the efforts of these investigators. Most of us have felt the fascination of moving to and fro over vast reaches of time, as imperially as the astronomer moves through space. Such flights are exhilarating. They involve us in no peril; we begin and end them in our armchair; they attach to us no responsibility. The power of generalizing, which even the humblest and most ignorant exercise daily, sheds upon us a peculiar satisfaction; but we must not value the generalizations we arrive at by the pleasurableness of the process. Counting by the hundred thousand years, individual man dwindles beyond the recall of the most powerful microscope. So we may well disregard an æon or two in speculating on the rate of progress between oligocene and neolithic conditions. But after mankind have plodded out of geology into history there is nothing more certain than that the masses have been pioneered by individuals. You can prove it wherever two or more persons meet—one inevitably leads.

As the race emerged from barbarism, the number and variety of individuals increased. Men in the mass are plastic; or, to change the figure, they are like reservoirs of latent energy, awaiting the leader who shall apply their force to a special work. In many cases the great man is far from being the product of his time, but he has some interior and unborrowed faculty for influencing, controlling, we may even say hypnotizing, his generation. It is idle to suppose that a Napoleon can be explained on the theory that he is the sum of a hundred, or ten thousand, of his average French contemporaries. He shared certain traits with them, just as he had organs and appetites common to all normal men; but it was precisely those uncommon attributes which were his and not theirs that made him Napoleon.

We may safely cultivate biography, therefore, not merely as an adjunct of history, but as one of history's mighty sources. In proportion as the materials concerning a given period or episode abound, it becomes easier to trace the significance of the great men who directed it—easier and most entrancing, for in this detective work we are shadowing Destiny itself. We see how some apparently trivial personal happening—Napoleon's lassitude due to a cold at Borodino, Frederick the Second's seasickness on starting on his crusade, McDowell's cholera morbus at the first battle of Bull Run—was the hazard on which Fate hung the issue of history. We see, further, that men and women are not abstractions—that what we regard as laws in human evolution are the result of the motives and deeds—motives and deeds—of human beings; and that a flaw or twist in a single individual may break the current of development or deflect it into an unexpected channel.

The lives of state builders and of state preservers and pilots offer, accordingly, a double attraction: they show us history at those moments when, ceasing to be abstract and impersonal, it turns upon us recognizable human features and works through the heart and brain of highly individualized genius. They show us also biography, when individual genius becomes so powerful that it diffuses itself through multitudes, yet is never more truly itself than in this diffusion.

THE RELATION OF BIOGRAPHY TO FICTION

On the other hand, biography touches fiction at many points. Novelists discovered long ago the allure which any period except the present—for the present has always been Time's black sheep—exerts over the imagination.

The three-legged stool was only that and nothing more to our Puritan ancestors; now it is a piece of old Plymouth or old Salem, glorified by that association, and by the possibility that Governor Bradford or Priscilla Mullens may have sat on it. There lies the spell which historical novelists have cast with stupendous effect; and, having the environment, they introduce into it the historical personages who once belonged there.

The novelist, by his trade, may take or reject what he pleases; so that, if he finds the facts of history intractable, he may change or omit them. Or, since his deepest interest, like the biographer's, is in persons and the unfolding of character, he may achieve a lifelike portrait. At best, however, historical personages, as they appear in fiction, can never escape from the suspicion of being so far modified by the novelist that they are no longer real.

As to the larger question of the relative value of fiction and biography, we would not dogmatize. We would no more promote biography by abolishing fiction—if it were possible—than we would magnify sculpture by dwarfing painting. And yet, if talents equal to those of the foremost novelists had been or were devoted to writing biography, the popularity—at least among cultivated readers—of the two branches of literature might be reversed. As I have said, the utmost achievement for the novelist is to create an illusion so perfect that the characters in his books shall seem to be real.

In other words, so far as concerns reality, the novelist leaves off where the biographer begins. And if the novelist has an apparent advantage in dealing with unruly facts, he is under the immense disadvantage of being restricted in his choice of characters. So true is this that, if all other records except the novels of the past century were to be destroyed, posterity five hundred years hence would have slight means of knowing the men and women through whom human evolution has really operated in our age. In no art has the process of vulgarization gone so far as in fiction. The novelist to-day dares not paint goodness or greatness; his upper limit is mediocrity; his lower is depravity, and he tends more and more to exploit the lower.

An art which, pretending to mirror life, instinctively shuts out a large province of life—an art which boasts that it alone can display human personality in all its varieties and yet becomes dumb before the highest manifestations of personality—has no right to rank among the truly universal arts—painting and sculpture, the Elizabethan drama and biography.

All the myriad novelists writing in English since 1850 have not created one character comparable to Abraham Lincoln or to Cavour nor have the romances imagined any hero to match Garibaldi. Or, to take contemporary examples, what novelist would venture to depict, even if his imagination could have conceived, a Theodore Roosevelt or a J. P. Morgan? For myself, if it were necessary, in a shipwreck, to choose between saving the Georgian novelists and Boswell's "Life of Johnson," I would unhesitatingly take Boswell.

THE ART OF BIOGRAPHY

Before concluding, let me recur to biography as an art. You cannot read far in this field without being struck by the great differences in the ability of biographers. One makes a brilliant subject dull, or a juicy subject dry; while a biographer of other quality holds you spellbound over the life story of some relatively unimportant person. Gradually you come to study the laws of the art; to determine how much depends upon the biographer and how much on the biographee; above all, to define just what portion of a given subject's life should be described. Remember that not a hundredth part of any life can be recorded. The biographer must select. But what? The significant, the individual, the revealing How shall those be settled? By the judgment of the biographer. Selection and perspective are the sun and moon of all art, and unless they shine for him, his portrait will be out of drawing. When, for instance, the writer on Havelock devotes almost as much space to his piety as to his military achievement, you recognize the faulty selection; or when another describes General Grant's later misfortune as the dupe of a financial sharper as amply as his Vicksburg campaign, you have a fine example of bungled perspective. With practice, you will learn how to recover some of the true features of the victims of such distortions.

Comparison, the mother of Criticism, will help you to ampler pleasures. I have already suggested comparing Woolman's, Franklin's and Mill's autobiographies; but the process can be carried forward in many directions. You can investigate what matters were regarded as essential for a biographer to tell at any period. Plutarch, for instance, has left a gallery of portraits of ancient statesmen and soldiers. Wherein would the method and results of a modern Plutarch differ from his? If Boswell, and not Xenophon, had written the familiar life of Socrates, what would he have added? What do you miss in quaint Izaak Walton's lives of Wotton and Donne and Herbert? Do we really know Napoleon better, for all the thousands of books about him, than we know Cæsar? How far does sameness of treatment in Vasari's "Lives" blur their individuality?

These and many other questions will stimulate you in any comparative reading of biography. They all refer to three deeper matters: differences in the skill of biographers; changes in the angle of curiosity from which the public regard celebrities; and, finally, the variation, slowly effectuated, in human Personality itself.

The outlook for biography never was brighter. Its votaries will practice it with a constantly increasing skill. The demand for veracity will not slacken. The public, grown more discerning, will read it with greater relish.

The fact that the persons and events whom the biographer depicts were real will lend to them an additional attractiveness.

Given life, the first impulse of life, the incessant, triumphant impulse, is to manifest itself in individuals. From the beginning there has never been a moment, or the fraction of a second, when the universe, or the tiniest part of it, became abstract. In the world of matter, not less than in the organic world of animals and plants, always and everywhere and forever—individuals! from atom to Sirius, nothing but individuals! Even in the protean transmutation of one thing into another, of life into death and death into life, individuality keeps pace with each changing stage.

Since the process of individualization is from lower to higher, from simple to complex, the acknowledged great men in history, or the persons who stand out from any mass, are endowed with unusual qualities, or with common qualities in an uncommon degree—an endowment which gives them more points of contact, more power, more interest, more charm. These are the men and women whom biography perpetuates. The master creations of fiction spring from the human brain; the subjects of biography are the very creations of God himself: the realities of God must forever transcend the fictions of man.

2

Lord Acton Cambridge Modern History

John Emerich Edward Dalberg Acton was born in Jan. 1834 in Naples into an English Roman Catholic émigré family.

His paternal grandfather, Sir John Francis Edward, had held several high offices in the Kingdom of Naples, including Commander in Chief of the Navy and Prime Minister.

Sir John Francis Edward Acton had in fact inherited his title as a baronet in 1791 upon the death of a distant cousin. This Sir John Acton's elder son, Richard, inherited the baronetcy in 1811. Sir Richard Acton entered into a marriage with a young lady of the House of Dalberg, the only daughter of a Duke Dalberg. The Dalberg's, as a family, were considered by some to be second only to the Habsburgs in eminence in the affairs of Austrian Europe. Duke Dalberg had himself been active in European diplomacy as part of the French representation to the Congress of Vienna. Upon Duke Dalberg's death in 1833 Sir Richard Acton and his wife assumed the name Dalberg-Acton.

Sir Richard died in Paris in 1837 and his twenty-three year old widow, and their child (now himself a baronet), relocated to the family's estates in Shropshire, England. In 1840 the young widow married Lord Leveson, heir to the Earl of Granville. This marrige brought young baronet Acton into a close association with the Leveson-Gowers and Cavendishes, both noted English political families.

Acton was educated in England, Scotland and Germany. In his later studies, at Munich, Acton was introduced to German historical methods by the celebrated liberal Roman Catholic scholar Johann Joseph Ignaz von Döllinger with whom he was afterwards to maintain a life-long friendship. Acton decided, as one of his life ambitions to attempt to write a great " History of Liberty " and began to assemble what eventually became a noted library of historical works in support of future scholarship.

Acton, who was himself of a liberal political outlook, maintained contacts with intellectual circles widely in Europe and north America. In 1859 he was returned as a Member of Parliament for Carlow, Shropshire, and subsequently adhered to the Liberal leader William Gladstone. Acton was not an active Member of the House and lost his seat in 1865. He had meanwhile (1859) succeeded John Henry Newman as editor of the English Roman Catholic periodical The Rambler. In 1862 Acton merger the Rambler with the Home and Foreign Review.

Acton was at one and the same time a sincere Roman Catholic and a holder of "liberal" views. The Home and Foreign Review was criticised by Cardinal Wiseman in 1862. In 1864 Döllinger appealed to a Munich Congress for a less hostile attitude to be taken by the Roman Catholic church to historical criticism-the then pope issued a declaration that the opinions of Catholic writers were subject to the authority of the Roman congregations. Acton subsequently resigned his editorship of Home and Foreign Review.

In 1865 Acton married a Bavarian Countess with whom, in time, he was to have a family of three daughters and a son. Some years later the prominent Liberal politician Gladstone, recently (1868) become Prime Minister, decided to recommend that his friend and advisor, Sir John Dalberg-Acton, be raised to the English peerage-the former baronet now became a baron with the title of Lord Acton in 1869.

Lord Acton found difficulty in agreeing with the doctrine of papal infallibility as defined at the time of the First Vatican Council in 1870 and came into conflict with church policy whilst continuing to regard his personal communion with Rome as "dearer than life."

From these times Lord Acton produced a number of particularly well regarded articles and essays and also helped to found the English Historical Review (1886) but, whilst these efforts may be seen as often being in line with Acton's interest in issues of liberty, his long intended masterwork-History of Liberty-does not seem to have neared completion.

Lord Acton continued as a valued political adviser to Gladstone and, in 1895, was appointed as Regius Professor of Modern History at the University of Cambridge. Following this appointment Lord Acton delivered an inaugural lecture on "The Study of History" which made a tremendous impression in the University due to the wealth of learning and erudition of which it gave evidence.

As Regius Professor of Modern History Lord Acton was central to the planning of what was intended to be an extensive and definitive multi-volume-Cambridge Modern History-to which, although this ambitious project remained uncompleted for a number of years, he made important editorial contributions.

Lord Acton died in June 1902, several of his courses of lectures were collected and published after his death.

Lord Acton's magnificent historical library was purchased by the philanthropist Andrew Carnegie and presented to the Liberal Statesman, and biographer of Gladstone, Viscount Morley who promptly transferred this gift to the University of Cambridge.

Ralph Waldo Emerson resigned as an Unitarian minister in 1832 and subsequently tried to establish himself as a lecturer and writer. His efforts in this direction included the self-financed publication of a pamphlet entitled "Nature" in 1836. This essay, only five hundred copies of which were printed (and these took some six years to be distributed), received little initial notice but effectively articulated the philosophical underpinnings of the subsequently widely influential New England Transcendentalism movement.

Emerson's first substantial publication was a volume of Essays that issued from the presses in 1841. There were twelve essays in this volume the very first being one entitled "History".

There is no great and no small

To the Soul that maketh all:

And where it cometh, all things are;

And it cometh everywhere.

I am owner of the sphere,

Of the seven stars and the solar year,

Of Caesar's hand, and Plato's brain,

Of Lord Christ's heart, and Shakspeare's strain.

There is one mind common to all individual men. Every man is an inlet to the same and to all of the same. He that is once admitted to the right of reason is made a freeman of the whole estate. What Plato has thought, he may think; what a saint has felt, he may feel; what at any time has be-fallen any man, he can understand. Who hath access to this universal mind is a party to all that is or can be done, for this is the only and sovereign agent.

Of the works of this mind history is the record. Its genius is illustrated by the entire series of days. Man is explicable by nothing less than all his history. Without hurry, without rest, the human spirit goes forth from the beginning to embody every faculty, every thought, every emotion, which belongs to it in appropriate events. But the thought is always prior to the fact; all the facts of history preexist in the mind as laws. Each law in turn is made by circumstances predominant, and the limits of nature give power to but one at a time. A man is the whole encyclopaedia of facts. The creation of a thousand forests is in one acorn, and Egypt, Greece, Rome, Gaul, Britain, America, lie folded already in the first man. Epoch after epoch, camp, kingdom, empire, republic, democracy, are merely the application of his manifold spirit to the manifold world.

This human mind wrote history, and this must read it. The Sphinx must solve her own riddle. If the whole of history is in one man, it is all to be explained from individual experience. There is a relation between the hours of our life and the centuries of time. As the air I breathe is drawn from the great repositories of nature, as the light on my book is yielded by a star a hundred millions of miles distant, as the poise of my body depends on the equilibrium of centrifugal and centripetal forces, so the hours should be instructed by the ages, and the ages explained by the hours. Of the universal mind each individual man is one more incarnation. All its properties consist in him. Each new fact in his private experience flashes a light on what great bodies of men have done, and the crises of his life refer to national crises. Every revolution was first a thought in one man's mind, and when the same thought occurs to another man, it is the key to that era.

Every reform was once a private opinion, and when it shall be a private opinion again, it will solve the problem of the age. The fact narrated must correspond to something in me to be credible or intelligible. We as we read must become Greeks, Romans, Turks, priest and king, martyr and executioner, must fasten these images to some reality in our secret experience, or we shall learn nothing rightly. What befell Asdrubal or Caesar Borgia is as much an illustration of the mind's powers and depravations as what has befallen us. Each new law and political movement has meaning for you. Stand before each of its tablets and say, 'Under this mask did my Proteus nature hide itself.' This remedies the defect of our too great nearness to ourselves. This throws our actions into perspective: and as crabs, goats, scorpions, the balance, and the waterpot lose their meanness when hung as signs in the zodiac, so I can see my own vices without heat in the distant persons of Solomon, Alcibiades, and Catiline.

It is the universal nature which gives worth to particular men and things. Human life as containing this is mysterious and inviolable, and we hedge it round with penalties and laws. All laws derive hence their ultimate reason; all express more or less distinctly some command of this supreme, illimitable essence. Property also holds of the soul, covers great spiritual facts, and instinctively we at first hold to it with swords and laws, and wide and complex combinations. The obscure consciousness of this fact is the light of all our day, the claim of claims; the plea for education, for justice, for charity, the foundation of friendship and love, and of the heroism and grandeur which belong to acts of self-reliance. It is remarkable that involuntarily we always read as superior beings. Universal history, the poets, the romancers, do not in their stateliest pictures — in the sacerdotal, the imperial palaces, in the triumphs of will or of genius — anywhere lose our ear, anywhere make us feel that we intrude, that this is for better men; but rather is it true, that in their grandest strokes we feel most at home. All that Shakspeare says of the king, yonder slip of a boy that reads in the corner feels to be true of himself. We sympathize in the great moments of history, in the great discoveries, the great resistances, the great prosperities of men; — because there law was enacted, the sea was searched, the land was found, or the blow was struck for us, as we ourselves in that place would have done or applauded.

We have the same interest in condition and character. We honor the rich, because they have externally the freedom, power, and grace which we feel to be proper to man, proper to us. So all that is said of the wise man by Stoic, or oriental or modern essayist, describes to each reader his own idea, describes his unattained but attainable self. All literature writes the character of the wise man. Books, monuments, pictures, conversation, are portraits in which he finds the lineaments he is forming. The silent and the eloquent praise him and accost him, and he is stimulated wherever he moves as by personal allusions. A true aspirant, therefore, never needs look for allusions personal and laudatory in discourse. He hears the commendation, not of himself, but more sweet, of that character he seeks, in every word that is said concerning character, yea, further, in every fact and circumstance, — in the running river and the rustling corn. Praise is looked, homage tendered, love flows from mute nature, from the mountains and the lights of the firmament.

These hints, dropped as it were from sleep and night, let us use in broad day. The student is to read history actively and not passively; to esteem his own life the text, and books the commentary. Thus compelled, the Muse of history will utter oracles, as never to those who do not respect themselves. I have no expectation that any man will read history aright, who thinks that what was done in a remote age, by men whose names have resounded far, has any deeper sense than what he is doing to-day.

The world exists for the education of each man. There is no age or state of society or mode of action in history, to which there is not somewhat corresponding in his life. Every thing tends in a wonderful manner to abbreviate itself and yield its own virtue to him. He should see that he can live all history in his own person. He must sit solidly at home, and not suffer himself to be bullied by kings or empires, but know that he is greater than all the geography and all the government of the world; he must transfer the point of view from which history is commonly read, from Rome and Athens and London to himself, and not deny his conviction that he is the court, and if England or Egypt have any thing to say to him, he will try the case; if not, let them for ever be silent. He must attain and maintain that lofty sight where facts yield their secret sense, and poetry and annals are alike.

The instinct of the mind, the purpose of nature, betrays itself in the use we make of the signal narrations of history. Time dissipates to shining ether the solid angularity of facts. No anchor, no cable, no fences, avail to keep a fact a fact. Babylon, Troy, Tyre, Palestine, and even early Rome, are passing already into fiction. The Garden of Eden, the sun standing still in Gibeon, is poetry thenceforward to all nations. Who cares what the fact was, when we have made a constellation of it to hang in heaven an immortal sign? London and Paris and New York must go the same way. "What is History," said Napoleon, "but a fable agreed upon?" This life of ours is stuck round with Egypt, Greece, Gaul, England, War, Colonization, Church, Court, and Commerce, as with so many flowers and wild ornaments grave and gay. I will not make more account of them. I believe in Eternity. I can find Greece, Asia, Italy, Spain, and the Islands, — the genius and creative principle of each and of all eras in my own mind.

We are always coming up with the emphatic facts of history in our private experience, and verifying them here. All history becomes subjective; in other words, there is properly no history; only biography. Every mind must know the whole lesson for itself, — must go over the whole ground. What it does not see, what it does not live, it will not know. What the former age has epitomized into a formula or rule for manipular convenience, it will lose all the good of verifying for itself, by means of the wall of that rule. Somewhere, sometime, it will demand and find compensation for that loss by doing the work itself. Ferguson discovered many things in astronomy which had long been known. The better for him.

History must be this or it is nothing. Every law which the state enacts indicates a fact in human nature; that is all. We must in ourselves see the necessary reason of every fact, — see how it could and must be. So stand before every public and private work; before an oration of Burke, before a victory of Napoleon, before a martyrdom of Sir Thomas More, of Sidney, of Marmaduke Robinson, before a French Reign of Terror, and a Salem hanging of witches, before a fanatic Revival, and the Animal Magnetism in Paris, or in Providence. We assume that we under like influence should be alike affected, and should achieve the like; and we aim to master intellectually the steps, and reach the same height or the same degradation, that our fellow, our proxy, has done.

All inquiry into antiquity, — all curiosity respecting the Pyramids, the excavated cities, Stonehenge, the Ohio Circles, Mexico, Memphis, — is the desire to do away this wild, savage, and preposterous There or Then, and introduce in its place the Here and the Now. Belzoni digs and measures in the mummy-pits and pyramids of Thebes, until he can see the end of the difference between the monstrous work and himself. When he has satisfied himself, in general and in detail, that it was made by such a person as he, so armed and so motived, and to ends to which he himself should also have worked, the problem is solved; his thought lives along the whole line of temples and sphinxes and catacombs, passes through them all with satisfaction, and they live again to the mind, or are now.

A Gothic cathedral affirms that it was done by us, and not done by us. Surely it was by man, but we find it not in our man. But we apply ourselves to the history of its production. We put ourselves into the place and state of the builder. We remember the forest-dwellers, the first temples, the adherence to the first type, and the decoration of it as the wealth of the nation increased; the value which is given to wood by carving led to the carving over the whole mountain of stone of a cathedral. When we have gone through this process, and added thereto the Catholic Church, its cross, its music, its processions, its Saints' days and image-worship, we have, as it were, been the man that made the minster; we have seen how it could and must be. We have the sufficient reason.

The difference between men is in their principle of association. Some men classify objects by color and size and other accidents of appearance; others by intrinsic likeness, or by the relation of cause and effect. The progress of the intellect is to the clearer vision of causes, which neglects surface differences. To the poet, to the philosopher, to the saint, all things are friendly and sacred, all events profitable, all days holy, all men divine. For the eye is fastened on the life, and slights the circumstance. Every chemical substance, every plant, every animal in its growth, teaches the unity of cause, the variety of appearance.

Upborne and surrounded as we are by this all-creating nature, soft and fluid as a cloud or the air, why should we be such hard pedants, and magnify a few forms? Why should we make account of time, or of magnitude, or of figure? The soul knows them not, and genius, obeying its law, knows how to play with them as a young child plays with graybeards and in churches. Genius studies the causal thought, and, far back in the womb of things, sees the rays parting from one orb, that diverge ere they fall by infinite diameters. Genius watches the monad through all his masks as he performs the metempsychosis of nature. Genius detects through the fly, through the caterpillar, through the grub, through the egg, the constant individual; through countless individuals, the fixed species; through many species, the genus; through all genera, the steadfast type; through all the kingdoms of organized life, the eternal unity. Nature is a mutable cloud, which is always and never the same. She casts the same thought into troops of forms, as a poet makes twenty fables with one moral. Through the bruteness and toughness of matter, a subtle spirit bends all things to its own will. The adamant streams into soft but precise form before it, and, whilst I look at it, its outline and texture are changed again. Nothing is so fleeting as form; yet never does it quite deny itself. In man we still trace the remains or hints of all that we esteem badges of servitude in the lower races; yet in him they enhance his nobleness and grace; as Io, in Aeschylus, transformed to a cow, offends the imagination; but how changed, when as Isis in Egypt she meets Osiris-Jove, a beautiful woman, with nothing of the metamorphosis left but the lunar horns as the splendid ornament of her brows!

The identity of history is equally intrinsic, the diversity equally obvious. There is at the surface infinite variety of things; at the centre there is simplicity of cause. How many are the acts of one man in which we recognize the same character! Observe the sources of our information in respect to the Greek genius. We have the civil history of that people, as Herodotus, Thucydides, Xenophon, and Plutarch have given it; a very sufficient account of what manner of persons they were, and what they did. We have the same national mind expressed for us again in their literature, in epic and lyric poems, drama, and philosophy; a very complete form. Then we have it once more in their architecture, a beauty as of temperance itself, limited to the straight line and the square, — a builded geometry. Then we have it once again in sculpture, the "tongue on the balance of expression," a multitude of forms in the utmost freedom of action, and never transgressing the ideal serenity; like votaries performing some religious dance before the gods, and, though in convulsive pain or mortal combat, never daring to break the figure and decorum of their dance. Thus, of the genius of one remarkable people, we have a fourfold representation: and to the senses what more unlike than an ode of Pindar, a marble centaur, the peristyle of the Parthenon, and the last actions of Phocion?

Every one must have observed faces and forms which, without any resembling feature, make a like impression on the beholder. A particular picture or copy of verses, if it do not awaken the same train of images, will yet superinduce the same sentiment as some wild mountain walk, although the resemblance is nowise obvious to the senses, but is occult and out of the reach of the understanding. Nature is an endless combination and repetition of a very few laws. She hums the old well-known air through innumerable variations.

Nature is full of a sublime family likeness throughout her works; and delights in startling us with resemblances in the most unexpected quarters. I have seen the head of an old sachem of the forest, which at once reminded the eye of a bald mountain summit, and the furrows of the brow suggested the strata of the rock. There are men whose manners have the same essential splendor as the simple and awful sculpture on the friezes of the Parthenon, and the remains of the earliest Greek art. And there are compositions of the same strain to be found in the books of all ages. What is Guido's Rospigliosi Aurora but a morning thought, as the horses in it are only a morning cloud. If any one will but take pains to observe the variety of actions to which he is equally inclined in certain moods of mind, and those to which he is averse, he will see how deep is the chain of affinity.

A painter told me that nobody could draw a tree without in some sort becoming a tree; or draw a child by studying the outlines of its form merely, — but, by watching for a time his motions and plays, the painter enters into his nature, and can then draw him at will in every attitude. So Roos "entered into the inmost nature of a sheep." I knew a draughtsman employed in a public survey, who found that he could not sketch the rocks until their geological structure was first explained to him. In a certain state of thought is the common origin of very diverse works. It is the spirit and not the fact that is identical. By a deeper apprehension, and not primarily by a painful acquisition of many manual skills, the artist attains the power of awakening other souls to a given activity.

It has been said, that "common souls pay with what they do; nobler souls with that which they are." And why? Because a profound nature awakens in us by its actions and words, by its very looks and manners, the same power and beauty that a gallery of sculpture, or of pictures, addresses.

Civil and natural history, the history of art and of literature, must be explained from individual history, or must remain words. There is nothing but is related to us, nothing that does not interest us, — kingdom, college, tree, horse, or iron shoe, the roots of all things are in man. Santa Croce and the Dome of St. Peter's are lame copies after a divine model. Strasburg Cathedral is a material counterpart of the soul of Erwin of Steinbach. The true poem is the poet's mind; the true ship is the ship-builder. In the man, could we lay him open, we should see the reason for the last flourish and tendril of his work; as every spine and tint in the sea-shell preexist in the secreting organs of the fish. The whole of heraldry and of chivalry is in courtesy. A man of fine manners shall pronounce your name with all the ornament that titles of nobility could ever add.

The trivial experience of every day is always verifying some old prediction to us, and converting into things the words and signs which we had heard and seen without heed. A lady, with whom I was riding in the forest, said to me, that the woods always seemed to her to wait, as if the genii who inhabit them suspended their deeds until the wayfarer has passed onward: a thought which poetry has celebrated in the dance of the fairies, which breaks off on the approach of human feet. The man who has seen the rising moon break out of the clouds at midnight has been present like an archangel at the creation of light and of the world. I remember one summer day, in the fields, my companion pointed out to me a broad cloud, which might extend a quarter of a mile parallel to the horizon, quite accurately in the form of a cherub as painted over churches, — a round block in the centre, which it was easy to animate with eyes and mouth, supported on either side by wide-stretched symmetrical wings. What appears once in the atmosphere may appear often, and it was undoubtedly the archetype of that familiar ornament. I have seen in the sky a chain of summer lightning which at once showed to me that the Greeks drew from nature when they painted the thunderbolt in the hand of Jove. I have seen a snow-drift along the sides of the stone wall which obviously gave the idea of the common architectural scroll to abut a tower.

By surrounding ourselves with the original circumstances, we invent anew the orders and the ornaments of architecture, as we see how each people merely decorated its primitive abodes. The Doric temple preserves the semblance of the wooden cabin in which the Dorian dwelt. The Chinese pagoda is plainly a Tartar tent. The Indian and Egyptian temples still betray the mounds and subterranean houses of their forefathers. "The custom of making houses and tombs in the living rock," says Heeren, in his Researches on the Ethiopians, "determined very naturally the principal character of the Nubian Egyptian architecture to the colossal form which it assumed. In these caverns, already prepared by nature, the eye was accustomed to dwell on huge shapes and masses, so that, when art came to the assistance of nature, it could not move on a small scale without degrading itself. What would statues of the usual size, or neat porches and wings, have been, associated with those gigantic halls before which only Colossi could sit as watchmen, or lean on the pillars of the interior?"

The Gothic church plainly originated in a rude adaptation of the forest trees with all their boughs to a festal or solemn arcade, as the bands about the cleft pillars still indicate the green withes that tied them. No one can walk in a road cut through pine woods, without being struck with the architectural appearance of the grove, especially in winter, when the bareness of all other trees shows the low arch of the Saxons. In the woods in a winter afternoon one will see as readily the origin of the stained glass window, with which the Gothic cathedrals are adorned, in the colors of the western sky seen through the bare and crossing branches of the forest. Nor can any lover of nature enter the old piles of Oxford and the English cathedrals, without feeling that the forest overpowered the mind of the builder, and that his chisel, his saw, and plane still reproduced its ferns, its spikes of flowers, its locust, elm, oak, pine, fir, and spruce.

The Gothic cathedral is a blossoming in stone subdued by the insatiable demand of harmony in man. The mountain of granite blooms into an eternal flower, with the lightness and delicate finish, as well as the aerial proportions and perspective, of vegetable beauty.

In like manner, all public facts are to be individualized, all private facts are to be generalized. Then at once History becomes fluid and true, and Biography deep and sublime. As the Persian imitated in the slender shafts and capitals of his architecture the stem and flower of the lotus and palm, so the Persian court in its magnificent era never gave over the nomadism of its barbarous tribes, but travelled from Ecbatana, where the spring was spent, to Susa in summer, and to Babylon for the winter.

In the early history of Asia and Africa, Nomadism and Agriculture are the two antagonist facts. The geography of Asia and of Africa necessitated a nomadic life. But the nomads were the terror of all those whom the soil, or the advantages of a market, had induced to build towns. Agriculture, therefore, was a religious injunction, because of the perils of the state from nomadism. And in these late and civil countries of England and America, these propensities still fight out the old battle in the nation and in the individual. The nomads of Africa were constrained to wander by the attacks of the gad-fly, which drives the cattle mad, and so compels the tribe to emigrate in the rainy season, and to drive off the cattle to the higher sandy regions. The nomads of Asia follow the pasturage from month to month. In America and Europe, the nomadism is of trade and curiosity; a progress, certainly, from the gad-fly of Astaboras to the Anglo and Italo-mania of Boston Bay. Sacred cities, to which a periodical religious pilgrimage was enjoined, or stringent laws and customs, tending to invigorate the national bond, were the check on the old rovers; and the cumulative values of long residence are the restraints on the itineracy of the present day. The antagonism of the two tendencies is not less active in individuals, as the love of adventure or the love of repose happens to predominate. A man of rude health and flowing spirits has the faculty of rapid domestication, lives in his wagon, and roams through all latitudes as easily as a Calmuc. At sea, or in the forest, or in the snow, he sleeps as warm, dines with as good appetite, and associates as happily, as beside his own chimneys. Or perhaps his facility is deeper seated, in the increased range of his faculties of observation, which yield him points of interest wherever fresh objects meet his eyes. The pastoral nations were needy and hungry to desperation; and this intellectual nomadism, in its excess, bankrupts the mind, through the dissipation of power on a miscellany of objects. The home-keeping wit, on the other hand, is that continence or content which finds all the elements of life in its own soil; and which has its own perils of monotony and deterioration, if not stimulated by foreign infusions.

Every thing the individual sees without him corresponds to his states of mind, and every thing is in turn intelligible to him, as his onward thinking leads him into the truth to which that fact or series belongs.

The primeval world, — the Fore-World, as the Germans say, — I can dive to it in myself as well as grope for it with researching fingers in catacombs, libraries, and the broken reliefs and torsos of ruined villas.

What is the foundation of that interest all men feel in Greek history, letters, art, and poetry, in all its periods, from the Heroic or Homeric age down to the domestic life of the Athenians and Spartans, four or five centuries later? What but this, that every man passes personally through a Grecian period. The Grecian state is the era of the bodily nature, the perfection of the senses, — of the spiritual nature unfolded in strict unity with the body.

In it existed those human forms which supplied the sculptor with his models of Hercules, Phoebus, and Jove; not like the forms abounding in the streets of modern cities, wherein the face is a confused blur of features, but composed of incorrupt, sharply defined, and symmetrical features, whose eye-sockets are so formed that it would be impossible for such eyes to squint, and take furtive glances on this side and on that, but they must turn the whole head. The manners of that period are plain and fierce. The reverence exhibited is for personal qualities, courage, address, self-command, justice, strength, swiftness, a loud voice, a broad chest. Luxury and elegance are not known. A sparse population and want make every man his own valet, cook, butcher, and soldier, and the habit of supplying his own needs educates the body to wonderful performances. Such are the Agamemnon and Diomed of Homer, and not far different is the picture Xenophon gives of himself and his compatriots in the Retreat of the Ten Thousand. "After the army had crossed the river Teleboas in Armenia, there fell much snow, and the troops lay miserably on the ground covered with it. But Xenophon arose naked, and, taking an axe, began to split wood; whereupon others rose and did the like." Throughout his army exists a boundless liberty of speech. They quarrel for plunder, they wrangle with the generals on each new order, and Xenophon is as sharp-tongued as any, and sharper-tongued than most, and so gives as good as he gets. Who does not see that this is a gang of great boys, with such a code of honor and such lax discipline as great boys have?

The costly charm of the ancient tragedy, and indeed of all the old literature, is, that the persons speak simply, — speak as persons who have great good sense without knowing it, before yet the reflective habit has become the predominant habit of the mind. Our admiration of the antique is not admiration of the old, but of the natural. The Greeks are not reflective, but perfect in their senses and in their health, with the finest physical organization in the world. Adults acted with the simplicity and grace of children. They made vases, tragedies, and statues, such as healthy senses should,— — that is, in good taste. Such things have continued to be made in all ages, and are now, wherever a healthy physique exists; but, as a class, from their superior organization, they have surpassed all. They combine the energy of manhood with the engaging unconsciousness of childhood. The attraction of these manners is that they belong to man, and are known to every man in virtue of his being once a child; besides that there are always individuals who retain these characteristics. A person of childlike genius and inborn energy is still a Greek, and revives our love of the Muse of Hellas. I admire the love of nature in the Philoctetes. In reading those fine apostrophes to sleep, to the stars, rocks, mountains, and waves, I feel time passing away as an ebbing sea. I feel the eternity of man, the identity of his thought. The Greek had, it seems, the same fellow-beings as I. The sun and moon, water and fire, met his heart precisely as they meet mine. Then the vaunted distinction between Greek and English, between Classic and Romantic schools, seems superficial and pedantic. When a thought of Plato becomes a thought to me, — when a truth that fired the soul of Pindar fires mine, time is no more. When I feel that we two meet in a perception, that our two souls are tinged with the same hue, and do, as it were, run into one, why should I measure degrees of latitude, why should I count Egyptian years?

The student interprets the age of chivalry by his own age of chivalry, and the days of maritime adventure and circumnavigation by quite parallel miniature experiences of his own. To the sacred history of the world, he has the same key. When the voice of a prophet out of the deeps of antiquity merely echoes to him a sentiment of his infancy, a prayer of his youth, he then pierces to the truth through all the confusion of tradition and the caricature of institutions.

Rare, extravagant spirits come by us at intervals, who disclose to us new facts in nature. I see that men of God have, from time to time, walked among men and made their commission felt in the heart and soul of the commonest hearer. Hence, evidently, the tripod, the priest, the priestess inspired by the divine afflatus.

Jesus astonishes and overpowers sensual people. They cannot unite him to history, or reconcile him with themselves. As they come to revere their intuitions and aspire to live holily, their own piety explains every fact, every word.

How easily these old worships of Moses, of Zoroaster, of

Menu, of Socrates, domesticate themselves in the mind. I cannot find any antiquity in them. They are mine as much as theirs.

I have seen the first monks and anchorets without crossing seas or centuries. More than once some individual has appeared to me with such negligence of labor and such commanding contemplation, a haughty beneficiary, begging in the name of God, as made good to the nineteenth century Simeon the Stylite, the Thebais, and the first Capuchins.

The priestcraft of the East and West, of the Magian, Brahmin, Druid, and Inca, is expounded in the individual's private life. The cramping influence of a hard formalist on a young child in repressing his spirits and courage, paralyzing the understanding, and that without producing indignation, but only fear and obedience, and even much sympathy with the tyranny, – is a familiar fact explained to the child when he becomes a man, only by seeing that the oppressor of his youth is himself a child tyrannized over by those names and words and forms, of whose influence he was merely the organ to the youth. The fact teaches him how Belus was worshipped, and how the Pyramids were built, better than the discovery by Champollion of the names of all the workmen and the cost of every tile. He finds Assyria and the Mounds of Cholula at his door, and himself has laid the courses.

Again, in that protest which each considerate person makes against the superstition of his times, he repeats step for step the part of old reformers, and in the search after truth finds like them new perils to virtue. He learns again what moral vigor is needed to supply the girdle of a superstition. A great licentiousness treads on the heels of a reformation. How many times in the history of the world has the Luther of the day had to lament the decay of piety in his own household! "Doctor," said his wife to Martin Luther, one day, "how is it that, whilst subject to papacy, we prayed so often and with such fervor, whilst now we pray with the utmost coldness and very seldom?"

The advancing man discovers how deep a property he has in literature, – in all fable as well as in all history. He finds that the poet was no odd fellow who described strange and impossible situations, but that universal man wrote by his pen a confession true for one and true for all. His own secret biography he finds in lines wonderfully intelligible to him, dotted down before he was born. One after another he comes up in his private adventures with every fable of Aesop, of Homer, of Hafiz, of Ariosto, of Chaucer, of Scott, and verifies them with his own head and hands.

The beautiful fables of the Greeks, being proper creations of the imagination and not of the fancy, are universal verities. What a range of meanings and what perpetual pertinence has the story of Prometheus! Beside its primary value as the first chapter of the history of Europe, (the mythology thinly veiling authentic facts, the invention of the mechanic arts, and the migration of colonies,) it gives the history of religion with some closeness to the faith of later ages. Prometheus is the Jesus of the old mythology. He is the friend of man; stands between the unjust "justice" of the Eternal Father and the race of mortals, and readily suffers all things on their account. But where it departs from the Calvinistic Christianity, and exhibits him as the defier of Jove, it represents a state of mind which readily appears wherever the doctrine of Theism is taught in a crude, objective form, and which seems the self-defence of man against this untruth, namely, a discontent with the believed fact that a God exists, and a feeling that the obligation of reverence is onerous. It would steal, if it could, the fire of the Creator, and live apart from him, and independent of him.

The Prometheus Vinctus is the romance of skepticism. Not less true to all time are the details of that stately apologue. Apollo kept the flocks of Admetus, said the poets. When the gods come among men, they are not known. Jesus was not; Socrates and Shakspeare were not. Antaeus was suffocated by the gripe of Hercules, but every time he touched his mother earth, his strength was renewed. Man is the broken giant, and, in all his weakness, both his body and his mind are invigorated by habits of conversation with nature. The power of music, the power of poetry to unfix, and, as it were, clap wings to solid nature, interprets the riddle of Orpheus. The philosophical perception of identity through endless mutations of form makes him know the Proteus. What else am I who laughed or wept yesterday, who slept last night like a corpse, and this morning stood and ran?

And what see I on any side but the transmigrations of Proteus? I can symbolize my thought by using the name of any creature, of any fact, because every creature is man agent or patient. Tantalus is but a name for you and me. Tantalus means the impossibility of drinking the waters of thought which are always gleaming and waving within sight of the soul. The transmigration of souls is no fable. I would it were; but men and women are only half human. Every animal of the barn-yard, the field, and the forest, of the earth and of the waters that are under the earth, has contrived to get a footing and to leave the print of its features and form in some one or other of these upright, heaven-facing speakers. Ah! brother, stop the ebb of thy soul, — ebbing downward into the forms into whose habits thou hast now for many years slid. As near and proper to us is also that old fable of the Sphinx, who was said to sit in the road-side and put riddles to every passenger. If the man could not answer, she swallowed him alive.

If he could solve the riddle, the Sphinx was slain. What is our life but an endless flight of winged facts or events! In splendid variety these changes come, all putting questions to the human spirit. Those men who cannot answer by a superior wisdom these facts or questions of time, serve them. Facts encumber them, tyrannize over them, and make the men of routine the men of sense, in whom a literal obedience to facts has extinguished every spark of that light by which man is truly man. But if the man is true to his better instincts or sentiments, and refuses the dominion of facts, as one that comes of a higher race, remains fast by the soul and sees the principle, then the facts fall aptly and supple into their places; they know their master, and the meanest of them glorifies him.

See in Goethe's Helena the same desire that every word should be a thing. These figures, he would say, these Chirons, Griffins, Phorkyas, Helen, and Leda, are somewhat, and do exert a specific influence on the mind. So far then are they eternal entities, as real to-day as in the first Olympiad. Much revolving them, he writes out freely his humor, and gives them body tohis own imagination. And although that poem be as vague and fantastic as a dream, yet is it much more attractive than the more regular dramatic pieces of the same author, for the reason that it operates a wonderful relief to the mind from the routine of customary images, — awakens the reader's invention and fancy by the wild freedom of the design, and by the unceasing succession of brisk shocks of surprise.

The universal nature, too strong for the petty nature of the bard, sits on his neck and writes through his hand; so that when he seems to vent a mere caprice and wild romance, the issue is an exact allegory. Hence Plato said that "poets utter great and wise things which they do not themselves understand." All the fictions of the Middle Age explain themselves as a masked or frolic expression of that which in grave earnest the mind of that period toiled to achieve. Magic, and all that is ascribed to it, is a deep presentiment of the powers of science. The shoes of swiftness, the sword of sharpness, the power of subduing the elements, of using the secret virtues of minerals, of understanding the voices of birds, are the obscure efforts of the mind in a right direction. The preternatural prowess of the hero, the gift of perpetual youth, and the like, are alike the endeavour of the human spirit "to bend the shows of things to the desires of the mind."

In Perceforest and Amadis de Gaul, a garland and a rose bloom on the head of her who is faithful, and fade on the brow of the inconstant. In the story of the Boy and the Mantle, even a mature reader may be surprised with a glow of virtuous pleasure at the triumph of the gentle Genelas; and, indeed, all the postulates of elfin annals, — that the fairies do not like to be named; that their gifts are capricious and not to be trusted; that who seeks a treasure must not speak; and the like, — I find true in Concord, however they might be in Cornwall or Bretagne.

Is it otherwise in the newest romance? I read the Bride of Lammermoor. Sir William Ashton is a mask for a vulgar temptation, Ravenswood Castle a fine name for proud poverty, and the foreign mission of state only a Bunyan disguise for honest industry. We may all shoot a wild bull that would toss the good and beautiful, by fighting down the unjust and sensual. Lucy Ashton is another name for fidelity, which is always beautiful and always liable to calamity in this world.

But along with the civil and metaphysical history of man, another history goes daily forward, — that of the external world,

— in which he is not less strictly implicated. He is the compend of time; he is also the correlative of nature. His power consists in the multitude of his affinities, in the fact that his life is intertwined with the whole chain of organic and inorganic being. In old Rome the public roads beginning at the Forum proceeded north, south, east, west, to the centre of every province of the empire, making each market-town of Persia, Spain, and Britain pervious to the soldiers of the capital: so out of the human heart go, as it were, highways to the heart of every object in nature, to reduce it under the dominion of man. A man is a bundle of relations, a knot of roots, whose flower and fruitage is the world. His faculties refer to natures out of him, and predict the world he is to inhabit, as the fins of the fish foreshow that water exists, or the wings of an eagle in the egg presuppose air. He cannot live without a world. Put Napoleon in an island prison, let his faculties find no men to act on, no Alps to climb, no stake to play for, and he would beat the air and appear stupid. Transport him to large countries, dense population, complex interests, and antagonist power, and you shall see that the man Napoleon, bounded, that is, by such a profile and outline, is not the virtual Napoleon. This is but Talbot's shadow;

"His substance is not here:
For what you see is but the smallest part
And least proportion of humanity;
But were the whole frame here,
It is of such a spacious, lofty pitch,
Your roof were not sufficient to contain it."

HENRY VI

Columbus needs a planet to shape his course upon. Newton and Laplace need myriads of ages and thick-strewn celestial areas. One may say a gravitating solar system is already prophesied in the nature of Newton's mind. Not less does the brain of Davy or of Gay-Lussac, from childhood exploring the affinities and repulsions of particles, anticipate the laws of organization. Does not the eye of the human embryo predict the light? the ear of Handel predict the witchcraft of harmonic sound? Do not the constructive fingers of Watt, Fulton, Whittemore, Arkwright, predict the fusible, hard, and temperable texture of metals, the properties of stone, water, and wood? Do not the lovely attributes of the maiden child predict the refinements and decorations of civil society? Here also we are reminded of the action of man on man. A mind might ponder its thought for ages, and not gain so much self-knowledge as the passion of love shall teach it in a day. Who knows himself before he has been thrilled with indignation at an outrage, or has heard an eloquent tongue, or has shared the throb of thousands in a national exultation or alarm? No man can antedate his experience, or guess what faculty or feeling a new object shall unlock, any more than he can draw to-day the face of a person whom he shall see to-morrow for the first time.

I will not now go behind the general statement to explore the reason of this correspondency. Let it suffice that in the light of these two facts, namely, that the mind is One, and that nature is its correlative, history is to be read and written.

Thus in all ways does the soul concentrate and reproduce its treasures for each pupil. He, too, shall pass through the whole cycle of experience. He shall collect into a focus the rays of nature. History no longer shall be a dull book. It shall walk incarnate in every just and wise man. You shall not tell me by languages and titles a catalogue of the volumes you have read. You shall make me feel what periods you have lived. A man shall be the Temple of Fame. He shall walk, as the poets have described that goddess, in a robe painted all over with wonderful events and experiences; — his own form and features by their exalted intelligence shall be that variegated vest. I shall find in him the Foreworld; in his childhood the Age of Gold; the Apples of Knowledge; the Argonautic Expedition; the calling of Abraham; the building of the Temple; the Advent of Christ; Dark Ages; the Revival of Letters; the Reformation; the discovery of new lands; the opening of new sciences, and new regions in man. He shall be the priest of Pan, and bring with him into humble cottages the blessing of the morning stars and all the recorded benefits of heaven and earth.

Is there somewhat overweening in this claim? Then I reject all I have written, for what is the use of pretending to know what we know not? But it is the fault of our rhetoric that we cannot strongly state one fact without seeming to belie some other. I hold our actual knowledge very cheap. Hear the rats in the wall, see the lizard on the fence, the fungus under foot, the lichen on the log. What do I know sympathetically, morally, of either of these worlds of life? As old as the Caucasian man, — perhaps older, — these creatures have kept their counsel beside him, and there is no record of any word or sign that has passed from one to the other. What connection do the books show between the fifty or sixty chemical elements, and the historical eras? Nay, what does history yet record of the metaphysical annals of man? What light does it shed on those mysteries which we hide under the names Death and Immortality? Yet every history should be written in a wisdom which divined the range of our affinities and looked at facts as symbols. I am ashamed to see what a shallow village tale our so-called History is. How many times we must say Rome, and Paris, and Constantinople! What does Rome know of rat and lizard? What are Olympiads and Consulates to these neighbouring systems of being? Nay, what food or experience or succour have they for the Esquimaux seal-hunter, for the Kanaka in his canoe, for the fisherman, the stevedore, the porter?

Broader and deeper we must write our annals, — from an ethical reformation, from an influx of the ever new, ever sanative conscience, — if we would trulier express our central and wide-related nature, instead of this old chronology of selfishness and pride to which we have too long lent our eyes. Already that day exists for us, shines in on us at unawares, but the path of science and of letters is not the way into nature. The idiot, the Indian, the child, and unschooled farmer's boy, stand nearer to the light by which nature is to be read, than the dissector or the antiquary.

3

Jacques Barzun From Dawn to Decadence

Jacques Barzun was born in 1907 and grew up in Paris and Grenoble, where his great-grandfather, a university professor, had settled to teach during the mid-19th century. In Paris, his parents' house was one of the centers of the new 'modernist' movements in the arts at the turn of the century, and so, the boy's earliest adult friends included Apollinaire, the poet, who taught him how to read time on his watch, and Marie Laurencein, who made his portrait. Other constant visitors were the Cubist painters Gleizes and Duchamp, the musician Varése, and such foreigners as Richard Aldington and Stefan Zweig.

Barzun's father is supposed to have disputed with another aspirant poet over the honor of having invented 'simultaneous' poetry!

His early education was taken at the Lycée Janson de Sailly, after which he experienced life behind the lines in the First World War. His father came to the United States on a diplomatic mission during the war and decided Jacques should attend college there. He entered Columbia University in 1920 where he studied law and history over several years. His upbringing in the arts led him increasingly to the study of cultural history, then a new branch of history.

Soon after graduation, he was appointed lecturer, and in due course became professor in 1937. In 1955 he was named Dean of the Graduate Faculties and three years later, Dean of Faculties and Provost. Concurrently, he occupied the chair of Seth Low Professor of History and Extraordinary Fellow of Churchill College at the University of Cambridge. He resigned from administrative work in 1967 and was named University Professor.

For seven decades he has written and edited critical and historical studies on a wide variety of subjects. They include *Race: a Study in Modern Superstition* (1937), *Darwin, Marx, Wagner* (1941), *Romanticism and the Modern Ego* (1945), *The Teacher in America* (1945), *The House of Intellect* (1959), *Classic, Romantic, and Modern* (1961), *Science: The Glorious Entertainment* (1964), *The American University* (1968), *Berlioz and the Romantic Century* (3d ed. 1969), *The Use and Abuse of Art* (1974), and *Begin Here: The Forgotten Conditions of Teaching and Learning* (1991).

Some of Mr. Barzun's approximately thirty books-particularly *Teacher in America* and *The House of Intellect*-were bestsellers that influenced debate about culture far beyond the realm of academic history. A more recent, and very widely acclaimed, bestseller is *From Dawn to Decadence: 500 Years of Western Cultural Life, 1500 to the Present* (2000).

In this later work Barzun divides the period 1500-2000 in western cultural history into four large segments. The first segment takes us from Luther's Protestant revolution to Newton-from the early sixteenth century to the end of the seventeenth century. Part two opens with the ascent of Louis XIV and the rise of the nation state; it ends with the Enlightenment and the French Revolution. Part three, which opens with a section called "The Work of Mind-and-Heart," details the Romantic reaction-that is to say, the Romantic reactions, for they were many and disparate-to Enlightenment rationalism. Here Mr. Barzun takes his story from the time of Goethe and Wordsworth to the pre-World-War-I period he calls the Cubist Decade. Part four brings the story up to the year 2000.

Barzun guides the reader through conflicting views of history, highlighting the existence of particular themes in the last five hundred years of Western cultural life. Some of these include SELF-CONSCIOUSNESS (he uses the capitalisation himself), a "mental state" of individuality without limits; ANALYSIS, or "the breaking of wholes into parts," a fundamental process of science but new to art; SPECIALISM, with its threefold appearance in intellectual, scientific and educational circles; EMANCIPATION, "indeed the immediate appeal of all revolutions"; PRIMITIVISM, the desire for a break from the demands of urban life and technology and a return to simpler modes of living; and INDIVIDUALISM, an effect of emancipation and cause of self-consciousness. Unlike historians with an agenda, Barzun does not force his account to conform to these themes, as a statistician might skew data to support a hypothetical trend. Instead he notes their reappearance and discusses its relation to precedents.He is convinced that our age, despite its extraordinary technological capabilities, is an Alexandrian age: a time of cultural sunset, depleted energies and moral confusion. His summary of what he calls "our present decadence" shows that he does not regard decadence as a neutral historical fact but as a cultural, moral, and political disaster of the first order.

As one would expect, the sources of decadence are many and varied. Mr. Barzun shows how, from one perspective, the symptoms of decadence can be understood as resulting from the hypertrophy of those very traits that defined the West: primitivism, emancipation, self-consciousness, individualism, and so on. What appear as motors for cultural development can, when pursued ruthlessly and without regard to other virtues, degenerate into engines of decadence and decline. Mr. Barzun devotes the last sections of his book to showing how decadence has triumphed in various facets of modern life. There is, first of all, the spiritual paralysis that results from willing contradictory things. These days, Mr. Barzun observes, "any doctrine or program that claims the merit of going against common sense has presumption in its favor." Western nations spend billions on public schooling for all, urged along by the public cry for Excellence. At the same time the society pounces on any show of superiority as elitism. The same nations deplore violence and sexual promiscuity among the young, but pornography and violence in films and books, shops and clubs, on television and the Internet, and in the lyrics of pop music cannot be suppressed, in the interests of "the free market of ideas."

The confusion generated by such contradictions attends every aspect of cultural endeavor. In the arts, it leads to the rise of anti-art, embodied on one side by the nihilistic pranks of Marcel Duchamp, on another by Picasso. Mr. Barzun is right that "When people accept futility and the absurd as normal, the culture is decadent." But futility and absurdity only seem normal to a damaged sensibility. Of course, it is not only in the realm of culture that confusion reigns. The realms of social relations and politics are equally beset. One result is what Mr. Barzun refers to as the "Great Switch," "the reversal of Liberalism into its opposite." If Liberalism originally "triumphed on the principle that the best government is that which governs least," today "for all the western nations political wisdom has recast the ideal of liberty into liberality." The universalization and extension of the welfare state has nurtured a culture of entitlement. What began in an access of largess ends in an explosion of regulation and hectoring scrutiny.

The titles of the book's last two sections indicate the tenor of Barzun's overall assessment: "Embracing the Absurd" and "Demotic Life and Times." On a more general level, the very notion of rights in Western society has devolved into farce, with everyone demanding his voice be heard. All this takes place under the rousing rebel yell of democracy, when the fundamental principle of democracy is *majority* rule. This last advent, socially speaking, creates a tyranny of the common man over his gifted counterpart—in short, it is the lamentable rise of the "demotic," not "democratic," in fashion, music, and the arts—a decline expedited by the Lowest Common Denominator strategies propagated by the monolithic advertising and television industries

Although the picture Mr. Barzun paints is one of cultural desolation, he nevertheless manages to end on a note of cautious optimism. Even if present trends continue and society becomes more routinized and culturally sterile, human ingenuity can surely be counted upon to precipitate a rebellion against the spread of bureaucratized futility. Sooner or later, some few intrepid souls will turn with new curiosity to the neglected past and use it "to create a new present," discovering along the way "what a joy it is to be alive." The forces of decadence that Mr. Barzun describes are formidably potent. But decadence is no more inevitable than progress.

4

Popular European History pages at Age-of-the-Sage

The preparation of these pages was influenced to some degree by a particular "Philosophy of History" as suggested by this quote from the famous Essay "History" by Ralph Waldo Emerson:-

There is one mind common to all individual men...

Of the works of this mind history is the record. Its genius is illustrated by the entire series of days. Man is explicable by nothing less than all his history. Without hurry, without rest, the human spirit goes forth from the beginning to embody every faculty, every thought, every emotion, which belongs to it in appropriate events. But the thought is always prior to the fact; all the facts of history preexist in the mind as laws. Each law in turn is made by circumstances predominant, and the limits of nature give power to but one at a time. A man is the whole encyclopaedia of facts. The creation of a thousand forests is in one acorn, and Egypt, Greece, Rome, Gaul, Britain, America, lie folded already in the first man. Epoch after epoch, camp, kingdom, empire, republic, democracy, are merely the application of his manifold spirit to the manifold world.

Ralph Waldo Emerson resigned as an Unitarian minister in 1832 and subsequently tried to establish himself as a lecturer and writer. His efforts in this direction included the self-financed publication of a pamphlet entitled "Nature" in 1836. This essay, only five hundred copies of which were printed (and these took some six years to be distributed), received little initial notice but effectively articulated the philosophical underpinnings of the subsequently widely influential New England Transcendentalism movement.

Emerson's first substantial publication was a volume of Essays that issued from the presses in 1841. There were twelve essays in this volume the very first being one entitled "History".

There is one mind common to all individual men. Every man is an inlet to the same and to all of the same. He that is once admitted to the right of reason is made a freeman of the whole estate. What Plato has thought, he may think; what a saint has felt, he may feel; what at any time has be-fallen any man, he can understand. Who hath access to this universal mind is a party to all that is or can be done, for this is the only and sovereign agent.

Of the works of this mind history is the record. Its genius is illustrated by the entire series of days. Man is explicable by nothing less than all his history. Without hurry, without rest, the human spirit goes forth from the beginning to embody every faculty, every thought, every emotion, which belongs to it in appropriate events. But the thought is always prior to the fact; all the facts of history preexist in the mind as laws. Each law in turn is made by circumstances predominant, and the limits of nature give power to but one at a time. A man is the whole encyclopaedia of facts. The creation of a thousand forests is in one acorn, and Egypt, Greece, Rome, Gaul, Britain, America, lie folded already in the first man. Epoch after epoch, camp, kingdom, empire, republic, democracy, are merely the application of his manifold spirit to the manifold world.

This human mind wrote history, and this must read it. The Sphinx must solve her own riddle. If the whole of history is in one man, it is all to be explained from individual experience. There is a relation between the hours of our life and the centuries of time. As the air I breathe is drawn from the great repositories of nature, as the light on my book is yielded by a star a hundred millions of miles distant, as the poise of my body depends on the equilibrium of centrifugal and centripetal forces, so the hours should be instructed by the ages, and the ages explained by the hours. Of the universal mind each individual man is one more incarnation. All its properties consist in him. Each new fact in his private experience flashes a light on what great bodies of men have done, and the crises of his life refer to national crises. Every revolution was first a thought in one man's mind, and when the same thought occurs to another man, it is the key to that era. Every reform was once a private opinion, and when it shall be a private opinion again, it will solve the problem of the age. The fact narrated must correspond to something in me to be credible or intelligible. We as we read must become Greeks, Romans, Turks, priest and king, martyr and executioner, must fasten these images to some reality in our secret experience, or we shall learn nothing rightly. What befell Asdrubal or Caesar Borgia is as much an illustration of the mind's powers and depravations as what has befallen us. Each new law and political movement has meaning for you. Stand before each of its tablets and say, 'Under this mask did my Proteus nature hide itself.' This remedies the defect of our too great nearness to ourselves. This throws our actions into perspective: and as crabs, goats, scorpions, the balance, and the waterpot lose their meanness when hung as signs in the zodiac, so I can see my own vices without heat in the distant persons of Solomon, Alcibiades, and Catiline.

It is the universal nature which gives worth to particular men and things. Human life as containing this is mysterious and inviolable, and we hedge it round with penalties and laws. All laws derive hence their ultimate reason; all express more or less distinctly some command of this supreme, illimitable essence. Property also holds of the soul, covers great spiritual facts, and instinctively we at first hold to it with swords and laws, and wide and complex combinations. The obscure consciousness of this fact is the light of all our day, the claim of claims; the plea for education, for justice, for charity, the foundation of friendship and love, and of the heroism and grandeur which belong to acts of self-reliance. It is remarkable that involuntarily we always read as superior beings. Universal history, the poets, the romancers, do not in their stateliest pictures — in the sacerdotal, the imperial palaces, in the triumphs of will or of genius — anywhere lose our ear, anywhere make us feel that we intrude, that this is for better men; but rather is it true, that in their grandest strokes we feel most at home. All that Shakspeare says of the king, yonder slip of a boy that reads in the corner feels to be true of himself. We sympathize in the great moments of history, in the great discoveries, the great resistances, the great prosperities of men; — because there law was enacted, the sea was searched, the land was found, or the blow was struck for us, as we ourselves in that place would have done or applauded.

We have the same interest in condition and character. We honor the rich, because they have externally the freedom, power, and grace which we feel to be proper to man, proper to us. So all that is said of the wise man by Stoic, or oriental or modern essayist, describes to each reader his own idea, describes his unattained but attainable self. All literature writes the character of the wise man. Books, monuments, pictures, conversation, are portraits in which he finds the lineaments he is forming. The silent and the eloquent praise him and accost him, and he is stimulated wherever he moves as by personal allusions. A true aspirant, therefore, never needs look for allusions personal and laudatory in discourse. He hears the commendation, not of himself, but more sweet, of that character he seeks, in every word that is said concerning character, yea, further, in every fact and circumstance, — in the running river and the rustling corn. Praise is looked, homage tendered, love flows from mute nature, from the mountains and the lights of the firmament.

These hints, dropped as it were from sleep and night, let us use in broad day. The student is to read history actively and not passively; to esteem his own life the text, and books the commentary. Thus compelled, the Muse of history will utter oracles, as never to those who do not respect themselves. I have no expectation that any man will read history aright, who thinks that what was done in a remote age, by men whose names have resounded far, has any deeper sense than what he is doing to-day.

The world exists for the education of each man. There is no age or state of society or mode of action in history, to which there is not somewhat corresponding in his life. Every thing tends in a wonderful manner to abbreviate itself and yield its own virtue to him. He should see that he can live all history in his own person. He must sit solidly at home, and not suffer himself to be bullied by kings or empires, but know that he is greater than all the geography and all the government of the world; he must transfer the point of view from which history is commonly read, from Rome and Athens and London to himself, and not deny his conviction that he is the court, and if England or Egypt have any thing to say to him, he will try the case; if not, let them for ever be silent. He must attain and maintain that lofty sight where facts yield their secret sense, and poetry and annals are alike.

The instinct of the mind, the purpose of nature, betrays itself in the use we make of the signal narrations of history. Time dissipates to shining ether the solid angularity of facts. No anchor, no cable, no fences, avail to keep a fact a fact. Babylon, Troy, Tyre, Palestine, and even early Rome, are passing already into fiction. The Garden of Eden, the sun standing still in Gibeon, is poetry thenceforward to all nations. Who cares what the fact was, when we have made a constellation of it to hang in heaven an immortal sign? London and Paris and New York must go the same way. "What is History," said Napoleon, "but a fable agreed upon?" This life of ours is stuck round with Egypt, Greece, Gaul, England, War, Colonization, Church, Court, and Commerce, as with so many flowers and wild ornaments grave and gay. I will not make more account of them. I believe in Eternity. I can find Greece, Asia, Italy, Spain, and the Islands, — the genius and creative principle of each and of all eras in my own mind.

We are always coming up with the emphatic facts of history in our private experience, and verifying them here. All history becomes subjective; in other words, there is properly no history; only biography. Every mind must know the whole lesson for itself, — must go over the whole ground. What it does not see, what it does not live, it will not know. What the former age has epitomized into a formula or rule for manipular convenience, it will lose all the good of verifying for itself, by means of the wall of that rule. Somewhere, sometime, it will demand and find compensation for that loss by doing the work itself. Ferguson discovered many things in astronomy which had long been known. The better for him.

History must be this or it is nothing. Every law which the state enacts indicates a fact in human nature; that is all. We must in ourselves see the necessary reason of every fact, — see how it could and must be. So stand before every public and private work;

before an oration of Burke, before a victory of Napoleon, before a martyrdom of Sir Thomas More, of Sidney, of Marmaduke Robinson, before a French Reign of Terror, and a Salem hanging of witches, before a fanatic Revival, and the Animal Magnetism in Paris, or in Providence. We assume that we under like influence should be alike affected, and should achieve the like; and we aim to master intellectually the steps, and reach the same height or the same degradation, that our fellow, our proxy, has done.

All inquiry into antiquity, — all curiosity respecting the Pyramids, the excavated cities, Stonehenge, the Ohio Circles, Mexico, Memphis, — is the desire to do away this wild, savage, and preposterous There or Then, and introduce in its place the Here and the Now. Belzoni digs and measures in the mummy-pits and pyramids of Thebes, until he can see the end of the difference between the monstrous work and himself. When he has satisfied himself, in general and in detail, that it was made by such a person as he, so armed and so motived, and to ends to which he himself should also have worked, the problem is solved; his thought lives along the whole line of temples and sphinxes and catacombs, passes through them all with satisfaction, and they live again to the mind, or are now.

A Gothic cathedral affirms that it was done by us, and not done by us. Surely it was by man, but we find it not in our man. But we apply ourselves to the history of its production. We put ourselves into the place and state of the builder. We remember the forest-dwellers, the first temples, the adherence to the first type, and the decoration of it as the wealth of the nation increased; the value which is given to wood by carving led to the carving over the whole mountain of stone of a cathedral. When we have gone through this process, and added thereto the Catholic Church, its cross, its music, its processions, its Saints' days and image-worship, we have, as it were, been the man that made the minster; we have seen how it could and must be. We have the sufficient reason.

The difference between men is in their principle of association. Some men classify objects by color and size and other accidents of appearance; others by intrinsic likeness, or by the relation of cause and effect. The progress of the intellect is to the clearer vision of causes, which neglects surface differences. To the poet, to the philosopher, to the saint, all things are friendly and sacred, all events profitable, all days holy, all men divine. For the eye is fastened on the life, and slights the circumstance. Every chemical substance, every plant, every animal in its growth, teaches the unity of cause, the variety of appearance.

Upborne and surrounded as we are by this all-creating nature, soft and fluid as a cloud or the air, why should we be such hard pedants, and magnify a few forms? Why should we make account of time, or of magnitude, or of figure? The soul knows them not, and genius, obeying its law, knows how to play with them as a young child plays with graybeards and in churches. Genius studies the causal thought, and, far back in the womb of things, sees the rays parting from one orb, that diverge ere they fall by infinite diameters. Genius watches the monad through all his masks as he performs the metempsychosis of nature. Genius detects through the fly, through the caterpillar, through the grub, through the egg, the constant individual; through countless individuals, the fixed species; through many species, the genus; through all genera, the steadfast type; through all the kingdoms of organized life, the eternal unity. Nature is a mutable cloud, which is always and never the same. She casts the same thought into troops of forms, as a poet makes twenty fables with one moral.

Through the bruteness and toughness of matter, a subtle spirit bends all things to its own will. The adamant streams into soft but precise form before it, and, whilst I look at it, its outline and texture are changed again. Nothing is so fleeting as form; yet never does it quite deny itself. In man we still trace the remains or hints of all that we esteem badges of servitude in the lower races; yet in him they enhance his nobleness and grace; as Io, in Aeschylus, transformed to a cow, offends the imagination; but how changed, when as Isis in Egypt she meets Osiris-Jove, a beautiful woman, with nothing of the metamorphosis left but the lunar horns as the splendid ornament of her brows!

The identity of history is equally intrinsic, the diversity equally obvious. There is at the surface infinite variety of things; at the centre there is simplicity of cause. How many are the acts of one man in which we recognize the same character! Observe the sources of our information in respect to the Greek genius. We have the civil history of that people, as Herodotus, Thucydides, Xenophon, and Plutarch have given it; a very sufficient account of what manner of persons they were, and what they did. We have the same national mind expressed for us again in their literature, in epic and lyric poems, drama, and philosophy; a very complete form. Then we have it once more in their architecture, a beauty as of temperance itself, limited to the straight line and the square, — a builded geometry. Then we have it once again in sculpture, the "tongue on the balance of expression," a multitude of forms in the utmost freedom of action, and never transgressing the ideal serenity; like votaries performing some religious dance before the gods, and, though in convulsive pain or mortal combat, never daring to break the figure and decorum of their dance. Thus, of the genius of one remarkable people, we have a fourfold representation: and to the senses what more unlike than an ode of Pindar, a marble centaur, the peristyle of the Parthenon, and the last actions of Phocion?

Every one must have observed faces and forms which, without any resembling feature, make a like impression on the beholder. A particular picture or copy of verses, if it do not awaken the same train of images, will yet superinduce the same sentiment as some wild mountain walk, although the resemblance is nowise obvious to the senses, but is occult and out of the reach of the understanding. Nature is an endless combination and repetition of a very few laws. She hums the old well-known air through innumerable variations.

Nature is full of a sublime family likeness throughout her works; and delights in startling us with resemblances in the most unexpected quarters. I have seen the head of an old sachem of the forest, which at once reminded the eye of a bald mountain summit, and the furrows of the brow suggested the strata of the rock. There are men whose manners have the same essential splendor as the simple and awful sculpture on the friezes of the Parthenon, and the remains of the earliest Greek art. And there are compositions of the same strain to be found in the books of all ages. What is Guido's Rospigliosi Aurora but a morning thought, as the horses in it are only a morning cloud. If any one will but take pains to observe the variety of actions to which he is equally inclined in certain moods of mind, and those to which he is averse, he will see how deep is the chain of affinity.

A painter told me that nobody could draw a tree without in some sort becoming a tree; or draw a child by studying the outlines of its form merely, — but, by watching for a time his motions and plays, the painter enters into his nature, and can then draw him at will in every attitude. So Roos "entered into the inmost nature of a sheep." I knew a draughtsman employed in a public survey, who found that he could not sketch the rocks until their geological structure was first explained to him. In a certain state of thought is the common origin of very diverse works. It is the spirit and not the fact that is identical. By a deeper apprehension, and not primarily by a painful acquisition of many manual skills, the artist attains the power of awakening other souls to a given activity.

It has been said, that "common souls pay with what they do; nobler souls with that which they are." And why? Because a profound nature awakens in us by its actions and words, by its very looks and manners, the same power and beauty that a gallery of sculpture, or of pictures, addresses.

Civil and natural history, the history of art and of literature, must be explained from individual history, or must remain words. There is nothing but is related to us, nothing that does not interest us, — kingdom, college, tree, horse, or iron shoe, the roots of all things are in man. Santa Croce and the Dome of St. Peter's are lame copies after a divine model. Strasburg Cathedral is a material counterpart of the soul of Erwin of Steinbach. The true poem is the poet's mind; the true ship is the ship-builder. In the man, could we lay him open, we should see the reason for the last flourish and tendril of his work; as every spine and tint in the sea-shell preexist in the secreting organs of the fish. The whole of heraldry and of chivalry is in courtesy. A man of fine manners shall pronounce your name with all the ornament that titles of nobility could ever add.

The trivial experience of every day is always verifying some old prediction to us, and converting into things the words and signs which we had heard and seen without heed. A lady, with whom I was riding in the forest, said to me, that the woods always seemed to her to wait, as if the genii who inhabit them suspended their deeds until the wayfarer has passed onward: a thought which poetry has celebrated in the dance of the fairies, which breaks off on the approach of human feet. The man who has seen the rising moon break out of the clouds at midnight has been present like an archangel at the creation of light and of the world. I remember one summer day, in the fields, my companion pointed out to me a broad cloud, which might extend a quarter of a mile parallel to the horizon, quite accurately in the form of a cherub as painted over churches, — a round block in the centre, which it was easy to animate with eyes and mouth, supported on either side by wide-stretched symmetrical wings. What appears once in the atmosphere may appear often, and it was undoubtedly the archetype of that familiar ornament. I have seen in the sky a chain of summer lightning which at once showed to me that the Greeks drew from nature when they painted the thunderbolt in the hand of Jove. I have seen a snow-drift along the sides of the stone wall which obviously gave the idea of the common architectural scroll to abut a tower.

By surrounding ourselves with the original circumstances, we invent anew the orders and the ornaments of architecture, as we see how each people merely decorated its primitive abodes. The Doric temple preserves the semblance of the wooden cabin in which the Dorian dwelt. The Chinese pagoda is plainly a Tartar tent. The Indian and Egyptian temples still betray the mounds and subterranean houses of their forefathers. "The custom of making houses and tombs in the living rock," says Heeren, in his Researches on the Ethiopians, "determined very naturally the principal character of the Nubian Egyptian architecture to the colossal form which it assumed. In these caverns, already prepared by nature, the eye was accustomed to dwell on huge shapes and masses, so that, when art came to the assistance of nature, it could not move on a small scale without degrading itself. What would statues of the usual size, or neat porches and wings, have been, associated with those gigantic halls before which only Colossi could sit as watchmen, or lean on the pillars of the interior?"

The Gothic church plainly originated in a rude adaptation of the forest trees with all their boughs to a festal or solemn arcade, as the bands about the cleft pillars still indicate the green withes that tied them. No one can walk in a road cut through pine woods, without being struck with the architectural appearance of the grove, especially in winter, when the bareness of all other trees shows the low arch of the Saxons. In the woods in a winter afternoon one will see as readily the origin of the stained glass window, with which the Gothic cathedrals are adorned, in the colors of the western sky seen through the bare and crossing branches of the forest. Nor can any lover of nature enter the old piles of Oxford and the English cathedrals, without feeling that the forest overpowered the mind of the builder, and that his chisel, his saw, and plane still reproduced its ferns, its spikes of flowers, its locust, elm, oak, pine, fir, and spruce.

The Gothic cathedral is a blossoming in stone subdued by the insatiable demand of harmony in man. The mountain of granite blooms into an eternal flower, with the lightness and delicate finish, as well as the aerial proportions and perspective, of vegetable beauty. In like manner, all public facts are to be individualized, all private facts are to be generalized. Then at once History becomes fluid and true, and Biography deep and sublime. As the Persian imitated in the slender shafts and capitals of his architecture the stem and flower of the lotus and palm, so the Persian court in its magnificent era never gave over the nomadism of its barbarous tribes, but travelled from Ecbatana, where the spring was spent, to Susa in summer, and to Babylon for the winter.

In the early history of Asia and Africa, Nomadism and Agriculture are the two antagonist facts. The geography of Asia and of Africa necessitated a nomadic life. But the nomads were the terror of all those whom the soil, or the advantages of a market, had induced to build towns. Agriculture, therefore, was a religious injunction, because of the perils of the state from nomadism. And in these late and civil countries of England and America, these propensities still fight out the old battle in the nation and in the individual. The nomads of Africa were constrained to wander by the attacks of the gad-fly, which drives the cattle mad, and so compels the tribe to emigrate in the rainy season, and to drive off the cattle to the higher sandy regions. The nomads of Asia follow the pasturage from month to month.

In America and Europe, the nomadism is of trade and curiosity; a progress, certainly, from the gad-fly of Astaboras to the Anglo and Italo-mania of Boston Bay. Sacred cities, to which a periodical religious pilgrimage was enjoined, or stringent laws and customs, tending to invigorate the national bond, were the check on the old rovers; and the cumulative values of long residence are the restraints on the itineracy of the present day. The antagonism of the two tendencies is not less active in individuals, as the love of adventure or the love of repose happens to predominate. A man of rude health and flowing spirits has the faculty of rapid domestication, lives in his wagon, and roams through all latitudes as easily as a Calmuc. At sea, or in the forest, or in the snow, he sleeps as warm, dines with as good appetite, and associates as happily, as beside his own chimneys. Or perhaps his facility is deeper seated, in the increased range of his faculties of observation, which yield him points of interest wherever fresh objects meet his eyes. The pastoral nations were needy and hungry to desperation; and this intellectual nomadism, in its excess, bankrupts the mind, through the dissipation of power on a miscellany of objects. The home-keeping wit, on the other hand, is that continence or content which finds all the elements of life in its own soil; and which has its own perils of monotony and deterioration, if not stimulated by foreign infusions.

Every thing the individual sees without him corresponds to his states of mind, and every thing is in turn intelligible to him, as his onward thinking leads him into the truth to which that fact or series belongs.

The primeval world, — the Fore-World, as the Germans say, — I can dive to it in myself as well as grope for it with researching fingers in catacombs, libraries, and the broken reliefs and torsos of ruined villas.

What is the foundation of that interest all men feel in Greek history, letters, art, and poetry, in all its periods, from the Heroic or Homeric age down to the domestic life of the Athenians and Spartans, four or five centuries later? What but this, that every man passes personally through a Grecian period. The Grecian state is the era of the bodily nature, the perfection of the senses, — of the spiritual nature unfolded in strict unity with the body.

In it existed those human forms which supplied the sculptor with his models of Hercules, Phoebus, and Jove; not like the forms abounding in the streets of modern cities, wherein the face is a confused blur of features, but composed of incorrupt, sharply defined, and symmetrical features, whose eye-sockets are so formed that it would be impossible for such eyes to squint, and take furtive glances on this side and on that, but they must turn the whole head. The manners of that period are plain and fierce.

The reverence exhibited is for personal qualities, courage, address, self-command, justice, strength, swiftness, a loud voice, a broad chest. Luxury and elegance are not known. A sparse population and want make every man his own valet, cook, butcher, and soldier, and the habit of supplying his own needs educates the body to wonderful performances. Such are the Agamemnon and Diomed of Homer, and not far different is the picture Xenophon gives of himself and his compatriots in the Retreat of the Ten Thousand. "After the army had crossed the river Teleboas in Armenia, there fell much snow, and the troops lay miserably on the ground covered with it. But Xenophon arose naked, and, taking an axe, began to split wood; whereupon others rose and did the like." Throughout his army exists a boundless liberty of speech. They quarrel for plunder, they wrangle with the generals on each new order, and Xenophon is as sharp-tongued as any, and sharper-tongued than most, and so gives as good as he gets. Who does not see that this is a gang of great boys, with such a code of honor and such lax discipline as great boys have?

The costly charm of the ancient tragedy, and indeed of all the old literature, is, that the persons speak simply, — speak as persons who have great good sense without knowing it, before yet the reflective habit has become the predominant habit of the mind. Our admiration of the antique is not admiration of the old, but of the natural. The Greeks are not reflective, but perfect in their senses and in their health, with the finest physical organization in the world. Adults acted with the simplicity and grace of children. They made vases, tragedies, and statues, such as healthy senses should,— — that is, in good taste. Such things have continued to be made in all ages, and are now, wherever a healthy physique exists; but, as a class, from their superior organization, they have surpassed all. They combine the energy of manhood with the engaging unconsciousness of childhood. The attraction of these manners is that they belong to man, and are known to every man in virtue of his being once a child; besides that there are always individuals who retain these characteristics.

A person of childlike genius and inborn energy is still a Greek, and revives our love of the Muse of Hellas. I admire the love of nature in the Philoctetes. In reading those fine apostrophes to sleep, to the stars, rocks, mountains, and waves, I feel time passing away as an ebbing sea. I feel the eternity of man, the identity of his thought. The Greek had, it seems, the same fellow-beings as I. The sun and moon, water and fire, met his heart precisely as they meet mine. Then the vaunted distinction between Greek and English, between Classic and Romantic schools, seems superficial and pedantic. When a thought of Plato becomes a thought to me, — when a truth that fired the soul of Pindar fires mine, time is no more. When I feel that we two meet in a perception, that our two souls are tinged with the same hue, and do, as it were, run into one, why should I measure degrees of latitude, why should I count Egyptian years?

The student interprets the age of chivalry by his own age of chivalry, and the days of maritime adventure and circumnavigation by quite parallel miniature experiences of his own. To the sacred history of the world, he has the same key. When the voice of a prophet out of the deeps of antiquity merely echoes to him a sentiment of his infancy, a prayer of his youth, he then pierces to the truth through all the confusion of tradition and the caricature of institutions.

Rare, extravagant spirits come by us at intervals, who disclose to us new facts in nature. I see that men of God have, from time to time, walked among men and made their commission felt in the heart and soul of the commonest hearer. Hence, evidently, the tripod, the priest, the priestess inspired by the divine afflatus.

Jesus astonishes and overpowers sensual people. They cannot unite him to history, or reconcile him with themselves. As they come to revere their intuitions and aspire to live holily, their own piety explains every fact, every word.

How easily these old worships of Moses, of Zoroaster, of Menu, of Socrates, domesticate themselves in the mind. I cannot find any antiquity in them. They are mine as much as theirs.

I have seen the first monks and anchorets without crossing seas or centuries. More than once some individual has appeared to me with such negligence of labor and such commanding contemplation, a haughty beneficiary, begging in the name of God, as made good to the nineteenth century Simeon the Stylite, the Thebais, and the first Capuchins.

The priestcraft of the East and West, of the Magian, Brahmin, Druid, and Inca, is expounded in the individual's private life. The cramping influence of a hard formalist on a young child in repressing his spirits and courage, paralyzing the understanding, and that without producing indignation, but only fear and obedience, and even much sympathy with the tyranny, — is a familiar fact explained to the child when he becomes a man, only by seeing that the oppressor of his youth is himself a child tyrannized over by those names and words and forms, of whose influence he was merely the organ to the youth. The fact teaches him how Belus was worshipped, and how the Pyramids were built, better than the discovery by Champollion of the names of all the workmen and the cost of every tile. He finds Assyria and the Mounds of Cholula at his door, and himself has laid the courses.

Again, in that protest which each considerate person makes against the superstition of his times, he repeats step for step the part of old reformers, and in the search after truth finds like them new perils to virtue. He learns again what moral vigor is needed to supply the girdle of a superstition. A great licentiousness treads on the heels of a reformation. How many times in the history of the world has the Luther of the day had to lament the decay of piety in his own household! "Doctor," said his wife to Martin Luther, one day, "how is it that, whilst subject to papacy, we prayed so often and with such fervor, whilst now we pray with the utmost coldness and very seldom?"

The advancing man discovers how deep a property he has in literature, — in all fable as well as in all history. He finds that the poet was no odd fellow who described strange and impossible situations, but that universal man wrote by his pen a confession true for one and true for all. His own secret biography he finds in lines wonderfully intelligible to him, dotted down before he was born. One after another he comes up in his private adventures with every fable of Aesop, of Homer, of Hafiz, of Ariosto, of Chaucer, of Scott, and verifies them with his own head and hands.

The beautiful fables of the Greeks, being proper creations of the imagination and not of the fancy, are universal verities. What a range of meanings and what perpetual pertinence has the story of Prometheus! Beside its primary value as the first chapter of the history of Europe, (the mythology thinly veiling authentic facts, the invention of the mechanic arts, and the migration of colonies,) it gives the history of religion with some closeness to the faith of later ages. Prometheus is the Jesus of the old mythology. He is the friend of man; stands between the unjust "justice" of the Eternal Father and the race of mortals, and readily suffers all things on their account. But where it departs from the Calvinistic Christianity, and exhibits him as the defier of Jove, it represents a state of mind which readily appears wherever the doctrine of Theism is taught in a crude, objective form, and which seems the self-defence of man against this untruth, namely, a discontent with the believed fact that a God exists, and a feeling that the obligation of reverence is onerous. It would steal, if it could, the fire of the Creator, and live apart from him, and independent of him. The Prometheus Vinctus is the romance of skepticism. Not less true to all time are the details of that stately apologue. Apollo kept the flocks of Admetus, said the poets. When the gods come among men, they are not known. Jesus was not; Socrates and Shakspeare were not.

Antaeus was suffocated by the gripe of Hercules, but every time he touched his mother earth, his strength was renewed. Man is the broken giant, and, in all his weakness, both his body and his mind are invigorated by habits of conversation with nature. The power of music, the power of poetry to unfix, and, as it were, clap wings to solid nature, interprets the riddle of Orpheus. The philosophical perception of identity through endless mutations of form makes him know the Proteus. What else am I who laughed or wept yesterday, who slept last night like a corpse, and this morning stood and ran? And what see I on any side but the transmigrations of Proteus? I can symbolize my thought by using the name of any creature, of any fact, because every creature is man agent or patient. Tantalus is but a name for you and me. Tantalus means the impossibility of drinking the waters of thought which are always gleaming and waving within sight of the soul.

The transmigration of souls is no fable. I would it were; but men and women are only half human. Every animal of the barn-yard, the field, and the forest, of the earth and of the waters that are under the earth, has contrived to get a footing and to leave the print of its features and form in some one or other of these upright, heaven-facing speakers. Ah! brother, stop the ebb of thy soul, — ebbing downward into the forms into whose habits thou hast now for many years slid. As near and proper to us is also that old fable of the Sphinx, who was said to sit in the road-side and put riddles to every passenger. If the man could not answer, she swallowed him alive. If he could solve the riddle, the Sphinx was slain. What is our life but an endless flight of winged facts or events! In splendid variety these changes come, all putting questions to the human spirit. Those men who cannot answer by a superior wisdom these facts or questions of time, serve them. Facts encumber them, tyrannize over them, and make the men of routine the men of sense, in whom a literal obedience to facts has extinguished every spark of that light by which man is truly man. But if the man is true to his better instincts or sentiments, and refuses the dominion of facts, as one that comes of a higher race, remains fast by the soul and sees the principle, then the facts fall aptly and supple into their places; they know their master, and the meanest of them glorifies him.

See in Goethe's Helena the same desire that every word should be a thing. These figures, he would say, these Chirons, Griffins, Phorkyas, Helen, and Leda, are somewhat, and do exert a specific influence on the mind. So far then are they eternal entities, as real to-day as in the first Olympiad. Much revolving them, he writes out freely his humor, and gives them body tohis own imagination. And although that poem be as vague and fantastic as a dream, yet is it much more attractive than the more regular dramatic pieces of the same author, for the reason that it operates a wonderful relief to the mind from the routine of customary images, — awakens the reader's invention and fancy by the wild freedom of the design, and by the unceasing succession of brisk shocks of surprise.

The universal nature, too strong for the petty nature of the bard, sits on his neck and writes through his hand; so that when he seems to vent a mere caprice and wild romance, the issue is an exact allegory. Hence Plato said that "poets utter great and wise things which they do not themselves understand." All the fictions of the Middle Age explain themselves as a masked or frolic expression of that which in grave earnest the mind of that period toiled to achieve. Magic, and all that is ascribed to it, is a deep presentiment of the powers of science. The shoes of swiftness, the sword of sharpness, the power of subduing the elements, of using the secret virtues of minerals, of understanding the voices of birds, are the obscure efforts of the mind in a right direction. The preternatural prowess of the hero, the gift of perpetual youth, and the like, are alike the endeavour of the human spirit "to bend the shows of things to the desires of the mind."

In Perceforest and Amadis de Gaul, a garland and a rose bloom on the head of her who is faithful, and fade on the brow of the inconstant. In the story of the Boy and the Mantle, even a mature reader may be surprised with a glow of virtuous pleasure at the triumph of the gentle Genelas; and, indeed, all the postulates of elfin annals, — that the fairies do not like to be named; that their gifts are capricious and not to be trusted; that who seeks a treasure must not speak; and the like, — I find true in Concord, however they might be in Cornwall or Bretagne.

Is it otherwise in the newest romance? I read the Bride of Lammermoor. Sir William Ashton is a mask for a vulgar temptation, Ravenswood Castle a fine name for proud poverty, and the foreign mission of state only a Bunyan disguise for honest industry. We may all shoot a wild bull that would toss the good and beautiful, by fighting down the unjust and sensual. Lucy Ashton is another name for fidelity, which is always beautiful and always liable to calamity in this world.

But along with the civil and metaphysical history of man, another history goes daily forward, — that of the external world, — in which he is not less strictly implicated. He is the compend of time; he is also the correlative of nature. His power consists in the multitude of his affinities, in the fact that his life is intertwined with the whole chain of organic and inorganic being. In old Rome the public roads beginning at the Forum proceeded north, south, east, west, to the centre of every province of the empire, making each market-town of Persia, Spain, and Britain pervious to the soldiers of the capital: so out of the human heart go, as it were, highways to the heart of every object in nature, to reduce it under the dominion of man. A man is a bundle of relations, a knot of roots, whose flower and fruitage is the world. His faculties refer to natures out of him, and predict the world he is to inhabit, as the fins of the fish foreshow that water exists, or the wings of an eagle in the egg presuppose air. He cannot live without a world. Put Napoleon in an island prison, let his faculties find no men to act on, no Alps to climb, no stake to play for, and he would beat the air and appear stupid. Transport him to large countries, dense population, complex interests, and antagonist power, and you shall see that the man Napoleon, bounded, that is, by such a profile and outline, is not the virtual Napoleon. This is but Talbot's shadow;

"His substance is not here:

For what you see is but the smallest part

And least proportion of humanity;

But were the whole frame here,

It is of such a spacious, lofty pitch,

Your roof were not sufficient to contain it."

Henry VI

Columbus needs a planet to shape his course upon. Newton and Laplace need myriads of ages and thick-strewn celestial areas. One may say a gravitating solar system is already prophesied in the nature of Newton's mind. Not less does the brain of Davy or of Gay-Lussac, from childhood exploring the affinities and repulsions of particles, anticipate the laws of organization. Does not the eye of the human embryo predict the light? the ear of Handel predict the witchcraft of harmonic sound? Do not the constructive fingers of Watt, Fulton, Whittemore, Arkwright, predict the fusible, hard, and temperable texture of metals, the properties of stone, water, and wood? Do not the lovely attributes of the maiden child predict the refinements and decorations of civil society? Here also we are reminded of the action of man on man. A mind might ponder its thought for ages, and not gain so much self-knowledge as the passion of love shall teach it in a day. Who knows himself before he has been thrilled with indignation at an outrage, or has heard an eloquent tongue, or has shared the throb of thousands in a national exultation or alarm? No man can antedate his experience, or guess what faculty or feeling a new object shall unlock, any more than he can draw to-day the face of a person whom he shall see to-morrow for the first time.

I will not now go behind the general statement to explore the reason of this correspondency. Let it suffice that in the light of these two facts, namely, that the mind is One, and that nature is its correlative, history is to be read and written.

Thus in all ways does the soul concentrate and reproduce its treasures for each pupil. He, too, shall pass through the whole cycle of experience. He shall collect into a focus the rays of nature. History no longer shall be a dull book. It shall walk incarnate in every just and wise man. You shall not tell me by languages and titles a catalogue of the volumes you have read. You shall make me feel what periods you have lived. A man shall be the Temple of Fame. He shall walk, as the poets have described that goddess, in a robe painted all over with wonderful events and experiences; — his own form and features by their exalted intelligence shall be that variegated vest. I shall find in him the Foreworld; in his childhood the Age of Gold; the Apples of Knowledge; the Argonautic Expedition; the calling of Abraham; the building of the Temple; the Advent of Christ; Dark Ages; the Revival of Letters; the Reformation; the discovery of new lands; the opening of new sciences, and new regions in man. He shall be the priest of Pan, and bring with him into humble cottages the blessing of the morning stars and all the recorded benefits of heaven and earth.

Is there somewhat overweening in this claim? Then I reject all I have written, for what is the use of pretending to know what we know not? But it is the fault of our rhetoric that we cannot strongly state one fact without seeming to belie some other. I hold our actual knowledge very cheap. Hear the rats in the wall, see the lizard on the fence, the fungus under foot, the lichen on the log. What do I know sympathetically, morally, of either of these worlds of life? As old as the Caucasian man, — perhaps older, — these creatures have kept their counsel beside him, and there is no record of any word or sign that has passed from one to the other. What connection do the books show between the fifty or sixty chemical elements, and the historical eras? Nay, what does history yet record of the metaphysical annals of man? What light does it shed on those mysteries which we hide under the names Death and Immortality? Yet every history should be written in a wisdom which divined the range of our affinities and looked at facts as symbols. I am ashamed to see what a shallow village tale our so-called History is. How many times we must say Rome, and Paris, and Constantinople! What does Rome know of rat and lizard? What are Olympiads and Consulates to these neighbouring systems of being? Nay, what food or experience or succour have they for the Esquimaux seal-hunter, for the Kanaka in his canoe, for the fisherman, the stevedore, the porter?

Broader and deeper we must write our annals, — from an ethical reformation, from an influx of the ever new, ever sanative conscience, — if we would trulier express our central and wide-related nature, instead of this old chronology of selfishness and pride to which we have too long lent our eyes. Already that day exists for us, shines in on us at unawares, but the path of science and of letters is not the way into nature. The idiot, the Indian, the child, and unschooled farmer's boy, stand nearer to the light by which nature is to be read, than the dissector or the antiquary.

5

Fernand Braudel Mediterranean Studies Annales School

Fernand Braudel is seen by many as having been the greatest historian of the twentieth century-his influence on the study of history since the publication of his first major work fifty years ago has been remarkably pervasive.

He was born in August 1902 into a family of peasant backgound in Lorraine, Northeastern France. He was sickly as a child and, because of this, was raised during his early years in the contryside at his grandmother's small farm. The family moved to Paris in 1908 where his father had obtained a teaching post in mathematics. After completing his history education at the Sorbonne in Paris, where he was particularly attracted to economic and social history and to the study of ancient Greece. Braudel spent 10 years after 1923 teaching in high schools in Algeria, then a French colony.

His true intellectual formation began in Algeria where he decided that wished to enter upon an academic career in history-this required that he work to obtain a Doctoral qualification. He turned from studying the past of Lorraine, (which he came to consider to be too full of political problems that would grate upon his fiery French nationalism), to that of Spain, and he began to contemplate a traditional historical thesis on the Mediterranean policy of Philip II between 1559 and 1574; by 1927 he was publishing reviews of books on Spanish history.

Braudel, by this time, had been greatly impressed by the new approach to history of Lucien Febvre, based on the science of human geography, as exemplified in a book written in 1913 but not published until 1922, La Terre et l'évolution humaine, translated as A Geographical Introduction to History (London, 1932). Braudel read the book in 1924. As usual his approach was cautious: it was three years before he began to write to Febvre, and their close personal friendship did not begin for another ten years. Meanwhile, in his first reply to Braudel, Febvre had planted a serious doubt about Braudel's subject of research:

Philip II and the Mediterranean, a good subject. But why not the Mediterranean and Philip II? A much larger subject. For between these two protagonists, Philip and the middle sea, the division is not equal.

In 1929 Lucien Febvre and Marc Bloch, who were then professors based at Strasbourg, established a journal called "Annals of economic and social history" (Annales d'histoire économique et sociale). As a Journal Annales was intended to promote a new and more open approach to history in a provocatively colloquial style, an approach defined mostly by its search for "a larger and a more human history", by its denial of all historical barriers and by its rejection of the traditional history of politics and government in favour of a deeper analysis of social and economic forces with the goal of departing from traditional political and military history to explore economic and social history, and to focus more on a long term perspective.

Braudel had become a successful schoolteacher and was recognised as an expert in his chosen area. In 1932 he returned to Paris and was nominated to a series of more and more prestigious lycées; in 1933 he married one of his earliest pupils from Algiers. In 1935 he made a decision that was to change his life: he accepted the offer of a five-year secondment to the new university being established with French help at São Paolo, Brazil. In the winter Braudel returned to Europe and worked in the archives of the great Mediterranean trading cities, such as Venice and Dubrovnik (Ragusa). He was an innovative researcher in two respects, conceptual and practical. He made the move from government archives to commercial archives, and by chance he invented the 'microfilming' of documentation, which he used in order to copy two or three thousand documents a day, to be read during the university year in Brazil.

Braudel afterwards said that it was whilst in Brazil that he became "intelligent"-it is possible that inherent challenges to his own background and cultural heritage posed by living in a non European society changed his outlook in important ways.

In 1937 he was offered, and he accepted, a post with a much lower salary at the main research centre in Paris, the École Pratique des Hautes Études, in one of the two nonscientific sections, the IVe Section (historical and philological sciences).

Lucien Febvre, who was now employed a professor of history at Collège de France, visited South America in 1937. He gave a series of lectures in Buenos Aires and, arising out of the earlier contacts between himself and Braudel, arrangements were made by Braudel for Febvre to also spend some time in Bahia, Rio de Janiero and São Paulo in Brazil. During this visit and the subsequent two-week voyage where Braudel and his wife travelled home from Brazil-with Lucien Febvre being a fellow passenger-the two historians became close friends.

Febvre became something of an intellectual adviser and confidant to Braudel, who, in his new work at the École Pratique des Hautes Études attempted to depart from traditional event-based historiography to focus more on economic and social history in a long-term perspective.

Braudel enrolled in the French army in 1939 and, following the defeat of his country, was captured by the Germans in 1940. He took advantage of his captivity to attempt to write what would become his masterwork *The Mediterranean and the Mediterranean World in the Age of Philip II*. During several years, as a prisoner in Germany, he wrote on schoolboy booklets with only a very few books to which he could make some reference, (even these few books were denied him when his place captivity was changed from Mainz to near Lübeck in 1942!). Braudel shared his captivity with some twenty other prisoners and often had only a corner of a table, or even just a plank, to lean his work upon.

Despite these circumstances he constructed a work that combined a vast chronological and historical sweep with a mass of minute details, covering the entire Mediterranean world from the Renaissance to the sixteenth century. He managed this extraordinary feat by tapping into the vast knowledge he had accumulated over years of research. He sent the filled booklets to Lucien Febvre after one another. By the end of the war the work was substantiually finished as a first draft, it was rewritten, with critical advice supplied by Febvre, until it was finally presented in 1947 as a thesis of over one thousand pages.

In these times Braudel hoped for a professoral position at the University of Paris but was unsuccessful. He was, however, awarded a Doctorate on the basis of this thesis.

The Mediterranean and the Mediterranean World in the Age of Philip II, was first published in 1949 under its French title *La Méditerranée et le monde méditerranéen à l'époque de Philippe II*; with a second revised and reorganised edition being published in 1966, in preparation for the American edition of 1973. It made Braudel an international reputation. The rising generation of historical scholars were brought up to believe in the words of its preface: the old history of events was indeed dead, "the action of a few princes and rich men, the trivia of the past, bearing little relation to the slow and powerful march of history... those statesmen were, despite their illusions, more acted upon than actors."

In their place Braudel offered not "the traditional geographical introduction to history that often figures to so little purpose at the beginning of so many books, with its description of the mineral deposits, types of agriculture and typical flora, briefly listed and never mentioned again, as if the flowers did not come back every spring, the flocks of sheep migrate every year, or the ships sail on a real sea that changes with the seasons," but a whole new way of looking at the past, in which the historian re-created a lost reality through a feat of historical imagination based on detailed knowledge of the habits and techniques of the ploughman, the shepherd, the potter, and the weaver, the skills of the vintage and the olive press, the milling of corn, the keeping of records of bills of lading, tides and winds.

It began to seem as important for a historian to be able to ride a horse or sail a ship as to sit in a library. Only the third section of Braudel's book returned to the history of events, "surface disturbances, crests of foam that the tides of history carry on their strong backs." Braudel taught us to see that historical time was divided into three forms of movement—geographical time, social time, and individual time—but that beyond all this the past was a unity and a reality. All these movements belonged together- "history can do more than study walled gardens"-this was the ultimate expression of the intellectual ambitions of the Annales school.

Braudel's picture invites us to consider the Mediterranean in its broadest geographical context, inclusive of the great civilisations of Iraq and Egypt, the steppes of Russia, the forests of Germany, and the deserts of the Sahara. For him Mediterranean history is an aspect of world history. Within the context of human history he emphasises two themes-Technology and Exchange. Human history is a history of technological mastery and the development of the skills basic to ancient civilisation: fire and water technology, pottery, weaving, metalworking, seafaring and finally writing. This emphasis on the physical realities of early civilisations brings out the actual quality of life with a vividness that no amount of reading other books can achieve. As to the importance of exchange, especially long-distance exchange: "Our sea was from the very dawn of its protohistory a witness to those imbalances productive of exchange which would set the rhythm of its entire life." It is imbalance that creates exchange and therefore leads to progress. These two ideas, first formulated in *The Mediterranean and the Mediterranean World in the Age of Philip II* and subsequently explored in depth in for the preindustrial world in *Civilization and Capitalism*, are applied in the *Memory and the Mediterranean* to the ancient Mediterranean with magnificent effect.

Memory and the Mediterranean begins with the history of the Mediterranean seabed itself-the layers of clay, sand, and limestone from which the Egyptians carved their ancient tombs and with which the megalithic temples in Malta were built. What follows is the epic story of how the Phoenicians, the Etruscans, the Greeks and Romans, and the great river civilizations of Mesopotamia and Egypt struggled and thrived in this demanding but gloriously beautiful world bordered and shaped by the Mediterranean.

Lucien Febvre died in 1956, and Braudel inherited the direction of both the "VIe section de l'Ecole pratique des hautes études" and the journal Annales. In the first institution he created and fostered one of the most extraordinary collections of talent in the twentieth century through his appointments: to mention only the most famous of his colleagues, they included the historians Georges Duby, Jacques Le Goff, Emmanuel Le Roy Ladurie and Maurice Aymard; the philosophers Roland Barthes and Michel Foucault; the psychologists Jacques Lacan and Georges Devereux; the sociologist Pierre Bourdieu; the anthropologist Claude Lévi-Strauss; and the classical scholars Jean-Pierre Vernant and Pierre Vidal-Naquet. Braudel worked hard to create a separate institution or building where all his colleagues could work together, and where a succession of foreign visitors could be invited as associate professors; this idea, begun about 1958, did not achieve physical shape until the opening of the Maison des Sciences de l'Homme in 1970.

The new history of the sixties turned away from the factual certainties of economic and descriptive social history, and explored the "history of mentalities." It held that the historical world was created out of perceptions, not out of events, and we needed to recognise that the whole of history was a construct of human impressions.

Braudel's reply to this development was long in coming and remains incomplete; it was his last great projected work, The Identity of France. Three volumes were published before his death, comprising the first two parts on geography and demography and economy: these were for him traditional territory. With the third and fourth he would be entering new territory by writing about the state, culture, and society, and in the fourth about "France outside France."

In these volumes Braudel took the view that the peasant was the key to the history of France, and a true history of mentalities could only be written in the longue durée and from a long perspective.

In 1968 Braudel was giving a lecture series in Chicago when he was recalled to face—at the age of sixty-two—the revolutionary student movement. Like many radical professors he was sympathetic but uncomprehending of the anarchic streak in youthful protest; his interventions were paternalistic and not well received, and later he condemned the revolution because it made people less rather than more happy.

More dangerous still for Braudel was the reaction, which brought the conservatives under Pompidou to power, and which placed the blame, not on their own resistance to change, but on those who had tried to encourage change. Had not the "events" of 1968 proved the importance of the history of events? Where now was the long perspective? Conservatives claimed that either the new history (whatever it was) was responsible for the "events," or it was disproved by them. The claim was successful in blocking Braudel's access to government circles almost for the first time in his career.

Fernand Braudel retired in 1972 and, after more than ten years of retirement, died in November 1985 at Châteauvallon, on the Côte d'Azur, in Southern France.

6

Jakob Burckhardt Renaissance—Cultural History

Jakob Burckhardt, later famous as a Renaissance Cultural historian, was born in Basel, where his father was a minister in the Reformed church, in May 1818. He himself embarked upon a theological course in 1837 but changed to historical studies being educated therein at the universities of Basel and Berlin (1839-43).

Whilst at Berlin he attended lectures delivered by Leopold von Ranke. He also spent some of 1841 at Bonn where he was influenced by the Art Historian Franz Kugler.

With the exception of three years (1855-58), during which he taught at the Zürich Polytechnic Institute, he spent the following half century (1843-93) as lecturer and, (from 1858), as professor of the history of art and civilization at the University of Basel. It was in this later period that Burckhardt lost his faith but did not advertise this out of respect for his pious family.

Burckhardt is known to posterity as the father of cultural history. While earlier historians had concentrated on political and military history, Burckhardt discussed the total life of the people, including religion, art and literature. He wrote "And all things are sources-not only books, but the whole of life and every kind of spiritual manifestation." At the age of nineteen Burckhardt had made a trip to into the Italian peninsula and subsequently maintained that he had found there "a core of commitment around which his fantasies could crystalise." His later career as an historian was to reflect this early fascination with aspects of the history of the Italian peninsula.

Burckhardt's first important work was The Age of Constantine the Great (1852; trans. 1949), a study of the Roman Empire in the 4th century AD, in which he analyzed the decay of classical civilization and the triumph of Christianity.

"What was intended was not a history of the life and death of Constantine, nor yet an encyclopedia of all worth-while information pertaining to his period. Rather were the significant and essential characteristics of the contemporary world to be outlined and shaped into a perspicious view of the world."

Burckhardt's Age of Constantine was followed by The Cicerone: A Guide to the Works of Art in Italy (1855; trans. 1873), which became extremely popular, The Civilization of the Renaissance in Italy (1860; trans. 1878), his most famous work, and the History of the Renaissance in Italy (1867).

It is The Civilization of the Renaissance in Italy on which his reputation chiefly rests. In this work Burckhardt traced the cultural patterns of transition from the medieval period to the awakening of the modern spirit and creativity of the Renaissance. He saw the transition as one from a society in which people were primarily members of a class or community to a society that idealized the self-conscious individual.

The term Renaissance suggesting a re-birth of individualistic accomplishment after a long intermission since the Classical Age. The term itself had been coined in this regard by the French historian Jules Michelet circa 1855-8.

A much quoted passage from The Civilization of the Renaissance in Italy depicts a dramatic alteration in the outlook of many persons:-

"both sides of human consciousness-the side turned to the world and that turned inward-lay, as it were, beneath a common veil, dreaming or half awake. The veil was woven of faith, childlike prejudices, and illusion; seen through it, world and history appeared in strange hues; man recognized himself only as a member of a race, a nation, a party, a corporation, a family, or in some other general category. It was in Italy that this veil first melted into thin air, and awakened an objective perception and treatment of the state and all things of this world in general; but by its side, and with full power, there also arose the subjective; man becomes a self-aware individual and recognises himself as such." At the time Burkhardt wrote The Civilization of the Renaissance in Italy there was little in the way of accepted knowledge about what we today regard as "the Renaissance."

His work was accepted as demonstrating that the shift from corporate medieval society to the modern spirit occurred in "Renaissance" Italy in the 14th and 15th century and, to a great extent, moulded the modern concept of the European Renaissance as a necessary and positive break with the outlook and society that preceded it.

Burckhardt's work remains one of the most important on the subject of the Renaissance. The Dutch historian Johan Huizinga called it, "that transcendent masterpiece." The first three parts of the book are held to be especially good-readable and interesting, profound and philosophical.

Whilst certain people flourished as individuals during the Renaissance and, in cases, were responsible for artistic, literary or scientific achievements that are recognised as representing advances in their fields it was often the case that other people were somewhat socially displaced by the advent of the new, individualistic, milieu and found it to be something they were effectively "compelled to endure."

The new tendency to cultivate an individualistic personality and to seek to achieve, as an individual, resulted in many kinds of self-expression some of them aggressive. It was in these times that the Italian peninsula featured a number of "tyrant rulers" and bands of often ill disciplined mercenary soldiers known as *condottieri* who participated in diverse local wars contested between the rulers of Italian states.

It often happened that an individuals desire to achieve greatness as a ruler or to become famous as a *condottieri* tended to disrupt the chances of a peaceful existence being enjoyed many other persons. Several historians had opportunity to record "striking and terrible" enterprises that were embarked upon because of a "burning desire to do something great and memorable."

Individuality reached its zenith, according to Burckhardt, in the Renaissance humanists, who turned their backs on Christianity, revered the ancients, and tried to live and write like the ancients.

Similarly in the visual arts for most of the next three hundred years, the great artistic personalities of the sixteenth centuries [Michelangelo, Leonardo, Raphael, Titian] loomed so large that their predecessors seemed to belong to a forgotten era. When they were finally rediscovered, people still acknowledged the high Renaissance as the turning point by referring to all painters before Raphael as 'the Primitives.'

Burckhardt established the thesis that Renaissance art represented a break with the past, wherein representation became scientific, realistic, individualistic and humane; the visual analogue to the birth of the modern sensibility, one which left behind the superstitious mindset of the Dark Ages.

With qualifications, that thesis remains more or less the rule in the present, and is one reason that museums, such as the Uffizi in Florence, generally display works of art chronologically: so multitudes of students and aficionados can follow, with their own eyes, the elevation of art from its Gothic, one dimensional, iconic forms to its Renaissance, three dimensional, individualistic representations.

If qualified historians no longer speak of the Dark Ages, they still refer to the period before the fourteenth century as the Middle Ages or the Mediaeval Era-with most of the pejorative connotations of the Dark Ages still implied. They echo the writers and historians of the early Renaissance, of Dante and Petrarch and Alberti, who argued that the Renaissance generation broke with the superstitions of the past, recovered the best of the Classical world, and ushered in a new dawn of modernity.

Despite his interest in the dramatic, often extravagantly violent or sensual, Renaissance era Burckhardt himself lived a life of quiet routine in Basel. He refused many flattering invitations to take up academic appointments in other Universities and also declined invitations to give lectures. He showed no particular enthusiasm for the encouragements that were sometimes offered by family or friends that he enter into married life.

"To each eye, perhaps, the outlines of a great civilization present a different picture. In the wide ocean upon which we venture, the possible ways and directions are many; and the same studies which have served for my work might easily, in other hands, not only receive a wholly different treatment and application, but lead to essentially different conclusions."

Jacob Burckhardt retired from teaching in 1893 and died in Basel August 1897.

7

Thomas Carlyle The French Revolution, A History

Thomas Carlyle was born in December 1795 at Ecclefechan in southern Scotland as the eldest of an eventual nine children with which the second marriage of a James Carlyle was blessed. This James Carlyle earned his living as a stonemason but later farmed on a small scale.

The family were raised within a strict but affectionate Calvinist religious tradition and, as Thomas showed a great aptitude for learning at Annandale grammar school, his father decided to support his being educated as a divinity student at the University of Edinburgh.

At Edinburgh Carlyle distinguished himself in Mathematics and was offered a fairly well paid teaching position at Annan in 1814 that prompted him to 'temporarily' leave aside his intentions to become a minister of religion. Over the immediately subsequent years Carlyle continued in his intention to eventually become a minister but in the meantime taught Mathematics at Annan and then Kirkcaldy. This later posting brought Carlyle into association, and close friendship, with Edward Irving. Irving had a small personal library from which Carlyle was able to read books concerning history and French literature. Carlyle ålso considered entering into marriage with a Margaret Gordon but her friends used their influence against such an engagement.

Carlyle was dissatisfied with teaching as a profession and in 1818, when Irving left Annan, Carlyle resigned and moved to Edinburgh. Carlyle now entered a period of economic privation where he briefly attempted to study law and then became a private tutor whilst also writing articles for the Edinburgh Encyclopedia. These were also months of spiritual crisis from which Carlyle emerged with a faith that led him approach the world with a measure indignation and defiance. In June 1821, in Leith Walk, Edinburgh, he had experienced a striking spiritual rebirth. Put briefly and prosaically, it consisted in a sudden clearing away of doubts as to the beneficent organization of the universe; a semi-mystical conviction that he was free to think and work, and that honest effort and striving would not be thwarted by what he called the "Everlasting No."

During these times Carlyle taught himself the German language building on an introductory course taken whilst at Edinburgh University and was able to participate in the rising tendency for people widely in Europe to recognise that there were several important new intellectual currents arising out of German thought. He also made an intensive study of German literature and was particularly drawn to the works of Johann Wolfgang von Goethe.

Through his friendship with Irving Carlyle gained a well paid tutorship that lasted from January 1822 to July 1824. He nonetheless found the time to prepare a translation of Goethe's Wilhelm Meisters Lehrjahre (1796) that was published as Wilhelm Meister's Apprenticeship in 1824. Carlyle also wrote a Life of Schiller which appeared first in serial form in 1823-4 in the London Magazine and was published as a book in 1825.

Carlyle felt that it might be possible for him to launch his talents on a broader stage and, after travels in London, decided that his best option was to settle back in his native district where he could live simply and still achieve a great deal in the line of interpreting German thought for English consumption. He also wrote for the Edinburgh Review, a literary periodical.

In 1826 Carlyle married Jane Baillie Welsh, whom he had first met through his friend Irving in 1821. Miss Welsh was a talented writer who, at 25, was some six years younger than Carlyle.

Miss Welsh had inherited property from her father, a doctor, in 1819 yet at the time of their marriage Miss Welsh and Carlyle agreed that Miss Welsh's mother should benefit from the income of the Welsh family property for her lifetime. Carlyle was personally intent on trying to develop his talents as a principled, rather than popular, writer moreso than on gaining a greater level of income. The young couple embarked on life together with some expectation of being obliged to live frugally and possibly well below the level of material security in which Miss Welsh had been raised.

The couple lived modestly in Edinburgh where they attracted the favourable notice of literary society. Carlyle interested himself in transcendentalism and mysticism. He was unsuccessful in an attempt to gain a professorship at St. Andrews although his application had received the support of influential friends.

After 1828 the Carlyles lived in a modest house located on a farm in Craigenputtock, Scotland, that was owned by Mrs. Welsh. Here Carlyle wrote a philosophical satire, Sartor Resartus (The Tailor Retailored), which despite the "passion" that he had put into it was found to be difficult to profitably place with a publisher.

In late 1831 and into 1832 the Carlyles attempted to establish themselves in London. Despite gaining introductions to some personalities in the London literary scene, including John Stuart Mill, the Carlyle's were unable to see their way to actually settling down to live there. The Carlyle's finances were assisted in these difficult times by loans from Lord Jeffrey the editor of the Edinburgh Review.

The couple returned to Craigenputtock in 1832 and Carlyle began to make more headway in Edinburgh literary circles. He found inspiration amidst the contents of the Advocate's Library for his celebrated work "Diamond Necklace." Carlyle's satire "Sartor Resartus" was published between 1833 and 1834 in Fraser's Magazine but was not particularly well received by its readership.

It was in these times that Carlyle wrote some of his most distinguished essays and also established what proved to be a lifelong friendship with the American essayist Ralph Waldo Emerson following Emerson's visit of August 1833 to him in Scotland. Carlyle also began to study the history of the French Revolution.

Following on from this mixed success in Scotland the Carlyles decided to again try their luck in the English capital, this move being decided in large part by the readier availability of resources for historical study there.

In the summer of 1834 the Carlyles moved to the Chelsea, London, and this time Thomas Carlyle had more success as a man of letters becoming accepted in the literary circle that included the essayists Leigh Hunt and John Stuart Mill.

In London Carlyle's friendship with Mill was of practical benefit in that Mill had a collection of books relating to the French Revolution that were made available to Carlyle. When Carlyle had finished the manuscript of the first volume he lent it to Mill who happened to leave it at the house of a lady friend. The manuscript was subsequently regarded by an illiterate housekeeper to be a pile of waste paper, and was as such consumed by flames whilst at this house. Although Mill offered to pay a fairly handsome amount to Carlyle by way of compensation Carlyle who was most reluctant to take any of Mill's money was eventually persuaded into accepting a lesser sum that was, in his opinion, broadly appropriate to the loss of time that had been incurred.

It was in January 1837 that Carlyle finished his two volume "The French Revolution, A History." This study concentrated on the oppression of the poor, and was immediately successful upon its publication in that same year. Carlyle's "French Revolution" benefited by being favourably reviewed by Mill and by Thackeray. It is seen as not being fully in line with stricter modern standards of factual accuracy yet as being enhanced by the insight, sympathy and intuition about human life that Carlyle was able to portray upon a solid historical framework.

Following on from the publication of his work on the French Revolution Carlyle was sought after to give series of Lectures from which he earned a welcome income from 1837-41.

One of these series of lectures was published, in 1841, as On Heroes, Hero-Worship, and the Heroic in History. The central theme of this publication maintained that world civilization had developed as it had primarily because of the activities of heroes. This theme being different in tenor from the quasi-philosophic intuitions about the human condition, and its vagaries, that had featured strongly in his earlier work about the revolution in France.

Carlyle was by this time firmly established as one of the leading literary and intellectual figures in the London of the day. Amongst his later historical works are Life and Letters of Oliver Cromwell (1845) and his celebrated multi volume History of Frederick the Great that was published between 1858 and 1865. This later work was based on extensive researches that included a number of trips to Germany to survey battlefields and to obtain more source materials. The final work benefits from Carlyle's literary talents as well as from his extensive scholarship.

In 1865 Carlyle was elected to the rectorship of the University of Edinburgh. He was awarded the Prussian Order of Merit in 1874 due to the respect with which his History of Frederick the Great was regarded. In this same year Carlyle was offered a knighthood and pension by the British prime minister Disraeli but these were courteously declined.

Upon Carlyle's death in February 1881 it was made possible for his remains to be interred in Westminster Abbey but his wish to be buried beside his parents in Ecclefechan was respected.

Carlyle left property to fund bursaries at Edinburgh University and left his library to Harvard University.

8

Niall Ferguson

VIRTUAL HISTORY

The Pity of War

Niall Ferguson (pronounced "Neal") was born in Glasgow in April 1964 and was educated at Glasgow Academy.

As an adolescent in the 1970s, he felt that he wanted to write books but did not know what kind. He remembers that the decision turned on comparing Hamlet with the Thirty Years War.

He was writing essays about both of them, and loving both of them. But he began to think that Hamlet was really just one text, and therefore rather limited, whereas, he discovered with astonishment, Glasgow University's library contained hundreds of books on the Thirty Years War. (As he says, he seems not to have known how much literary criticism there was in the world.) One work of history he devoured with special excitement was Friedrich von Schiller's account of the Thirty Years War, a great 18th-century German's stirring reprisal of his country's 17th-century trauma. That glimpse of the historian's landscape as a place of infinite possibilities set Niall Ferguson on his way and also hinted at the particular themes of his career. Since he began by studying a war that took place mainly in Germany, it is not entirely surprising that most of his subsequent work has taken him to Germany or somewhere in the neighbourhood.

His accomplishments might suggest he has been hurtling toward success for two straight decades, but for a while he veered foolishly off course. At 17, when he arrived as a scholarship student at Magdalen College, he somehow forgot why he was there. He threw himself into a hectic social life, the Oxford Union, student theatre, anything except his studies. Soon he was so inadequate a student that (he now realizes) almost any other university in the world would have withdrawn his scholarship and sent him packing. But, as he says, Oxford forgives and Oxford forgets, if you prove yourself in the end.

Toward the close of his second year, as he was smoking a hookah on stage while dressed as the caterpillar in a production of Alice in Wonderland, he asked himself: What the hell am I doing here? More or less instantly, he turned into the scholar that nature had always intended him to be. He went into the library and, in a sense, never came out.

He does not lack a private life (he and his journalist wife, Sue Douglas, have three children) but the habit of deep research has remained with him ever since he ended his adolescence with his first serious assault on the Bodleian Library. Frantic catching-up won him a First that was good enough for a further scholarship, and soon he was heading toward a PhD. Cautiously, he chose subjects that would help him earn a living outside academe if he had to: economics and (because of its place in world business) Germany. He went off to Hamburg to study German inflation.

At Oxford since 1992 as Fellow and Tutor in Modern History, he was subsequently made Professor of Political and Financial History, a grand title devised to please him, express precisely what he does, and perhaps prevent him from considering offers elsewhere.

Niall Ferguson's major publications to date include:-*Paper and Iron: Hamburg Business and German Politics in the Era of Inflation, 1897-1927* (1995), which turned his doctoral thesis into a cool, measured account of the financial panics that drove the Germans crazy. Then he broke new ground with *The World's Banker: The History of the House of Rothschild* (1998), having been given first-ever access to the private archives (but only up to 1915) of the bank that played power-broker in half a dozen European countries for generations. He caused a sensation with *The Pity of War* (1998), an account of the origins, the strategies and the meaning of the First World War. And, after a brief pause for breath, he wrote a book that tries to show that there are different ways of explaining the relationship between economics and politics, *The Cash Nexus: Money and Power in the Modern World 1700-2000* (2001). A later work being *Empire: The Rise and Demise of the British World Order and the Lessons for Global Power;* and yet more recently *Colossus: The Price of America's Empire,* which is expected to be published in 2004.

It was not, however, through any of these that Ferguson first came to receive a measure of international notice as this was achieved through a rather more unusual work *Virtual History: Alternatives and Counterfactuals* (1997), which he conceived, edited and partly wrote-his involvement arising from his enthusiasm for what has been called counterfactual history-the spinning of elaborate theories about what might have happened.

Some reviewers treated *Virtual History* as no more than a clever parlour game, but Ferguson's subsequent writing demonstrates that it was close to the core of his life's work. Ferguson has been pressing toward a new and perhaps less confident kind of history. He wants historians to see any given period in the past as it was seen by those who lived it, rather than by those who know how it came out. One of his projects has been attacking historical determinism and putting in its place a more realistic (if far more complicated) principle of historical cause. It is precisely because historians don't much like to engage in what they consider idle speculation that this whole volume seems a little tentative. After justifying his idea in a long prologue that evokes chaos theory and other of-the-moment ideas Ferguson clears the stage for the first essay. By John Adamson, it is engagingly titled England without Cromwell: What if Charles I had avoided the Civil War?

Most of the essays are written by British historians and deal with aspects of British history. The essays consider, variously, what might have happened had there been no American Revolution, what might have been the result for Ireland and England had Home Rule been enacted in 1912, the results of Britain staying out of WWI (Niall Ferguson-*The Kaiser's European Union),* how England would have dealt with a Nazi invasion in 1940, what the impact on Europe would have been if Germany had defeated Russia in WWII, how America and Russia might have interacted had there been no Cold War, and the state of the world today had

Communism not collapsed. There is one 'American' scenario (and this by the only female essayist, Diane Kunz-*Camelot Continued*) which takes up the task of imagining what might have happened had Kennedy not been assassinated.

The next work of Ferguson's to attract widespread notice was *The Pity of War* which was an attempt to re-evaluate Britain's role in the First World War. Ferguson argues mainly that the destruction of that war, which claimed the lives of some nine million men, could well have been avoided. By his reckoning, the war between Germany and Austria on one side and Russia and France on the other was one thing: it was only through the decision of the British that a local war became a world war.

Much of Ferguson's analysis has to do with the decision that brought England into the war. He argues, for example, that Britain went to war because it misread German intentions: they saw Kaiser Wilhelm as another Napoleon, not understanding that Germany's main interests had always been focused on Eastern, rather than Western, Europe. He further argues that the proponents of sending an English army to France — which was the trigger that made a wider war inevitable — were a minority, and that it was only because of the lack of conviction of the rest of the cabinet ministers and party leaders that the fateful decision was made. Somewhat surprisingly, Ferguson argues that war with Germany was not even in England's economic interests, since a German overseas presence would only have worked to France's detriment, not Britain's.

Ferguson asserts that Britains decision to enter into this war was historically speaking the greatest error of the twentieth century. Britain was wrong to cross the channel and fight the Germans in 1914. It cost far too much, in blood and money, for the advantage gained. By the end of the 20th century, after all, the Germans had achieved exactly what they wanted in 1914, economic leadership of Europe.

By 2004,in addition to his Oxford visiting professorship, Ferguson also taught Financial History at the Stern School of Business at New York University and was a Senior Fellow of the Hoover Institution at Stanford University. In the fall of 2004 he is due to join the faculty at Harvard University.

9

Edward Gibbon

DECLINE AND FALL OF THE ROMAN EMPIRE

Edward Gibbon was born in Putney, (now part of London), in 1737 as the first child of Edward Gibbon, a Member of Parliament, and his wife. Seven children in all were born into the family and young Edward Gibbon, although a notably sickly child, was luckier than his siblings in that he was the only one to survive childhood.

Due to his poor health Gibbon had almost no formal schooling. Following his mother's death in 1747 his father chose to live a retired life in Hampshire leaving young Edward Gibbon to the care of an aunt and grandfather in Putney.

In this household Gibbon had a free access to his grandfather's library where, with his aunt's encouragement, he became an avid reader-an initial "indiscriminate appetite subsided by degrees in the historic line." His health continued to prevent his being consistently educated in any formal educational establishment obliging the family to arrange for private tutoring until, at age 15, his health suddenly improved and his father was thus able to enter him into Magdalen College at the University of Oxford.

Given his unconventional early life Gibbon traveled to Oxford at this time "with a stock of erudition which might have puzzled a doctor, and a degree of ignorance of which a schoolboy might have been ashamed." Gibbon came to hate Oxford, he did not like his tutors and they did not like him-he was afterwards to write of the fourteen months he spent there as being "the most idle and unprofitable of my whole life."

Whilst at Oxford Gibbon incurred his father's displeasure in June 1753 by adopting Roman Catholicism, (such conversion also automatically disbarred him from further attendance at Oxford University!), with the result that Gibbon was sent to Lausanne where he was to stay in the home of a Calvinist minister.

Gibbon senior intended that, through this arrangement, his son would come to abjure his recent conversion in faith.

Gibbon spent some five years in Switzerland, becoming thoroughly fluent in the French language to the extent that it displaced English as the language in which he thought. His father's intention that Gibbon be reconciled to Protestantism was fulfilled by Christmas of 1754.

During these years Gibbon studied Greek, Latin, Logic, and Mathematics; he met Voltaire in 1757 and in that same year fell in love with Suzanne Curchot, a daughter of a materially poor minister of religion. His father, however, objected to the match and Gibbon wrote "Without his consent I was destitute and helpless. I sighed as a lover, I obeyed as a son." (Suzanne Curchot subsequently married a man named Jacques Necker who later became a prominent banker and rose to be chief minister in the French state. A daughter of this marriage was later, as Madame de Stäel, prominent in European *Belles Lettres* and politics).

Following this return to England Gibbon was introduced to a literary circle supported by Lady Hervey and, in 1761, published an essay entitled *Essai sur l'étude de la littérature* that he had begun in Lausanne in 1758. His father had encouraged this publication hoping that it would bring Gibbon to public notice but it seemed to have more impact in continental circles than in England-it was not translated into English until 1764 when it appeared as an "Essay on the Study of Literature."

From 1759 to 1762 Gibbon held a commission in the Hampshire militia, reaching the rank of colonel. By this time Gibbon had determined to devote his life to scholarship and writing. He returned to the continent spending some time in Paris in the circle of d'Alembert and Diderot, then spent about a year in the Lausanne area before traveling to Rome in April of 1764. It was of a day in October of that year that Gibbon later wrote "as I sat musing amidst the ruins of the Capitol, while barefoot friars were singing vespers in the Temple of Jupiter, the idea of writing the decline and fall of the city first started to my mind."

Although the idea for what eventually became Gibbon's celebrated History of the Decline and Fall of the Roman Empire had thus occurred to him in October 1764 it was to be several years in gestation. Gibbon returned to England in June 1765 and between other claims on his time, including some alternative literary projects, had not progressed his eventual masterwork much beyond the planning and initial research stages in 1770 when difficult circumstances associated with his father's death precipitated further causes of delay.

It was only by late 1772 that Gibbon's project really seems to have been under way. Gibbon records that after a slow and hesitant start, that was complicated by a decision having to be made as to overall tone to be adopted, he proceeded more swiftly and without much in the way of alteration or correction.

In 1774 Gibbon was invited to join Dr Johnson's Club where he associated with many of the leading figures of London's literary scene. Johnson's friend and biographer, Boswell, has descibed Gibbon as "an ugly, affected, disgusting fellow" that being said Gibbon did have a reputation for not caring overmuch about cleanliness.

The first volume of Decline and Fall was published in February 1776 and met with a prompt and considerable acclaim. Sales were such that this volume actually went into three editions. Some serious controversy arose from objections to Gibbon's rather cynical and ironical treatment of the early growth of Christianity in its pages.

Gibbon was himself something of a Deist rather than a traditional Christian and, from an historian's perspective, believed that religious dissentions had greatly tended to weaken the Empire. The following sentiments about the Christian religion's effect on the Roman Empire appear after something of an eulogisation of Roman statesmen and Roman ethics in earlier days when it had been, in Christian eyes, a pagan Empire:-

"The theologian may indulge the pleasing task of describing Religion as she descended from Heaven, arrayed in her native purity. A more

melancholy duty is imposed on the historian. He must discover the inevitable mixture of error and corruption which she contracted in a long residence upon Earth, among a weak and degenerate race of beings."

".. life is the great object of religion, we may hear without surprise or scandal that the introduction, or least the abuse, of Christianity had some influence on the decline and fall of the Roman empire. The clergy successfully preached the doctrines of patience and pusillanimity; the active virtues of society were discouraged; and the last remains of military spirit were buried in the cloister. A large portion of public and private wealth were consecrated to the specious demands of charity and devotion, and the soldiers' pay was lavished on the useless multitudes of both sexes who could only plead the merits of abstinence and chastity. Faith, zeal, curiosity, and more earthly passions of malice and ambition kindled the flame of theological factions, whose conflicts were sometimes bloody and always implacable; the attention of the emperors was diverted from camps to synods; the Roman world was oppressed by a new species of tyranny, and the persecuted sects became the secret enemies of the country."

The above passages are open to being contrasted with a previous, pagan, situation where "The various modes of worship which prevailed in the Roman world, were all considered by the people, as equally true; by the philosopher; as equally false; and by the magistrate, as equally useful." Gibbon suggests that "Toleration produced not only a mutual indulgence, but even religious concord."

Two further volumes of the Decline and Fall, which bring to an end the period of the Western Empire (to about AD 480) appeared in April 1781 and these also sold well.

Gibbon summed up the Fall of the Roman Empire in the west as "the triumph of barbarism and religion!!!"

From 1774 Gibbon was a notably inactive (he did not speak even once) member of Parliament and also held other official duties and posts until Gibbon lost a remunerative post at the Board of Trade in events that were associated with the fall of Lord North's ministry. Gibbon, having also lost his seat, retired from politics and thereafter considered that, by sitting in Parliament, he had benefitted from "a school of civil prudence, the first and most essential virtue of an historian." In 1783 Gibbon sold up his possessions, with the exception of his library, and journeyed to take up residence in Lausanne where he lived in a substantial house with a charming garden and a wonderful view belonging to his close friend George Deyverdun. It was in this setting that Gibbon worked upon further volumes of Decline and Fall such that the last three volumes, treating with the final thousand or so years of the empire in the East, were completed by late June of 1787.

Gibbon wrote of the day of this completion "I will not dissemble the first emotions of joy on the recovery of my freedom, and, perhaps, the establishment of my fame. But my pride was soon humbled, and a sober melancholy was spread over my mind by the idea that I had taken an everlasting leave of an old and agreeable companion, and that whatsoever might be the future fate of my history, the life of the historian must be short and precarious."

For Gibbon it had always been reading and study that :-

"supplied each day, each hour, with a perpetual source of independent and rational pleasure,"

Although these last three volumes volumes were not all completed as late as June of 1787, (volume four had been actually completed in 1784 and volume five in 1786) it was not until later in 1787, after Gibbon traveled to England with them in manuscript form, that arrangements were made for their publication.

This took place in April 1788 and these last volumes enjoyed a success similar to that enjoyed by the earlier volumes.

Gibbon returned to Lausanne, where he was greatly affected in July 1789 by the death of George Deyverdun-it transpired that Gibbon was a beneficiary of Deyverdun's will to the effect that Gibbon was enabled to continue to reside in Deyverdun's house in Lausanne.

In 1789 Gibbon wrote his Memoirs of My Life and Writings. He returned to England in 1793 suffering from several medical complaints and was advised to undergo a number of operations later that same year-it happened that Gibbon's health continued to fail with the result that he died in January 1794.

Gibbon's Memoirs of My Life and Writings and also his Miscellaneous Works were published in 1796

10

The Decline and Fall of the Roman Empire

The famous opening lines of Gibbon's eventual million and a half word masterwork read:-

"In the second century of the Christian era, the Empire of Rome comprehended the fairest part of the earth, and the most civilized portion of mankind. The frontiers of that extensive monarchy were guarded by ancient renown and disciplined valor. The gentle but powerful influence of laws and manners had gradually cemented the union of the provinces. Their peaceful inhabitants enjoyed and abused the advantages of wealth and luxury. The image of a free constitution was preserved with decent reverence: the Roman senate appeared to possess the sovereign authority, and devolved on the emperors all the executive powers of government. During a happy period (A.D. 98-180) of more than fourscore years, the public administration was conducted by the virtue and abilities of Nerva, Trajan, Hadrian, and the two Antonines. It is the design of this, and of the two succeeding chapters, to describe the prosperous condition of their empire; and afterwards, from the death of Marcus Antoninus, to deduce the most important circumstances of its decline and fall; a revolution which will ever be remembered, and is still felt by the nations of th earth."

Gibbon's Decline and Fall is recognised as being written in a brilliant style and with a broad and tolerant grasp of the associated historical material.

Gibbon asserted that he had attempted, where possible, to access original source material rather than to rely on secondary sources. As he himself wrote "I have always endeavoured to draw from the fountainhead; my curiousity, as well as a sense of duty, has always urged me to study the originals; and if they have sometimes eluded my search, I have carefully marked the secondary evidence on whose faith a passage or a fact were reduced to depend."

Suzanne Curchot-Necker, who long continued as a friend of, and correspondent with, Gibbon, and who was herself familiar with many of the classics, expressed the opinion that the Roman historian Tacitus was the "model and perhaps the source" of much that went into Gibbon's masterwork.

Any emulation of a classical author, and any restatement of excerpts from the classics, tended to be welcomed by the educated public of the day who were themselves often well versed in the classics and could experience a certain pleasure in seeing familiar passages, that they had possibly been obliged to learn by heart, presented within an overall historical context.

Scholars tend to see the selection of Tacitus as a model as effectively implying an explicit rejection of a Christian world view by Gibbon as author. It is also seen as something of an identification with the world view of Tacitus, was particularly known for his cool, dis-enchanted, and penetrating, assessments of men and affairs.

Gibbon was a thoroughgoing scholar of the classics and considered that in these times had lived men of "sense and spirit most congenial to my own"-and saw in Tacitus a model of a "philosophic historian" who transcended prejudices and was able to invest his writings with a true critical spirit.

Gibbon is thought have reason to be grateful to Jean Mabillon (1632-1707), Bernard Montfasucon (1655-1741), and Ludovico Muratori (1672-1741) for their collections of facts and documents. He is also regarded as having himself accepted the "accepted wisdoms" of the day regarding disputed dates and the way in which certain texts should properly be read.

That being said more recent and more extensive scholarship

involving, in cases, familiarity with languages with which Gibbon was not familiar has tended to undermine the authority of some of the sources upon which Gibbon's own historical efforts relied.

Gibbon's treatment of the eastern Empire after 460 A.D. is seen as being set out in line with Gibbon's own view that its history was "a uniform tale of weakness and misery." This view is today seen as being somewhat unfair-whilst it is true that the eastern Empire was frequently under assault from any of a number of adversaries in nonetheless functioned for much of its thousand year existence as a focus of Greek civilisation and as a bulwark which effectively lessened the likelyhood of such adversaries being able to impact more directly upon western Europe.

11

Herodotus—Greek Historian

THE FATHER OF HISTORY

Herodotus, later famous as a Greek historian to the point of becoming known as the 'father of history', was born in Halicarnassus (now Bodrum, Turkey) in about 484 BC. Halicarnassus was at this time an ancient Greek colonial town subject to Persian overlordship.

As a son of a prominent family Herodotus received a good education sufficient to allow him to eventually gain an extensive familiarity with the literature of ancient Greece.

He seems to have travelled very extensively in the Greek and Persian worlds into which he had been born. When he was in his early thirties (circa 457 BC) some political difficulties between Herodotus' wider family and the rulers of Halicarnassus contributed to his living in exile for several years. During these times his initial destination seems to have been the the island of Samos but thereafter Herodotus traveled widely throughout virtually the entire ancient Middle East visiting Asia Minor, Babylonia, Egypt, and Greece.

Herodotus was centrally involved in the rebellious overthrow of the unpopular ruler of Halicarnassus and was thereby enabled to enjoy full rights of citizenship in his home city. He did not settle down there however but, circa 447 BC, went to Athens, then the center and focus of culture in the Greek world, where he won the admiration of the most illustrious men of Greece, including the great Athenian statesman Pericles. During a stay of some years in

Athens Herodotus seems to have been awarded a substantial sum, by a decree of the people, in appreciation of his literary talents.

Herodotus did not enjoy the status of citizenship, with associated enhancements in rights, in Athens and this may have contributed to his joining in (443 BC) with a new colonial settlement at Thurii in southern Italy where he could hope to be a citizen. Such colonies were widely sponsored by individual greek city states for commercial reasons and also to better provide for the employment of their citizens.

Herodotus settled down in Thurii and devoted his efforts to the completion of a great work entitled 'Inquiry' (the Greek word for which is History). Herodotus' wide-ranging work has subsequently been presented by scholars as a nine part work the first six of which are introductory and give rounded introductions to most of the peoples of the ancient world giving insights into their customs, legends, history, and traditions. The last three parts treat with the rivalries and conflicts between the Greek and Persian worlds from the early fifth century BC.

Herodotus' work presents the development of civilization as moving inexorably toward a great confrontation between Persia and Greece, which are presented as the centers, respectively, of Eastern and Western culture.

In preparing his History Herodotus' sources of information include the works of predecessors, but these are widely complemented through the knowledge that he gained from his own extensive travels. Although Herodotus' great work does in fact contain some factual inaccuracies, he does seem to have striven for accuracy.

The entire work being an ambitious attempt to present the historical context of the Greek rivalry with Persia that is rendered particularly appealing by such admirable qualities as the fullness with which Herodotus conveys his subject and the beauty of expression that he is able to impart to the Ionic dialect in which it is composed.

The whole being a grandly concieved narrative with appropriate episodic diversions that manage to elucidate the main theme without seeming to interrupt its flow.

Thomas Babington Macaulay said of Herodotus that he:-

"wrote as it is natural that he should write. He wrote for a nation susceptible, curious, lively, insatiably desirous of novelty and excitement."

Herodotus believed that the universe is ruled by Fate and Chance, and that nothing is stable in human affairs. Moral choice is still important, however, since arrogance (Hubris) brings down upon itself the retribution of the gods (Nemesis).

Herodotus' effective attempt to draw moral lessons from the study of great events formed the basis of the Greek and Roman historiographical tradition which he is held to have established.

Herodotus died in 425 BC.

12

Eric Hobsbawm

MARXIST HISTORIAN

Eric Hobsbawm was born in Alexandria to a middle-class Jewish family in June 1917. Between the world wars, the family moved first to Vienna and then to Berlin.

He long retained a memory of himself as a 14-year-old boy who read on a newspaper board the headline announcing the accession of the Third Reich. 'Anybody who saw Hitler's rise happen first-hand could not have helped but be shaped by it, politically,' he said. 'This is still there in me. That boy is still somewhere inside, always will be.'

Hobsbawm's parents both died during the Depression and he and his sister were taken in by his uncle, who worked for a Berlin branch of a Hollywood, USA, based firm. Soon thereafter, the family moved to England, following his uncle's job, and for three years, Hobsbawm experienced what he has rarely felt since-that history was happening without him. He was bored and dislocated by the transition from the intensities of pre-war Germany to the complacencies of a south London grammar school. It was not until he got to Cambridge that he sensed he could carry on with the conversations that he'd started in Berlin.

Hobsbawm has defined and explained the progress of the last century as mankind learning to 'live in expectation of apocalypse'. He responded to those intimations in himself by joining the Communist Party. He would, he says, certainly have become a member earlier, but that his uncle was 'rather stiff' on the subject.

'He used to say, "You kids don't know what you are letting yourselves in for".' Hobsbawm smiles now, seeing his life unspooling in that prophecy. 'He was right, of course.'

You could imagine that the gangling young émigré, uprooted and orphaned, might have been attracted to the certainties of the party as a surrogate family and consequently begin to explain the strength of the attachment as a powerfully emotional as well as an intellectual one. Looking back, he suggests that 'probably that kind of security was one of the appeals', but also that he 'never felt short of family... it was more that you just felt things were going to pieces, and you felt it needed a revolution to re-create it, to put it back together'.

After the war, these political commitments no longer seemed quite so innocent. Hobsbawm applied for a series of Oxbridge jobs, and was 'turned down right, left and centre' He fetched up instead, happily, at Birkbeck where the student body was part-time, lectures were held in the evenings and the challenge among the faculty was to keep its audience awake in the graveyard slot between eight and nine. Hobsbawm, by all accounts, achieved this effortlessly and sustained his intellectual energy after hours.

Hobsbawm considered that, given his sympathy for communism, he got into academia 'under the wire'; a year later, after the Berlin Airlift in 1948, his story, he believed, would have been markedly different.

Though he never proselytised unlike many of his comrades, Hobsbawm did not leave the party after 1956. It may be that partly because of his political affiliations, he did not get promotion to a professorship until 1970.

According to Hobsbawm the historian's task, "is not simply to discover the past but to explain it, and in doing so to provide a link with the present." For Hobsbawm, history is a cumulative, collective enterprise to uncover "the patterns and mechanisms" that have transformed the world.

Historians commonly have diverse viewpoints; indeed, partisanship or commitment (to Marxism and socialism, in Hobsbawm's case) this possibly injects new creative energy into research and prevents the field from turning inward and becoming ossified. Hobsbawm's later writings display a general pessimism and estrangement, arising from his sense of how far humanity had slipped from the nineteenth century and its expectations of civility and human progress.

The start of World War I in 1914 (even more than the Russian Revolution in 1917) represented, in Hobsbawm's estimation, the great historical turning point separating an age of human progress from one of increased barbarism.

Reflecting on mankind's trajectory from the Sarajevo of 1914 to the Sarajevo of the fall of Yugoslavia — total warfare, the state sanctioned genocides of Nazism and Stalinism, the annihilatory madness of the Cold War arms race, and the latest monstrosities — he declares his unwavering commitment to the ideas and values of the eighteenth-century Enlightenment as "one of the few things that stands between us and an accelerated descent into darkness."

The Enlightenment may not be fashionable ("a conspiracy of dead white men in periwigs," Hobsbawm jokes) but it is the only basis, he insists, on which "to build societies fit for all human beings to live in anywhere on this Earth, and for the assertion and defence of their human rights as persons." And "the worst of it is that we have got used to the inhuman. We have learned to tolerate the intolerable."

This commitment also throws light on the combative, inflexible tone of his Marxism, now curiously linked to a certain nostalgia for past civility. If Marxism no longer supplies Hobsbawm with a political vision, neither is it for him simply a theory of historical development, the best tool to be found for making sense of the past. With its positivist values and clear affirmation of progress in history, Marxism is central to his moral and cultural critique, linking him firmly to that "Enlightenment project" dedicated to rationalism and human improvement.

Whether or not we agree with Hobsbawm's historical judgments or share his fears for the future, his voice remains loud and clear.

Marx seemed to him the best guide for understanding the mechanisms of historical change in the modern world, and he repeatedly affirms that he has since then discovered no comparable analytic tool. His analysis of Marxist concepts and his subtle and flexible use of them in his writing — abundantly illustrated in several of these essays — has been enormously influential. In this collection, however, the most recent essay on "Marx and History" dates from 1983 and so it addresses neither recent critiques nor his personal reactions to the collapse of the Soviet Union and other recent changes that, in the eyes of many historians, have diminished the working class as an historical actor.

As the Communist walls were coming down in 1989, Hobsbawm was often asked to explain his continued commitment. Typically, he replied both as a conviction historian-'I think the movement has achieved at least one absolutely major thing, and that includes the Soviet Union, namely the defeat of fascism,'-and as a rose-tinted loyalist: 'I don't wish to be untrue to my past or comrades of mine, a lot of them dead, some of them killed by their own side, whom I've admired [as] models to follow, in their unselfishness.'

His landmark trilogy on the nineteenth century synthesised myriad competing social swells into great epochal waves: the Ages of Revolution, and of Capital, and of Empire. He has characterised his own time and tide as the Age of Extremes, the tempestuous force of which conspired to deposit him on the shore of the present as the Last Marxist; still, he refuses to believe himself beached. One old friend observes: 'Eric has long ago worked out his precise intellectual position and he's quite happy there, thank you very much.'

These four volumes are probably the most widely admired of his works — not simply because of their erudition and bold analysis, but for the author's conviction that historians must write large-scale interpretations of the past without minimizing its diversity and complexity and, at the same time, make them readable, jargon-free, and accessible to non-professionals. If more scholars have recently taken up the challenge of historical synthesis, it is due in.no small part to Hobsbawm's example.

13

Johan Huizinga

THE WANING OF THE MIDDLE AGES

Johan Huizinga, who was later to become famous for his studies concerning the Waning of the Middle Ages, was born in Groningen in 1872. He was educated there and in Leipzig, Germany. His initial academic training was as a linguist-he studied Dutch language and literature in Groningen from 1891 until 1897 when he wrote his doctoral dissertation under the supervision of the classical scholar J.S. Speyer (1849-1913) on the *Vidûsaka in Indian theatre*.

Huizinga shifted his interest towards historical studies however, with a particular emphasis on studies as a Cultural historian in line with the school established by Jacob Burckhardt. After teaching in Haarlem and Amsterdam, he became professor of history at the University of Groningen in 1905 and at the Leiden University in 1915.

His most famous work is *The Waning of the Middle Ages*, (published in 1919 trans. 1924), in which he argues that the late Middle Ages were a period of weariness, pessimism and decadence.

This work, which is celebrated for its excellent literary quality and historical penetration, focuses on the 14th and 15th centuries in France and the Low Countries as exemplifying the last phase of the Middle Ages and discusses many aspects of medieval life: philosophy, literature, painting, chivalry, love, etc. Huizinga describes how medieval piety often found expression in rituals and external forms.

The Middle Ages are also discusses in his collection of essays *Men and Ideas*. One of these called, "The Task of Cultural History," argues that history should resurrect the past, and should give the reader a sense of what it was like to be alive during a particular period. Huizinga deplores the modern tendency to write romanticized history and romanticized biography, to try to make history entertaining and amusing holding that "No literary effect in the world can compare to the pure, sober taste of history."

Other essays are collected in a volume called *Dutch Civilization in the Seventeenth Century and Other Essays*. Much of this book is written not for the general reader, but for fellow Dutchmen and contemporaries. His preoccupation with the Netherlands reminds one of Ortega's preoccupation with Spain. In an essay called, "The Aesthetic Element in Historical Thought," Huizinga declares that he has "faith in the importance of the aesthetic element in historical thinking," and that he opposes the idea that history should attempt to be scientific. "The historian tries to re-experience what was once experienced by men like ourselves....The true study of history involves our imagination and conjures up conceptions, pictures, visions." *In the Shadow of Tomorrow* isn't a historical work, but rather an analysis of Western civilization. It discusses the problems besetting the West, from moral anarchy to artistic decadence. Though it sometimes reminds one of Ortega's *Revolt of the Masses*, its less pertinent to our time than Ortega's work since much of it is a criticism of Fascism. It is, however, an interesting, brief and readable book, it argues that that modern education and the mass media both have harmful effects on culture: "Our time [is] faced by the discouraging fact that two highly vaunted achievements of civilization, universal education and modern publicity, instead of raising the level of culture, appear ultimately to produce certain symptoms of cultural devitalisation and degeneration."

In looking at modern art, Huizinga finds a trend toward the irrational in both modern literature and modern painting. Literature and painting are held to have become increasingly unintelligible-poetry is represented as having maintained throughout history "a certain connection with rational expression....It is not until the closing years of the [nineteenth] century that one sees poetry purposely steering its course away from reason."

Man and the Masses in America and also *Life and Thought in America;* are two books that are sometimes published together in one volume. They consider American history before 1925, and they also look at modern society in general, including newspapers, movies and literature. Special attention is paid to the economic forces that have shaped American history.

In many of Huizinga's works, he discusses the play element in culture. Finally, when his life was drawing to a close, and he was a prisoner of the Nazis, he collected his thoughts on this subject into a book called *Homo Ludens: A Study of the Play-Element in Culture. Homo Ludens* contains some very interesting ideas, but it presents these ideas in a rather dry and scholarly manner. He argues that play is one of fundamental facts of human life, and is at the root of poetry, music, philosophy-even jurisprudence and war. Anyone interested in plumbing the depths of human nature, anyone interested in the question of why people fight wars, create culture, etc., should take his ideas into account. Huizinga is discussing more than play, he is discussing human nature, the fundamental drives within human nature-"The spirit of playful competition is, as a social impulse, older than culture itself and pervades all life like a veritable ferment. Ritual grew up in sacred play; poetry was born in play and nourished on play; music and dancing were pure play....We have to conclude, therefore, that civilization is, in its earliest phases, played. It does not come *from* play...it arises *in* and *as* play, and never leaves it."

Other works include early studies of the literature and culture of India and a biography of Erasmus (1924).

From 1942 until his death in 1945 Johan Huizinga was held in detention by the Nazis.

14

Isaiah Berlin and the History of Ideas

Isaiah Berlin was born in Riga in the Russian Empire's baltic territories on June 6th, 1909. His father was a successful timber merchant and landowner and his maternal grandfather was a Hasidic rabbi of the ecstatic Lubavitch tradition. In these early years Isaiah Berlin was actually known as Shaya Berlin.

In 1915 Berlin's family moved to St. Petersburg where, some months later, he was an eyewitness to the Russian Social-Democratic revolution (March 1917) and the Bolshevik revolution (October 1917) events which, in his own opinion, changed him for life.

In 1920 the Berlin family moved back to Riga, now the capital of an independent Latvia, and then emigrated to London, where they had business interests.

As a boy Berlin had had some Jewish religious education, this was continued in London, where he had his bar mitzvah. It appears that his Jewish background proved to be an obstacle to his being accepted as a pupil at Westminster School with the result that his family sought his being educated at St. Paul's.

At St. Paul's Berlin proved to be only a fair student and, on that basis was denied admission to Balliol College, Oxford, but managed to gain a scholarship to Corpus Christi. At the end of a course in humane letters Berlin was awarded a "bad" first but he then took another course, in philosophy, in which he was awarded a "better" first.

At this stage of his life Berlin had no definite thoughts as to a career. He attended an unsuccessful interview for a journalistic position with the Manchester Guardian, he declined his father's invitation to join him in the family business as he felt he could not belong in that world, he also considered law until this continued indecision was eventually interrupted by an offer of a teaching post in philosophy at Oxford University.

Berlin became a lecturer in philosophy at New College in 1932 and was appointed a Fellow of All Souls College at a remarkably young age. He was also the first Jew to hold such a fellowship. Some of the leading analytic philosophers of the day including J.L. Austin, A.J. Ayer, Stuart Hampshire, Donald MacKinnon, and Donald Macnabb often attended meetings held in Berlin's rooms at All Souls College.

The outbreak of the Second World War led to Berlin being redeployed and sent to New York, where he worked for the British Information Service, and then to Washington, where his assignment was to report on the direction of opinions and moods in America.

After the war Berlin was seconded briefly to the British Embassy in Moscow where he was given a role in preparing commentary on the output of the Russian press. It was his first visit to Russia since his family had left for Riga in 1920. Berlin was advised by British diplomats that he would find extreme difficulty in speaking with anyone other than the officials assigned to him by the communist regime which had a tradition of attempting to discourage meetings between Soviet citizens and foreigners. It transpired that he was able to independently meet a number of Russian artists and writers, and he wrote that "it was like speaking to the victims of a shipwreck on a desert island, cut off for decades from civilization."

Berlin later wrote an article about his meetings with Russian writers in which he expressed a sympathetic regret for the conditions under which they were obliged to live due to the restrictions imposed by the Soviet regime on most forms of artistic expression.

Berlin spent the years from 1947 to 1958 as a writer and lecturer in Oxford and London, and also in the United States at Washington, and at the universities as Harvard, Princeton, Bryn

Mawr, and Chicago. In the 1950s, Berlin fell in love with Aline de Gunzbourg, a Frenchwoman who was the descendant of a noble Russian family whom he married in 1956.

Berlin was so beguiling a conversationalist that when Prime Minister Harold MacMillan nominated him in 1957 for the queen's list he noted that the knighthood should be bestowed "for talking."

From 1957 to 1967, Sir Isaiah held the prestigious Chichele Chair in Social and Political Theory. As the first president of Wolfson College from 1966 to 1975, he was instrumental in attracting a strong faculty to a new school at Oxford.

His best-known essay in the United States, "The Hedgehog and the Fox," a 1953 study of Tolstoy's view of history as embodied in "War and Peace." is regarded as a classic of political inquiry and literary criticism. In this essay, which became part of a great body of work by Sir Isaiah on Russian thinkers of the 19th century, he drew a distinction between two human types: those, like the fox, who pursue many ends, often unrelated, even contradictory, and those, like the hedgehog, who relate everything to a single universal organizing principle.

Sir Isaiah's 1959 essay, "Two Concepts of Liberty," is considered a major contribution to political theory. In it, he made a distinction between negative liberty, that which the individual must be allowed to enjoy without state interference, and positive liberty, that which the state permits by imposing regulations that, by necessity, limit some freedoms in the name of greater liberty for all. He argued that both kinds of liberty were required for a just society.

Much of Berlin's writing might have been left lying in the basement of Headington House, his elegant Queen Anne residence in Oxford, had an enterprising young graduate student not come along to gather it together.

Sir Isaiah's lectures were often not published and his essays were scattered in so many magazines and journals that his body of work was inaccessible to most people. Henry Hardy, the graduate student, set out to collect it in four volumes that became five: "Russian Thinkers"(1978); "Concepts and Categories" (1978); "Against the Current" (1979); "Personal Impressions" (1980) and "The Crooked Timber of History," (1990).

In addition, Sir Isaiah was the author of five other books: "Karl Marx," (1939); "The Age of Enlightenment" (1956), "Four Essays on Liberty " (1969); "Vico and Herder"(1976); and "The Magus of the North: J.G. Hamann and the Origins of Modern Irrationalism" (1993).

Until the publication of the Hardy collections, Sir Isaiah had been known as a man who talked much but wrote little and had, in fact, been taken to task for not producing a major opus.

Sir Isaiah had begun to move away from analytic philosophy towards the history of ideas at the time of his return to academic life in Oxford after the Second World War. After his involvements with the earth shattering events of the war years analytic philosophy seemed to be a little disconnected from history and from the human lives lived in historical contexts. An initial opening of Berlin's interest to the whole area of the history of ideas, and of their influence, arising through his becoming familiar with the work of the Russian philosopher and revolutionary Alexander Herzen.

Herzen's writings about the history of social and political ideas made a tremendous impression on Isaiah Berlin and he increasingly involved himself in far-reaching related studies.

Sir Noel Annan, who wrote the introduction to Sir Isaiah's 1980 book, "Personal Impressions," observed: "Nobody in our time has invested ideas with such personality, given them a corporeal shape and breathed life into them more than Isaiah Berlin; and he succeeds in doing so because ideas for him are not mere abstractions. They live... in the minds of men and women, inspiring them, shaping their lives, influencing their actions and changing the course of history."

Sir Isaiah came to believe in the overriding importance of ideas. "When ideas are neglected by those who ought to attend to them -- that is to say, those who have been trained to think critically about ideas — they often acquire an unchecked momentum and an irresistible power over multitudes of men that may grow too violent to be affected by rational criticism," he wrote in "Two Concepts of Liberty." He added: "Over a hundred years ago, the German poet Heine warned the French not to underestimate the power of ideas: philosophical concepts nurtured in the stillness of a professor's study could destroy a civilization.... If professors can truly wield this fatal power, may it not be that only other professors, or, at least, other thinkers (and not governments or congressional committees) can alone disarm them? Our philosophers seem oddly unaware of these devastating effects of their activities."

A staunch advocate of pluralism in a century in which totalitarians and utopians claimed title to the one, single truth, Sir Isaiah considered the very notion that there could be one final answer to organizing human society a dangerous illusion that would lead to nothing but bloodshed, coercion, and deprivation of liberty.

The theme that runs throughout his work is his concern with liberty and the dignity of human beings, and he sought to emphasize that at all times, difficult, even tragic, tradeoffs had to be made. It was his view that man must forever choose among incommensurable and often incompatible values, that equality, for example, must at times be sacrificed to liberty.

Sir Isaiah did however believe that the "great man" can bring about significant historical change. He was also a critic of the concept of 'historical inevitability' and of a 'determinist interpretation of human affairs' :-

"Principally it seems to me to spring from a desire to resign from our responsibility, to cease from judging provided we be not judged ourselves and, above all, are not compelled to judge ourselves; from a desire to flee for refuge to some vast amoral, impersonal, monolthic whole, nature or history, or class, or race, or 'harsh realities of our time,' or 'the irresistible evolution of the social structure'..."

As an exponent of the history of ideas Sir Isaiah was awarded the Erasmus, Lippincott and Agnelli prizes and was also awarded the Order of Merit, Britain's highest honour for intellectual achievement.

Sir Isaiah was interested in the arts and was at various times Chairman of the Trustees of the National Gallery, a Trustee of the British Museum and a Director of the Royal Opera House, Covent

Garden. He was also a supporter of Zionism holding that Jews living as religious minorities in many states often effectively lived on a basis of compromise where they were tolerated, to varying degrees, rather than fully accepted as integral to the life of the state. Outside a Jewish state citizens who were Jewish by faith were thus usually denied a full living of their lives "in the light of day."

Sir Isaiah Berlin, philosopher and noted exponent of the history of ideas, revered for his intellect and cherished for his wit and his gift for friendship, died on Wednesday night, November 12th, 1997, of a heart attack in Oxford, England. He was 88.

Since Sir Isaiah's death his literary trustees have continued to make available books that are assembled from the many essays, lectures, and articles that are attributable to him. Two of these being 'Freedom and its Betrayal: Six Enemies of Human Liberty' and 'Liberty' this last being an expansion upon Sir Isaiah's "Four Essays on Liberty."

15

Thomas Babington Macaulay

Thomas Babington Macaulay was born on October 25th, 1800, at Rothley Temple, Leicestershire, as the son of former African Colonial Governor and anti-slavery philanthropist Zachary Macaulay.

Macaulay was a notably precocious child and something of an actual literary prodigy, he began to write poetry and a world history before he was ten years of age. He was later educated at Trinity College, Cambridge where he became known as a debater, as a brilliant conversationalist, and as a classical scholar.

In 1824 he gained a college prize for an essay on the character of William III. He was also awarded a fellowship at Trinity College. An anti-slavery address he gave in 1824 was reported upon by the favourably by the Edinburgh Review, one of the most notable literary magazines of the period.

His essay on the English poet John Milton was published (August 1825) in the Edinburgh Review and met with considerable acclaim, Macaulay was thereafter one of the best-known and most popular contributors to that publication.

Macaulay was called to the bar in 1826, and joined the northern circuit. He practiced little, preferring to follow literary pursuits and politics spending many hours watching the proceedings of the house of commons from the public gallery. It happened, however, that his family's business met with financial disaster-Macaulay was even forced to sell a Gold Medal he had won at Cambridge-and he was therafter obliged by his new circumstances to work seriously for his living.

In February 1830 he entered the House of Commons where he sat for the "pocket borough" of Calne that had been made available to him through the "no strings attached" patronage of Lord Landsdowne. Macaulay began to draw notice through the quality of his speeches including one delivered in support of the dramatically contentious parliamentary Reform Bill in March 1831 that was praised by Sir Robert Peel as containing portions "as beautiful as anything I have ever heard or read."

"...Renew the youth of the State. Save property, divided against itself. Save the multitude, endangered by its own ungovernable passions. Save the aristocracy, endangered by its own unpopular power. Save the greatest, and fairest, and most highly civilised community that ever existed, from calamities which may in a few days sweep away all the rich heritage of so many ages of wisdom and glory. The danger is terrible. The time is short. If this bill should be rejected, I pray to God that none of those who concur in rejecting it may ever remember their votes with unavailing remorse, amidst the wreck of laws, the confusion of ranks, the spoilation of property, and the dissolution of the social order...."

Following the passage of the Reform Bill of 1832 and a Whig (Liberal Party) victory in the following general election that was held before a now much broadened electorate, (and where many former "pocket boroughs" had been abolished), Macaulay was appointed a one of the commissioner of the Board of Control and took a special interest in Indian Affairs. He continued in these months to make time for some involvement in literary pursuits and was able to submit a number of essays to the Edinburgh Review.

In 1834 Macaulay became a member of the Supreme Council of India, created by the India Act of 1834; for which he was to be paid the then princely salary of £10,000 per annum. He spent four years in India, devoting his time chiefly to reforming the criminal code of the colony and to instituting an educational system based on that of Great Britain. In 1835 Macaulay began to seriously consider that he might someday attempt to write about the History of England.

In 1839, a year after his return, as a now well off man, to England, Macaulay resumed his political career and was elected to Parliament to represent an Edinburgh constituency. It was in this same year that Macaulay began to write his History of England. He served as secretary of war from 1839 to 1841 and, as such, had a seat in the British cabinet. The loss of office in 1841 being associated with the fall of the ministry in which he had served.

As he was now relatively free of political duties Macaulay was able to give more time to literary pursuits. In 1842 he finalised his Lays of Ancient Rome, this being a collection of poems in ballad form, retelling legends of the beginning of the Roman Republic. Three volumes of his Essays were published in 1843. His ongoing major historical work was now envisaged to eventually become a comprehensive history of England from the accession of King James II to 1832-this last being the year of the parlimentary reform act. The history would then extend from the "Revolution which brought the Crown into harmony with the Parliament" until the "Revolution which brought the Parliament into harmony with the nation."

Macaulay continued to devote time to politics, and served as a Liberal Party member of Parliament. The Liberals were returned to power in 1846, and Macaulay was appointed paymaster general for the armed forces. In the general election of July 1847, however, he was not returned to parliament and, given that his interest in politics had been waning and his interest in literary pursuits had been growing, now decided to concentrate on writing. He also adapted his pattern of life towards living a more retired life as a private citizen.

The first two volumes of the History of England from the Accession of James the Second were published in December 1848 and at once achieved a huge success. They were published in numerous editions in both Britain and the United States. The third chapter inherently contributed to the development of social history by presenting an highly contextually relevant extensive survey of English society in the year 1685 in terms of such things as population, cities, classes and tastes.

In 1852 Macaulay was again voted into Parliament for his former Edinburgh constituency, but declined to take up the offer of a place in the Cabinet. It transpired that he had developed a weakness in his heart causing him to decide to take little part in political activity and to continue to spend most of his time writing with the view of attempting to complete his History of England.

He worked to such effect that the third and fourth volumes of his history were published in November 1855, and achieved an even greater circulation than the first two. The volumes so far published were subsequently translated into several European languages and Macaulay received royalties in association with his efforts to the then prodigious amount of £20,000.

He was created Baron Macaulay of Rothley in 1857 but the continued failure of his health contributed to his never making a speech the house of lords. He resigned himself to the reality of his failing health and curtailed his next projected volume of his history to the close of the reign of William III. He died on December 28, 1859, in London and was buried in Westminster Abbey.

The last completed volume of his history, relating events until 1702, was published posthumously in 1861.

16

The History of England from the Accession of James the Second

Macaulay's masterwork achieved unprecedented levels of sales. The first two volumes sold to the extent of 13,000 sets in four months, volumes three and four achieved twice this figure in half the time. The publishers sold more than 140,000 sets of the entire history in Great Britain alone during the first twenty five years of its availability.

Macaulay work is today held to have weaknesses that detract from its many real merits. These weaknesses stem largely from Macaulay's approach to his subject which was that of a definite advocate of "progress." Macaulay's view of progress being closely aligned with an interpretation of history that saw many real achievements in British and World history as resulting from policies pursued by the Whig political interest.

In a speech delivered to the electors of Edinburgh in 1839, for example, his audience were left in no doubt as to Macaulay's devotion to the Whig party.

"...To the Whigs of the nineteenth century we owe it that the House of Commons has been purified. The abolition of the slave trade, the abolition of colonial slavery, the extension of popular education, the mitigation of the rigour of the penal code, all, all were effected by that party; of that party, I repeat, I am a member...."

The History of England from the Accession of James II opens with a declaration that Britain had recently been on a path of progress:

"...the history of our country during the last hundred and

sixty years is eminently the history of physical, of moral, and of intellectual improvement..."

For Macaulay an important aspect of such improvement was associated with the adoption of new industrial methods. As he had written in his famous essay "Southey's Colloquies on Society" (1830)

"...we must confess ourselves unable to find any satisfactory record of any great nation, past or present, in which he working classes have been in a more comfortable situation than in England during the last thirty years. When this island was thinly peopled, it was barbarous; there was little capital; and that little was insecure. It is now the richest and most highly civilised spot in the world...

...People live longer because they are better fed, better lodged, better clothed, and better attended in sickness, and these improvements are, owing to that increase of national wealth which the manufacturing system has produced..."

Macaulay effectively subscribed to a view of history where it was the Whigs, who had primarily sponsored many "progressive" reforms that had contibuted to the emergence of the British system of liberal parliamentary democracy that had, importantly, tended to facilitate the development of a commercial and industrial society. His history writing tended to acclaim those Whigs who had sought reforms and to decry those who had obstructed the passing of such reforms.

Macaulay's heroes were those who stood on the side of the developing powers of Parliament in the struggle to overcome the "autocratic powers of kingship."

Such heroes included those who had supported the signing of the Magna Carta (1215), the individually liberalising Protestant Reformation against the reactionary and despotic Catholic Church. In his treatment of the English Civil War Macaulay's sympathies lie with those who sought to uphold the authority of Parliament against the encroachments of Charles I. In terms of the events of 1688 Macaulay obviously approves of the Whig involvements in securing the departure of James II who is seen as being a champion of the exercise of a high degree of royal power.

Macaulay's writing of history shows a partisanship, often expressed in intemperate and excessive terms, in support of the Whigs and it also shows an high degree of certainty that the course of British history during the years in question had been one of progress.

For many readers there is something irritating about historical writings that seek to illustrate and to advocate rather than to understand and to elucidate. An obviously partisan approach can lead to a degree of distrust where the reader suspects that the author may not fairly presented the characters of individuals or adequately furnished a rounded presentation of the course of events. It is surely a definite drawback to the credibility of any historian for their readers to be brought to suspect that the work that they are considering may not present a broad and balanced picture.

Our own world is perhaps a more disillusioned place than that in which Macaulay lived. There have been realities brought home to us (depletion of resources, industrial pollution, also Communism and Fascism as awkwardly potent experimental? alternatives to liberal democracy) that may lead us to be a little envious of, and impatient with, Macaulay's own certain belief in liberal democracy as tending to ensure progress.

17

Friedrich Meinecke

COSMOPOLITANISM AND THE NATIONAL STATE

Friedrich Meinecke was born in October 1862 in the Prussian town of Salzwedel as the son of a post office worker. After studying History and Philosophy in Berlin and Bonn, he obtained his doctorate in 1886. He entered the Prussian archive service in 1887 and submitted his post-doctoral thesis in Berlin in 1896.

From 1893, he was editor, then from 1896 publisher of the 'Historische Zeitschrift' ('Historical Magazine'). In these times he was developing his interest in the history of ideas. In 1901, he was given a chair in Strasburg, and from 1906 he had a chair in Freiburg.

Meinecke's two volume biography of the army reformer von Boyen, appeared in 1896/99. His 'The Age of German Liberation', a study of the Prussian response to the French Revolution, appeared in 1906. The year 1907 saw the publication of one of Meinecke's most notable works 'Weltbürgertum und Nationalstaat. Studien zur Genesis das deutschen Nationalstaats,' ('The middle classes of the world and the national state. Studies on the genesis of the national state.'), which has appeared in english translations as Cosmopolitanism and the National State.

Prior to the appointment of Count Bismarck of Chancellor of Prussia in 1862 "the Germanies" had functioned, as a legacy of history, as a loosely structured Confederation of largely individually sovereign states under ancient aristocratic houses with Austria and Prussia being the most prominent of the German states. In his Cosmopolitanism and the National State Meinecke presents the history of the emergent German state from the Prussian period of reform to the formation of the Second German Empire by Bismarck as a steady development in which he brought to life and personified the concept of a national state.

Meinecke chronicles, and comments somewhat favourably on, the emergence of a German national state. Meinecke recognised that there had been a transition from (an eighteenth century) cultural cosmopolitanism towards a (ninetenth century) pride in nationality and a conception of the State as a natural expression of nationality-this tendency was not seen by him as being incompatible with an ideal international society. With this book Meinecke became well known, and together with Wilhelm Dilthey and Ernst Troeltsch became one of the founders of the political intellectual history.

In 1914, shortly after the outbreak of the First World War, which to start with was greeted by him with enthusiasm, Meinecke was awarded a Professorial position at Berlin's Friedrich Wilhelm University. As late as 1916, in an introduction to a new edition of Ranke's *Great Powers*, Meinecke depicted a situation where it was necessary that England's maritime supremacy be broken in order to provide the conditions necessary to a new equilibrium in world civilization that would feature equality, competition, and exchange.

As the conflict continued Meinecke was one of a minority of professors who supported a negotiated peace and internal reforms. With this, he was continuing his activities which had started in 1910 as a historical-political commentator, together with Friedrich Naumann, Max Weber and Ernst Troelsch, and which supported a renewal of liberalism within a social state. Only in this way could in his view the greater aim of internal unity within the nation be achieved. This made him support the Weimar democracy in 1918, despite the disgust of his own circle, 'not out of initial love for the republic, but for common sense reasons and a love of my fatherland'.

In 1924, he published his second important work on intellectual history "Idee der Staatsrason" which explored the concept of 'reasons of state' in modern history, through the examination of the attempts made to reconcile the often competing claims of ethics, power politics, values and causality from Machiavelli up to the present. In this, he disputed the idea of power politics which had been developed from 1848 by the national-liberal political historians, and, coupled with an appeal to 'reasons of state', a warning against rigorous power politics.

Meinecke taught in Berlin until 1932 when he retired at the age of 69. Something of an outsider, he was academically a supporter of a political intellectual history and had been politically a republican for practical reasons in the Weimar Republic.

In 1934, as a result of the Nazi take-over of power, he lost his position as chair of the 'Historische Reichskommission', a position he had held since 1928. In point of fact the entire 'Historische Reichskommission' was disbanded, despite its previously prestigious place in German letters, by order of the Nazi regime who sought to replace it with a *Reichinstitut fur Geshichte des neuen Deutshland* that was intended to produce historical data in line with the outlook of the new 'National Socialist' Germany. In 1935 Meinecke's position as publisher of the 'Historische Zeitschrift' came to an end.

Although he may have appeared to be a retired academic with little influence, he continued tirelessly to publish his works, for example in 1936 'Die Entstehung des Historismus' ('The origins of historicism') in which he questioned the fundamental rules and principles of the writings of history and of historical thinking. In 1946, at the age of 84, he finally produced his widely acknowledged book 'Die deutsche Katastrophe' ('The German catastrophe'). In this, he tries to explain the events of recent history with the help of the collective intellectual history of Germany since the 19th century. He saw German National Socialism as being an anomaly, ('the greatest disaster the German people have suffered but also their greatest shame'), that was not part of the pattern demonstrated in the past by Germany politically.

Meinecke re-examined the relation of National Socialism to German history and revised his earlier advocacy of power politics, concluding that such realpolitik represented 'the breakthrough of a Satanic principle into world-history'. The struggle between the two souls within Prussianism-the civilized and the militarist-had been perverted by the Nazis into a degrading worship of the omnipotent State, Meinecke even revised his earlier admiration for Bismarck and the cult of success, as well as his estimate of the function of the historian, calling for a renewed consciousness of the humanistic currents in German history. Above all, this return he demanded in his book to the idealism of the age of Goethe later came in for criticism and at times also for mockery. Meinecke was seen as having glossed over the death factories, the mass murder of the Jews, slave labor and other Nazi atrocities, and as arguing that Hitler derived his power from his "demonic personality," all of this was seen partially as a symptom of the inability of the middle-class intellectuals to take part in an appropriate discussion on the Nazi past.

In 1948, he was appointed Rector of the newly founded Free University in Dahlem (West Berlin) by the Allied occupation authorities and in 1948, as a symbol of the 'other Germany', was voted in as the first (honorary) rector of the Free University of Berlin, in 1951 the history department of this university was given his name. A reason for this was the fact that before 1945 he was rather an outsider in his profession.

A large number of pupils he taught later became important and well known in academic circles in both Europe and America. The prominence and influence of his pupils enhanced the reputation of Meinecke as a teacher. His career and political outlook have been frequently discussed as an example of the role of historians in German society from the period of Empire into the Nazi times. This has much to do with the fact that he was, from his generation, the only historian who experienced the changes in German history from 1914 to 1945 and 1948/49 and discussed them publicly.'

As well as one approach towards him which distinguishes Meinecke in his ability to change his opinions, a trait not usually seen in his fellow historians, which led him from being a monarchist from the heart to becoming a rational republican, there is another approach which is characterised by the continuity of this liberal ways of thinking.

He continued to exercise considerable intellectual influence on the historians of post-war Germany after his death in February 1954 in West Berlin.

18

Jules Michelet

HISTORY OF FRANCE

"The historian's first duties are sacrilege and the mocking of false gods. They are his indispensable instruments for establishing the truth."

Jules Michelet

Jules Michelet, who went on in life to become a famous French historian, was born in Paris in August 1798 into a family which had Huguenot traditions and where his father was precariously self-employed as a printer. As he grew to manhood Michelet was offered employment in the imperial printing office but his father, who had hopes for his evidently talented son, decided to keep him in school despite the relative poverty of his circumstances. The son fulfilled some of his father's expectations-he progressed from school to higher studies, in history. In 1821 he was appointed as a teacher of history. He married in 1824.

Between 1825 and 1827 Michelet produced a number of sketches, chronological tables, etc., of modern history. His *Introduction à l'histoire universelle,* published in 1831, displayed the peculiar romantic and visionary qualities which make him one the most stimulating of all historians. It also featured his tendency to indulge in historical suggestions which, although associated with solid facts, are not always trustworthy. The *Introduction à l'histoire universelle* was in fact partly inspired by the anti-rationalist approach of the philosopher Vico who had proclaimed the triumph of the imagination over analysis.

The events of 1830 which initiated the "liberal" monarchy of

Louis Philippe unmuzzled Michelet as a liberal, anti-clerical and very patriotic historian and writer, and also put him in a better position for study by obtaining for him the position of head of the Historical Section of the National Archives and a deputy-professorship under Guizot in the literary faculty of the Sorbonne.

Soon afterwards he began his chief and monumental work *Histoire de France* (History of France) in which he immersed himself in the narrative and stressed the development of France as a nation. It was in these years of his early thirties that Michelet seems to have begun to drift somewhat away from a previous acceptance of catholicism and royalism and towards more radical views.

The completion of the *Histoire de France* was to involved intermittently sustained efforts over more than thirty years from 1833 but Michelet also produced other many works during these years. Some of the earlier of these other works included *Oeuvres choisies de Vico,* the *Mémoires de Luther écrits par lui-même,* and the *Origines du droit française.*

In 1838 he was appointed professor at the Collège de France, where he held the chair of History and Ethics. He published, in 1839, his *Histoire romaine.* The results of his lectures appeared in the volumes *Le Prêtre, la femme, et la famille* (1843), and *Le Peuple* (1846).

In his *Le Peuple,* Michelet describes the spirit and qualities of the French working class. It is widely considered to be his best single volume. On its initial day of publication it sold a thousand copies and was immediately translated into English. It discussed various economic and political transformations as France and Europe shifted from an agrarian to an industrial society and examined the condition of the social classes. According to Michelet, modernization and industrialization were heightening political and ideological conflict. He called for a love of one's country to solve many of France's problems and placed faith in the innate goodness of the masses, seeing "the people" as the source of progress in history. *Le Peuple* looks to the people to unify France and make her great. Michelet believed they were the true custodians of the spirit of Joan of Arc, and that their revolution had been a revelation of the inherent nobility of humankind. Michelet visualized himself throughout his life as a champion of the people and, as the principles, (associated with disenchantment with Louis Phillipe's bourgeoise monarchy), that precipitated the outbreak of revolution of 1848 became more distinct and widely shared he was one of those who condensed and propagated them. When the revolutionism of 1848 actually broke out he devoted himself even more strenuously to his literary work.

One outcome of this period of unrest in France and Europe being the replacement of Louis Phillipe's monarchy by a republic headed by Louis Napoleon a putative nephew of Bonaparte.

Before many months passed Louis Napoleon, leader of the Second French Republic was accepted as the Emperor Napoleon III of France.

Given Michelet's sympathies for some radical aspects of the recent revolution, the government of Napoleon III suspended his popular lectures at the Collège de France in 1851. Michelet, though not in any way identified with the Second Republic administratively had refused to take the oaths of allegiance to the empire of Emperor Napoleon III, and lost his position at the National Archives.

A period of relative poverty now began for Michelet and his second wife.

The establishment of the new régime only kindled afresh his republican zeal. In the ensuing years until the fall of Napoleon III (1870), Michelet completed his enthusiastic *Histoire de la révolution française*.

His entering into marriage for a second time seems to have stimulated his literary powers. While his history studies made steady progress, a crowd of extraordinary little books accompanied them as subjects of his creative efforts. Two of the most acclaimed of these, *L'Oiseau* (1856) and *La Montagne* (1868), being on an area of interest he began to share with his new wife-natural science.

The authorship of these numerous titles, together with his major studies of French history took up a great deal of Michelet's time over the two decades after 1850. He lived partly in France and partly also in Italy and became habituated to the spending of the winter months at Hyères on the Riviera.

The term renaissance, meaning literally "rebirth," was first employed around 1855-8 by Jules Michelet to refer to the "discovery of the world and of man" in the 16th century. The great Swiss historian Jakob Burckhardt, in his classic *The Civilization of the Renaissance in Italy* (1860), expanded on Michelet's conception. Defining the Renaissance as the period between the Italian painters Giotto and Michelangelo, Burckhardt characterized the epoch as nothing less than the birth of modern humanity and consciousness after a long period of decay.

In 1867 Michelet's massive study *Histoire de France* was completed-its content now extending over some 19 volumes. Michelet was perhaps the first historian to devote himself to anything like a picturesque history of the middle ages, and his account is still the most vivid that exists. Its style, its emotional strength, and its powerful evocation make it a masterpiece of French literature. Michelet traced the biography of the nation as a whole, instead of concentrating on persons or groups of persons. His most convincing pages deal with the Middle Ages. Michelet had vast knowledge of factual detail and original documents-his inquiry into manuscript and printed authorities had been most laborious. This history, especially the latter part, views the past through Michelet's strong anti-clericalism and his leftist political prejudices, and is marred by emotional bias against the clergy, the nobility, and the monarchic institutions.

Dramatic, and sometimes bloody, events associated with the French Revolution are presented as unfortunate, but perhaps understandable, episodes that were associated with a crucial French mission to secure the liberty of the people at home and abroad.

Two chapters of the *Histoire de France,* present the most impressive of all romantic interpretations of Joan of Arc. Michelet dealt with Joan as an inspired girl from the people, as an incarnation of French patriotism. The chapters in question have been reprinted separately many times as a biography of the Maid of Orleans and such a separate presention have been referred to by some French people as "our national Bible".

Uncompromisingly hostile as Michelet was to the empire of Napoleon III, its downfall in the Franco-Prussian War of 1870-1, and the accompanying disasters of the country, once more stimulated him to activity. Not only did he write letters and pamphlets during the struggle, but when it was over he set himself to complete the vast task which his two great histories had almost covered by a *Histoire du XIX siècle*. He did not, however, live to carry it further than Waterloo.

The new republic that followed the downfall of Napoleon III was not altogether a restorarion for Michelet. His professorship, at the Collège de France of which he contended that he had never properly been deprived, was not given back to him.

He died at Hyères in February 1874.

In many ways Michelet's *Le Peuple* and other historical works expressed the romanticism of his age and reflected the credo of the liberal petite bourgeoisie. He believed in the federation of the social classes and not their disappearance, in the nation state, in improved relations between capital and labour, in Deism, in anti-clericalism, and in the infallibility of the people.

Although the Marxists criticized him because of his faith in the reconciliation of classes and the permanence of the nation state, the twentieth historian Lucien Febvre, a founder of the *Annales* school, viewed his work as an inspiration for a new variety of history because of Michelet's concern for "a total history" and "la longue durée" in history. Consequently, there has been a revival of interest in Michelet, an historian whose works reflect many of the changes, conflicts, trends, and hopes of the nineteenth century. Thus, he has had a significant impact on French historiography in both the nineteenth and twentieth centuries-an influence which continues to shape much popular historical thinking in France.

Michelet is indeed regarded by many in France as the countries greatest 'national' historian.

19

Leopold von Ranke

HISTORICISM

"You have reckoned that history ought to judge the past and to instruct the contemporary world as to the future. The present attempt does not yield to that high office. It will merely tell how it really was."
Leopold von Ranke

The son of an attorney, and a scion of an old Luther theological family, Leopold von Ranke was born in Wiehe, Thuringia, in December 1795 and later became a famous German historian and educator. Thuringia was then part of the Kingdom of Saxony but was awarded to Prussia by the peace terms of 1815 at the close of the Napoleonic wars.

Ranke attended the famous Pforta private school and, after further study at the Universities of Leipzig and Halle, he worked as a schoolmaster teaching Greek and Roman classics at the Gymnasium in Frankfort-on-the-oder; this post being one held within the Prussian system. It was only whilst employed as a schoolmaster at Frankfurt that he began to consider attempting to become seriously involved in historical studies initially with the view to improving his knowledge of the classical ages in order to be a better teacher.

His first book, History of the Latin and Teutonic Nations, 1494-1514 (1824) written at Frankfort, included an appended section entitled *Zur Kritik neuerer Geschictschreiber* (critique of modern historical writing) that presented a convincing criticism of contemporary historiography condemning its reliance on tradition and proposed, instead, Ranke's own more objective method. Ranke's aim was to reconstruct the unique periods of the past as they actually were and to avoid injecting the history of former times with the spirit of the present; this approach to historiography is known as historicism.

Ranke intended that his method would be applicable to modern history-Barthold Niebuhr had already pioneered a scientific method of historical investigation to be applied to ancient history. As a student Ranke had studied, and been greatly impressed by Niebuhr's *Roman History*-he acknowledged a debt to Niebuhr whose approach had been a source of backround inspiration.

Ranke distrusted historical textbooks and turned, at every convenient opportunity, to the study of more original sources. This method Ranke later developed to feature a primarily reliance on the "narratives of eye-witnesses and the most genuine immediate documents." He considered that "the strict presentation of the facts, contingent and unattractive though they may be, is undoubtedly the supreme law."

Ranke's *Zur Kritik neuerer Geschictschreiber* was favourably noticed by the Prussian minister of education and, in 1825, he was rewarded with a supernumerary professorship at the University of Berlin that initiated what were to become more than fifty years of association between Ranke and that University.

This appointment brought with it opportunities of access to the Prussian royal library.

Further studies resulted in Ranke's second book on the Ottomans and the Spanish monarchy and the quality of this work invited the continued favour of the Prussian authority which agreed to facilitate Ranke's studies being further undertaken in archives in Vienna. From these times (1827) Ranke was enabled, by the support of Gentz, to gain the protection of the powerful Austrian minister Metternich and this was to allow him very wide access to archived materials and thereby to gain very valuable information from Venetian and other sources located in Vienna.

Between 1828-31 Ranke pursued his lonely, sincere, and path-breaking studies, in the Italian peninsula where Metternich's influence had the power to open every door except those in the Vatican.

Most of these archived sources had not been seriously accessed by any historical scholar in the past and Ranke's researches in Vienna and the Italian peninsula provided the material for some of the most respected historical writing of the age.

The Prussian authority sought to employ Ranke's talents, for a time, in the editorship of the *Historische-Politische-Zeitschrift*, a periodical that was intended to help to defend the Prussian Government against the rising tide of liberal and democratic opinion. In this role, which lasted some four years, Ranke produced some of the best political thought that had appeared in the Germanies for a long time. Two famous essays *The Great Powers*, which surveys great power rivalry, and *A Political Conversation*, which treats with the nature of the state and its relationship with the citizen, date from this period.

A talent for historical and political scholarship proved, however, to be somewhat ill matched to the intended task of impairing the effectiveness of the expression of democratic aspirations.

Ranke was thus able to return to historical study and authorship.

His subsequent works cover the histories of the major European countries and include the History of the Popes During the 16th and 17th Centuries (1834-36), History of the Reformation in Germany (1839-47), Civil Wars and Monarchy in France in the 16th and 17th Centuries (1852).

He was awarded the security, and much enhanced salary, of a full professorship in Berlin in 1837 and was appointed as Prussian historiographer by King Frederick William IV in 1841.

He died in May, 1886 at the age of 91; the last ten years of his life having been given over to a *Weltgeschichte* (universal history) that Ranke had been able to bring, over nine volumes, to the end of the 15th century at the time of his death.

As a historian, Ranke attempted to put aside prevailing theories and prejudices and by the scrupulous use of primary sources to present an unvarnished picture of the facts. Nevertheless, because he viewed political power as the principal agent in history he tended to emphasize political history, dwelling upon the deeds of kings and leaders and ignoring economic and social forces.

A famous educator, he introduced the seminar as a method of teaching history and trained a generation of influential scholars. Since Ranke's time the seminar method of teaching history has become very widely adopted.

At the time of his death Ranke was regarded as the foremost historian in the world. Ranke's method of historicism has largely pioneered the modern insistence on rigorously analyzing firsthand documentation. He has variously been described as "The greatest German historian", "The father of the objective writing of history", and "The founder of the science of history."

Ranke does occasionally adopt a literary approach in his writing of history that tends to build up to a presentation of historical climaxes and also to build up certain historical figures whose contributions are deemed to be particularly significant. This adds to the readability and the drama of Ranke's works but it may not be strictly true that such literary effectiveness is fully in line with history "as it had really been."

Ranke aimed at an universal or world view of history, but his basic mood was nationalistic and conservative, accepting of monarchy and sincerely religious, the massive changes after the French Revolution are hardly discussed. Ranke seems to have seen the role of liberalism as being perhaps confined to the calling of the attention of statesmen to wrongs that needed correction.

His books on Prussian history contained, with no intention for it to be used for propaganda purposes, the seeds for a Prussian national German picture of history. This legacy compels one to critical reflection, but at the same time it points to a flourishing time in historical research at the Berlin University, started by Ranke, which above all Max Lenz and Friedrich Meinecke were able to continue.

"From the particular, one can carefully and boldly move up to the general; from general theories, there is no way of looking at the particular."

20

Simon Schama

A HISTORY OF BRITAIN

"Historians are left forever chasing shadows, painfully aware of their inability ever to reconstruct a dead world in its completeness however thorough or revealing their documentation. We are doomed to be forever hailing someone who has just gone around the corner and out of earshot." Simon Schama

"Afterword," Dead Certainties (1991).

Simon Schama was born in London in February 1945 into a Jewish family-both sets of grandparents had fled persecution, one from the remnants of the Ottoman empire, the other from Lithuania. Immigration, movement, cultural collision are part of his experience and are central themes in his work.

His father was a textile merchant who did well enough after the war for the family to move out to Essex, where they lived near Leigh-on-Sea. The young Schama enjoyed the non-kosher delights of Southend-he calls it "gloriously lurid" and salivates over the "flaccid, vinegar-saturated chips" and "cylinders of Day-Glo-pink rock candy"-and he eulogised the visual pleasures of the Thames estuary in Landscape and Memory. One of his father's periodic financial disasters necessitated a move back to London, to a more modest house in Golders Green, but Schama's intellectual progress was secure. He won a scholarship to Haberdashers' Aske's school, was captivated by a series of inspirational teachers, and shone at English and history, opting to study the latter at Christ's College, Cambridge, but never quite forgetting the former. His writing career and the way he commutes between art history and history reflect his fertile marriage of the two disciplines.

At Cambridge he fell under the spell of Plumb, whose 60's students-Linda Colley, Roy Porter, John Brewer-now dominate British historical thinking. Plumb instilled in his students the importance of style and a commitment to narrative; he "taught us that writing was not just an auxiliary to research, wanted people outside the academy to read history, wanted it to be entertaining," Schama has said.

Schama, with his starred first, immediately became a fellow at Christ's, but without tenure. He stayed for 10 years, his contract perpetually renewed, teaching, delivering a famously vivid set of lectures on the French revolution-complete with funny voices, waving arms and impersonations of Marat-and working on the book that became Patriots and Liberators, a fairly conventional treatment of the impact of the French revolution on Holland for which he was awarded the Wolfson Prize for History.

The expected tenured job at Cambridge never came, so in 1976 he took a fellowship at Brasenose, Oxford. He stayed for only four years before, tired of the teaching, the syllabus and the lottery that was the exam system ("I felt like a gerbil on a treadmill"), he headed for a professorship at Harvard, where a year earlier he had delivered a set of lectures on the Civilization of the Netherlands exploring themes that would later resurface in The Embarrassment of Riches, the 1987 history of the Dutch golden age that cemented his reputation and, some believe, is his most perfect fusion of historical narrative and cultural critique.

After The Embarrassment of Riches, Schama wrote Citizens: A Chronicle of the French Revolution. Commissioned by Penguin and written at breakneck speed, it was a triumph, admired everywhere except France where, in the revolution's bicentenary year, they found it hard to stomach his argument that from the beginning it had been the harbinger of terror, a "sacrament of blood". He was accused of Fukuyama-style revisionism, but denied the charge: he was, he insisted, no conservative, no apologist for the ancien regime; he told one interviewer he was on the right in the old Labour party, on the left in the new.

In 1991, his confidence and the urge to experiment growing, he produced Dead Certainties (Unwarranted Speculations), a curious hybrid of fact and fiction linking the death of General Wolfe in 1759 with the trial for murder of a Boston professor in 1849. It was bold, imaginative, daring-and almost universally disliked.

From 1995-98, Schama was art critic and cultural essayist for The New Yorker magazine. In 1996 he produced a television series called Landscape and Memory-fact, certainly, but fact presented in a uniquely imaginative, coruscating way. Reviewers entered their caveats and readers struggled with its sheer munificence-it posed as many questions as it answered-but the book sold well and won plaudits and prizes. Schama had become a phenomenon.

He is a populariser of history, but never dumbs down. His books are by no means easy reading. As his friend Antonia Fraser says: "If he wanted to achieve great popular success, he has a funny way of going about it." But his books do strike a chord and appeal to a large general audience; his wonderful titles, the breadth and humanity of his vision, the scale of his enterprise, the willingness to fail set him apart from other historians. He has become part of the cultural conversation in the US and the UK, and the plugged-in classes want to read him, or will at least buy his books with that intention.

The first batch of the 'A History of Britain' series of documentaries that were produced for the BBC to mark the Millenium were broadcast in autumn 2000. A second batch, screened spring 2001, took the story up to the end of the eighteenth century, and the series subsequently concluded with a look back at the last 200 years. The series was, in part, the odyssey of Schama as a returning exile, and in part a portrait of a society built on layers of immigration, exploring the tensions between sometimes competing cultural groups and the way identity is forged on the anvil of difference.

Everyone says that Schama is "brilliant", but the word is nuanced depending on who is saying it. His friends, of course, mean it. Take the historian Peter Hennessy, who has known him since they were at Cambridge together in the 60s. "He gets arcane matters to walk, in fact to dance, off the page," says Hennessy. "He was always like that, and to sustain that degree of verve over three decades is amazing. He was very precocious-I always knew he would be a star; he had brilliance and bubble, and nobody does narrative better than him."

A leading British historian who prefers not to be named also calls Schama "brilliant" and "engaging", but the meaning he gives those words is rather less flattering. "Academics tend to be quite sniffy about his work," he says. "He isn't engaged in quite the same project as the academic historian. He is concerned to present the past in a vivid fashion-which is not what academics are supposed to do. Their approach tends to be more analytical. He is in the tradition of Macaulay and principally concerned to evoke atmospheres. But the danger of that is that the imagination takes over; we just don't know enough about the past to be able to do it." Sometimes, perhaps, one can be a little too brilliant.

21

A.J.P. Taylor—Revisionism

THE ORIGINS OF THE SECOND WORLD WAR

(Alan John Percivale) A.J.P. Taylor was born in March, 1906, at Birkdale, Lancashire, England into a politically liberal family that enjoyed a definite affluence through involvements in the cotton industry-he was to be the only surviving child.

He showed early signs of intelligence as he began reading books and newspapers from a notably young age with a particular penchant for historical novels.

Due to his parent's opposition to the Great War then raging in Europe he was educated at Quaker schools (the Quaker Christian sect being committed to pacifism). He had a maternal uncle who was punished as a Conscientious Objector after refusing to obey government instructions that he serve in the army. His parents were moved by the example of the Russian Revolution to embrace Bolshevik sympathies-one Walton Newbold, a slightly notorious Conscientious Objector of Quaker background then 'on the run' from the authorities, who later became the first Communist Member of the British Parliament, was a clandestine visitor to the Taylor home.

As a thirteen-year-old in 1919 Taylor proved to be something of a rebellious influence in his last year at his preparatory school (The Downs School, Malvern) where, during a time when many pupils were laid low with the Mumps, he was responsible for transforming the student school Cabinet as approved of by the headmaster into a body which sought, amongst other things, to abolish corporal punishment. Taylor moved on to the Bootham School, York, and was, at the end of his time there (1924) awarded a scholarship by Oriel College, Oxford.

At Oxford he experienced something of a culture shock as he had decided 'Lancashire', 'Leftist', and 'irreligious' characteristics that were out of place in its plummy, conservative, and somewhat episcopalian groves of academe.

Whilst a student at Oxford Taylor became involved in various ways with support for the Communist Party. In the summer of 1925 Taylor, together with his mother and her political protege Henry Sara, (a sometime socialistic journalist who was a foundation member of the Communist Party of Great Britain), visited a Russia which was then experiencing the relatively balmy days of the New Economic Policy. In these weeks Taylor laid eyes on Lenin, heard Zinoviev speak, and met Kamenev and Litvinov.

Back in Oxford however Taylor's involvement with Communism was to be brief due to his disgust with what he saw as the party's do-nothing approach in the General Strike of 1926.

Taylor graduated from Oriel College with first-class honours in 1927. He considered that the course had just completed had primarily been structured to offer its participants, who might actually have no real interest in history, opportunities of gaining 'good' degrees that would enable them to secure prestigious jobs in the civil service or in commerce.

Uncertain about his path after graduation, he briefly clerked with his Conscientious Objector uncle (now a prominent left-wing solicitor-at-Law), but grew bored with the job. In 1928 he somewhat irregularly returned to Oriel for graduate work in history-he had no formal 'permission' to do so but just 'turned up.' His father was wealthy enough to finance further studies, Oriel College did not turn him away, Taylor himself imagined that this course might well lead to his becoming a schoolmaster.

Despite his own 'first class' degree qualification Taylor did not accept that he had actually as yet been trained as an historian. Whilst he had some familiarity with the French language a lecturer at Oriel advised him that he would have to achieve a good understanding of German if he really hoped to become an historian.

After Taylor had tried unsuccessfully for several possible openings in Germany a Professor mentioned a friend who was a professional colleague in Vienna and encouraged Taylor to apply to for a placement in that city.

Amongst other considerations Taylor was attracted by the reputation Vienna then had as being in the vanguard of European socialism-he applied, was awarded the opportunity of an interview, and was accepted. He subsequently kept up studies there for some two years-learning German mainly by reading german language works of history with, initially fairly constant, reference to a billingual dictionary.

The Viennese Radicals prior to 1848 had been initially agreed as his topic of study but Taylor found that studies in the "History of Ideas" did not suit him. His academic supervisor, Professor Pribram, suggested a study in diplomatic history concentrating on Anglo-Austrian relations between 1848 and 1866. At this time Taylor was in no way familiar with Diplomatic documentation. His autobiography records that:-

"I had never seen a diplomatic document before and simply plunged in at the deep end without any instruction. I did not know the difference between an original dispatch and a private letter. I had no idea how to weigh the reliability of historical evidence. I did not even know that I must note the number of each document, an ignorance which caused me much unnecessary labour. Nowadays graduate students are taught these things in their first seminars. I operated as though no one had worked in diplomatic archives before."

Some familiarity with the content of the archives was followed by Taylor again seeking to change his main subject of study as he thought that it would be interesting to focus on the international diplomacy surrounding the position of northern parts of the Italian peninsula in 1848-a time when Austrian governance there was being openly challenged by an array of 'Italian' interests.

Alongside these months of historical and diplomatic studies Taylor learned to ice-skate, to horse-ride, and also began to seriously frequent classical music recitals.

In 1930 Professor Pribram delivered that years Ford lectures at Oxford. Whilst at Oxford he heard from a friend of a lecturing appointment at Manchester University for which Taylor might be suitable. Taylor secured this assistant lecturership-he initially 'lectured' by reading out pre-prepared notes but eventually decided to lecture entirely from memory.

Manchester was already familiar to him as his family's roots were in the north east of England. He became active in trade-union politics, developing his talent for speaking to audiences by often addressing hundreds in town meetings. He also began writing reviews and essays for the Manchester Guardian (later The Guardian). In 1934 his first book, *The Italian Problem in European Diplomacy 1847-49,* was published.

The editor of the Manchester Guardian began to commission full articles from Taylor whilst pressing home the message that:- 'An article in the Guardian is no good unless people read it on the way to work.'

By these times Mussolini was in power in Italy and Hitler was in power in Germany-Europe had seriously begun to become a 'Europe of the Dictators' and the possibility of war led to the formation of variously directed anti-war movements.

Taylor's approach was pro-Russian, he considered that the British government were really hoping that Germany would be a future ally in keeping Soviet Russia at bay. Taylor thus opposed British rearmament as Britain was in his view anti-Russian. (He even proposed an alliance with Russia!). As early as February 1936, however, Taylor came to view Hitler's Germany as most likely to become open adversary in the future and began to support rearmament regardless of the present British governmentment policy of hoping for an accomodation with Germany whilst holding aloof from association with Soviet Russia.

In 1936 Taylor was appointed as full lecturer at Manchester with security of tenure. Although he was in many ways quite happy with his life in Manchester his friends encouragement that he consider questions of professional advancement, and his own realisation that this was pretty much expected of him, led to his applying for various positions at Oxford University.

In 1938, he became a fellow of Oxford's Magdalen College where he was to tutor in modern history. Although the academics of the 'City of the Dreaming Spires' considered that their University was a place where any academic person would dearly love to find employment Taylor found much there that appeared to him to be old-fashioned and parochial when he took up his new teaching position.

During the war Taylor, as a teacher of modern history, was regarded as helping to clarify why Britain was involved in the conflict. He was therefore not considered for military service but he did give lectures to servicemen about modern Europe and also featured on a weekly series radio broadcasts for the BBC.

In order to provide for home defence the government decided to organise units of Local Defence Volunteers later officially renamed the Home Guard and unofficially known as 'Dads Army.' Taylor joined early in the process of recruitment and found himself in the company of other volunteering academics such as C.S. Lewis.

Taylor's involvement with European matters led to his being approached by for help a prominent Hungarian exile named Michael Karolyi who later became a friend. Karolyi introduced Taylor to other central and eastern Europeans in British exile and this helped to broaden Taylor's understanding of the nationalities of central and eastern European.

In these times a colleague was approached by a major publisher to write a short history of modern Austria but this colleague did not feel that he could be successful as an author of a history on this subject with the result that Taylor embarked upon writing a constitutional and narrative history that was later published as *The Habsburg Monarchy 1815-1918*.

Hitler's invasion of Soviet Russia in 1941 opened up a vista that Taylor had hoped for before the war-an alliance between Britain and Russia as adversaries of Hitler's Germany. Before many months had passed Taylor was consulted, as a left-leaning expert on central and eastern Europe, by a clandestine Government sponsored agency called the Political Warfare Executive.

From 1943 Taylor was occasionally called upon to write leading articles for the Manchester Guardian. Before many months had passed the writing of most of its leading articles on foreign affairs were entrusted to him. His involvement with the Political Warfare Executive led to the writing of an article on Weimar Germany that was later expanded into a work entitled *The Course of German History* (1945) which became a best-seller. The line it took over an effective alliance between the Junkers and heavy industry from the times of Bismarck was not in accordance with established historical wisdom in Britain.

After the war ended, Taylor continued to write, including an extensive re-write of *The Habsburg Monarchy 1809-1918*, in the more vivid style that was now at his command due to his journalistic experience.

From early 1948 his standing as a left leaning academic friendly to Russia became somewhat open to question with the emergence of an increasing chilliness in relations between the former eastern and western allies. This chilliness proved to be the onset of the Cold War.

Taylor was invited to contribute a volume on international relations between 1848 and 1914 to an ongoing project that was intended to produce a twenty volume *Oxford History of Modern Europe*.

The proceedings of a UNESCO sponsored conference on Fascism that he attended in Monte Carlo included his preparing a document on Adolf Hitler that led him to see the German leader as an opportunist in his several policies rather than as a person who had consistently followed a definite evil plan.

In the summer of 1950 Taylor began a year of sabbatical leave that he intended to devote to research in diplomatic history. It happened, however, that he based himself in London where he was called upon by a former associate in radio broadcasting to appear as a panellist on a weekly BBC television programme of political discussion. A program called *In the News* was subsequently broadcast once a week and Taylor began to gain in celebrity and public notice.

At this time there were only a few hundred thousand TV sets in Britain, and these seem to have been taken up moreso by affluent and skilled working people than by the middle classes or intellectuals. Taylor began to find that he was increasingly recognised and addressed as "Alan". He was also building a perception of himself as a *Plain Man's Historian.*

Another outcome of this sabbatical year was *The Struggle for Mastery in Europe 1848-1918* (1954) a work of detailed diplomatic history which was very well received by reviewers and helped to soundly establish Taylor's academic reputation.

In 1953 Taylor was appointed as a special lecturer by the History Board at Oxford. This allowed him more opportunity for research whilst also involving a lessened burden of teaching duties.

In 1954 Taylor was invited to prepare to deliver the next series of Ford lectures (in 1956) at Oxford. The Ford lectures are widely thought to be the most prestigious lectures in history in the English speaking world.

The series of lectures involved were to be, in line with tradition, on English history: this was not Taylor's speciality but a friend suggested that Taylor, as a sometime opponent of government policy, lecture on a range of British people who had opposed the official government foreign policy in the past.

Taylor was well pleased with this suggestion and his extensive preparations for the Ford lectures also eventually resulted in a work that was published as *The Trouble Makers: Dissent Over British Foreign Policy 1792-1939 (1957).*

Unlike many previous Ford lecturers Taylor lectured over six, one-hour, sessions without the benefit of notes. He was also unlike many other lecturers in that the audience did not diminish as the series progressed such that the lectures had, almost unprecedently, to be maintained in a venue with adequate seating.

The impression this feat of presentation made upon observers resulted in Taylor being invited to feature in a series of half-hour TV programmes where he would be filmed lecturing, without benefit of notes, on historical topics. The first such series of three lectures on the Russian Revolution proved to be a success and this resulted in his being involved in one or two series of six of such lectures, each year, for each of the next ten years.

Following a conversation with the overall editor of the *Oxford History of Modern Europe* Taylor was accepted as the author of yet another volume in the series-this time on *English History 1914-1945*.

This acceptance incidentally led to the newspaper magnate Lord Beaverbrook became a sometime employer, and a friend, following a favourable review that Taylor had disinterestedly written in relation to Beaverbrook's historical work *Men and Power*. He had accepted this and other volumes for review in association with his researches towards *English History 1914-1945*. Taylor later counted Beaverbrook to have been the cleverest man he ever knew.

In these times the British Government had approved the building up of a stock of nuclear weapons and in 1958 Taylor made a first speech in favour of unilateral nuclear disarmament by Britain. Shortly thereafter an article in the *New Statesman* informed him of a group who were contemplating involvement in a campaign for nuclear disarmament. As a result Taylor was one of those in attendance at the very first meeting of the CND executive.

Other active persons of particular celebrity being Kingsley Martin, J.B. Priestly, E.P. Thompson, Bertrand Russell and Labour MP Michael Foot.

Taylor's *The Origins of the Second World War* written between 1957-61 proved to be vastly controversial. It challenged the then accepted view that Hitler had been an uniquely evil plotter of war by presenting a view of Hitler as an opportunist, who had enjoyed much popular support in Germany and Austria. Hitler's pushed for various reforms of diverse aspects of the peace settlement to the First World War hoping to secure concessions that would be satisfactory to Germanic sentiment.

When he came to power, Hitler inherited vast potential. By the twentieth century Germany's large population and industrial might gave the country a natural pre-eminence in west-central Europe, and the Versailles settlement of 1919 was an artificial absurdity that was bound to unravel. This unraveling could have been done rationally, as in the early stages of British and French appeasement over the Rhineland, Germany's *anschluss* with Austria, and so on; but after Munich, in 1938, it was increasingly bungled. Having appeased Berlin over more-contestable territorial issues, the British changed their stance and decided to fight over Danzig and the Polish Corridor, where the German case for revision was stronger. The result, Taylor maintained, was a war in Europe that nobody wanted and that personally dismayed Hitler. World War II was simply an accident: Hitler never imagined that the democracies would actually go to war over Poland, especially because London and Paris could do almost nothing to defend the Poles. Great Britain and France had in the past vacillated between policies of appeasement and resistance.

Taylor's own statements such as *"in principle and doctrine, Hitler was no more wicked and unscrupulous than many a contemporary statesman"* outraged very many people who thought of the racial imperialism, and of the death camps, that had been evident in the Second World War as being monstrously evil.

Taylor does however say of Hitler that *"in wicked acts he outdid them all."*

Fellow historian Hugh Trevor-Roper—Taylor's antagonist in the fierce debates over Hitler that roiled the intellectual world after Origins was published—once remarked, "The sad fact is that Taylor is really too independent to have any support from any Establishment." Taylor managed to annoy just about everybody in the British historical profession, and his interpretive daring, while sometimes strikingly original, often seemed willfully perverse to his peers and colleagues.

Taylor's initially 'outrageous' revisionism was increasingly, but not fully, accepted by British historians and by a majority amongst the rising generation of German historians.

English History 1914-1945 was finished in manuscript in July 1964. It was considered by Taylor to be technically the best book he had written and when published in paperback proved to be a bestseller

He loved to twit the United States, and often advocated an alliance between Britain and the USSR. "Anyone who claims to learn from history," he wrote with breathtaking assurance in 1967, "should devote himself to promoting an Anglo-Soviet alliance, the most harmless and pacific of all possible combinations."

In 1976 A.J.P. Taylor reached the age of seventy-this being the retirement age at Magdalen College. He accepted a visiting professorship at Bristol University which was maintained over the two years 1976-1978. He continued to be intermittently involved in television broadcasts and in lecturing after this time.

During his career he had written more than thirty books and was awarded several honorary Doctoral degrees (from the Universities of New Brunswick, York, Bristol, Warwick and Manchester). He died in September 1990 in London.

In retrospect we can say that A.J.P. Taylor was the best-known British historian of the twentieth century, certainly the most popular and probably the most influential. His books, particularly The Struggle for Mastery in Europe, The Origins of the Second World War, and English History 1914-1945 changed the way history was written and read. Most of all-and unlike any other historian before or since-Taylor made history accessible, controversial and enjoyable to a mass audience.

"I was born without ambition and this made the conventional rewards of life dust and ashes for me or not even that. History has always been my consuming passion: reading history, writing history, lecturing about history. I am afraid I enjoyed teaching history less: something I had to do in order to justify my academic position and of course also to bring in some money. Once I discovered that I could earn money more easily by becoming a journalist I slipped out of teaching history and I can almost say became an historian in my spare time. But I think I remained a good historian: careful about my sources, trying to set down the truth as I saw it. I have never belonged to a school of history, whether Marxism or Les Annales. I am a plain narrative historian and I hope I give the reader plenty of entertainment as well. For me writing history has been Fun on a high academic level. Add television lectures which combined history and entertainment and my enjoyment was complete. I would not have changed my professional life for any other in the world."

22

Antony Beevor

STALINGRAD

Berlin-The Downfall 1945

The award-winning military historian Antony Beevor was born in England in December 1946 and when he was small suffered from a condition called Perthes disease, which makes the hipbone go soft, with the result that medical treatment, between the ages of four and seven, required that he go on crutches.

His second level education was completed at Winchester College where he failed his A-level course due to what he regards as his own 'undirected bloody-mindedness'. From Winchester Beevor went to the Royal Military College, Sandhurst, where he studied under Sir John Keegan who was himself a recognised military historian. A regular officer 1967-70 with the 11th Hussars, he left the Army to write. He has had four novels published beginning with Violent Brink in 1975, and six works of non-fiction. They include *The Spanish Civil War* (1982); *Crete — The Battle and the Resistance* (1991), which was awarded a Runciman Prize, and *Paris After the Liberation, 1944-1949* (written with his wife Artemis Cooper-1994).

These early works gained some critical acceptance and seemed to offer some hope of material rewards but it was with Beevor's *Stalingrad,* first published in 1998, which won the first Samuel Johnson Prize, the Wolfson Prize for History and the Hawthornden Prize for Literature in 1999 that his celebrity as a military historian was firmly established. The British edition, a number one bestseller in both hardback and paperback, has so far sold over half a million copies. The book is also published in the United States and will be appearing in twenty-four foreign editions. Worldwide sales exceed 1.1 million. It was not in fact his own idea to endeavour to produce *Stalingrad* but had the subject suggested to him by a literary editor of some of his earlier works. Antony Beevor has said of this work that the tactical aspects of the story had been very well covered previously but that in terms of his own approach to the subject *'The challenge was to put back in the detail of human experience'*.

It is such reconstructions that Beevor has made his signature. Few describe with more sympathy and pathos the quotidian business of soldiering: the lore, the rituals, the sorrows, the joys-even the jokes.

"Those surrounded by danger do become intensely superstitious," Beevor explains. "Outsiders sometimes fail to understand that armies are very emotional organisations; on the surface is discipline and hierarchy but the emotions boiling underneath are terribly strong."

"Even the German army in its most murderous mode in Russia was appallingly sentimental. Appallingly because while the troops were celebrating Christmas in Stalingrad in 1942-and being terribly sentimental about their camaraderie, loyalty and their families at home-they were busily starving to death Russian prisoners, who were reduced to cannibalism."

Berlin – The Downfall 1945, published in 2002, was accompanied by a BBC Timewatch programme on his research into the subject. The book will also be appearing in twenty-four foreign editions. It has already been a No. 1 Bestseller in a number of countries apart from Britain.

Antony Beevor was made a Chevalier de l'Ordre des Arts et Lettres by the French government in 1997 and was elected a Fellow of the Royal Society of Literature in 1999. He was the 2002-2003 Lees-Knowles lecturer at Cambridge. In 2003, he received the first Longman-History Today Trustees' Award. He is a member of the management committee of the Society of Authors and the London Library. He is also Visiting Professor at the School of History, Classics and Archaeology at Birkbeck College, University of London. He lives in London with his wife and two children.

23

Adam Hart-Davis—Historian

LOCAL HEROES & WHAT THE ROMANS DID FOR US

Dr. Adam John Hart-Davis (born on July 4, 1943) is a British author, photographer, and broadcaster, well-known in the UK for presenting the television series Local Heroes and What the Romans Did for Us, the latter spawning several spin-off series involving the Victorians (What the Victorians Did for Us), the Tudors (What the Tudors Did for Us), and the Stuarts (What the Stuarts Did for Us). He was also a co-presenter of Tomorrow's World, and continues to present Science Shack.

Born and raised in Henley-on-Thames, he attended Eton College (receiving A and S-levels in Chemistry, Physics and Maths but failing his History O-level), before studying for an MA in chemistry at the University of Oxford. He later took a DPhil in organometallic chemistry at the University of York before doing three years of a post-doctoral thesis at the University of Alberta in Canada. Subsequently, he worked at the Oxford University Press, editing science texts and chess manuals.

His work in broadcasting began in 1977 when he joined Yorkshire Television as a researcher, working on material for the likes of Magnus Pyke, David Bellamy, Miriam Stoppard and Arthur C. Clarke.

In 1985 he was promoted to production work, producing Arthur C. Clarke's World of Strange Powers, the Fred Harris-fronted TV show Me & My Micro and the Johnny Ball-fronted Fun & Games amongst other things. He also devised and produced the highly popular school science show Scientific Eye which was widely viewed in the UK and in some thirty five other countries.

In the early 1990s he moved in front of the camera to present two series for the YTV region: Local Heroes and On the Edge (a scientific look at the east coast region).

Local Heroes involved him cycling around the country in his trademark fluorescent pink and yellow cycling clothes, seeking out places associated with the great innovators of science and technology.

He seems to have stumbled on the idea for this programme somewhat by accident-in the summer of 1990, feeling himself to be becoming a little older and little fatter, he had decided to pursue other ways of keeping fit than playing Squash so he bought a mountain bike choosing one in pink and yellow in order to be visible and stay alive:-

" One day I was staggering up the long hill from Birstall to Drighlington, when I spotted a blue plaque on what turned out to be Field Head Farm, almost overhanging the M62. Having discovered this was Joseph Priestley's birth place, I then found he had spent his teenage years with his Aunt at the Old Hall in Heckmondwicke, which had become my local pub, and had discovered oxygen as a result of watching the beer brewing in a brewery in Leeds."

Adam Hart-Davis felt sufficienty hooked by this brush with 'living history' as to tell all his colleagues about it — and with such enthusiasm that his boss suggested that he should make a television programme. This was the beginning of the Local Heroes series of programmes.

Local Heroes was subsequently transferred to BBC2, where its scope widened from the Yorkshire region towards a nationwide coverage, a different region being the subject of each episode.

Since then he has essentially become the face of the BBC's output on science and the history of science. At the same time he is heavily critical of the standard of science output on British television (including, to a certain extent, his own programmes), which he sees as dumbed-down.

He has written many books, including a history of the toilet, entitled Thunder, Flush and Thomas Crapper (Thomas Crapper being one of the pioneers of the toilet's development).

Adam is the youngest child of the publisher Sir Rupert Hart-Davis (1907-1999), his siblings being the historian, biographer and journalist Peter Duff Hart-Davis and Bridget Min Hart-Davis *aka* Lady Silsoe.

He has received eight honorary doctorates and is a fellow of the Royal Society of Arts. He is the partner of the psychologist Dr. Susan Blackmore. He lives with her and her family in the west of England.

24

Edward Augustus Freeman

[The following text is derived from the "classical" 11th Edition of the Encyclopedia Brittanica that was published in 1911.]

Edward Augustus Freeman (1823-1892), English historian, was born at Harborne, Staffordshire, on the 2nd of August 1823. He lost both his parents in infancy, was brought up by a grandmother, and was educated at private schools and by a private tutor. He was a studious and precocious boy, more interested in religious matters, history and foreign politics than in boyish things.

He obtained a scholarship at Trinity College, Oxford, and a second class in the degree examination, and was elected fellow of his college (1845). While at Oxford he was much influenced by the High Church movement, and thought seriously of taking orders, but abandoned the idea.

He married a daughter of his former tutor, the Rev. R. Gutch, in 1847, and entered on a life of study. Ecclesiastical architecture attracted him strongly. He visited many churches and began a practice, which he pursued throughout his life, of making drawings of buildings on the spot and afterwards tracing them over in ink. His first book, save for his share in a volume of English verse, was a *History of Architecture* (1849).

Though he had not then seen any buildings outside England, it contains a good sketch of the development of the art. It is full of youthful enthusiasm and is written in florid language. After some changes of residence he bought a house called Somerleaze, near Wells, Somerset, and settled there in 1860.

Freeman's life was one of strenuous literary work. He wrote many books, and countless articles for reviews, newspapers and other publications, and was a constant contributor to the *Saturday Review* until 1878, when he ceased to write for it for political reasons. His *Saturday Review* articles corrected many errors and raised the level of historical knowledge among the educated classes, but as a reviewer he was apt to forget that a book may have blemishes and yet be praiseworthy. For some years he was an active county magistrate. He was deeply interested in politics, was a follower of Mr Gladstone, and approved the Home Rule Bill of 1886, but objected to the later proposal to retain the Irish members at Westminster.

To be returned to Parliament was one of his few ambitions, and in 1868 he unsuccessfully contested Mid-Somerset. Foreign rather than domestic politics had the first place with him. Historical and religious sentiment combined with his destestation of all that was tyrannical to inspire him with hatred of the Turk and sympathy with the smaller and subject nationalities of eastern Europe. He took a prominent part in the agitation which followed "the Bulgarian atrocities"; his speeches were intemperate, and he was accused of uttering the words "Perish India!" at a public meeting in 1876. This, however, was a misrepresentation of his words. He was made a knight commander of the order of the Saviour by the king of Greece, and also received an order from the prince of Montenegro.

Freeman advanced the study of history in England in two special directions, by insistence on the unity of history, and by teaching the importance and right use of original authorities. History is not, he urges, to' be divided "by a middle wall of partition" into ancient and modern, nor broken into fragments as though the history of each nation stood apart. It is more than a collection of narratives; it is a science, "the science of man in his political character."

The historical student, then, cannot afford to be indifferent to any part of the record of man's political being; but as his abilities for study are limited, he will, while reckoning all history to be within his range, have his own special range within which he will master every detail (*Rede Lecture).* Freeman's range included Greek,

Roman and the earlier part of English history, together with some portions of foreign medieval history, and he had a scholarly though general knowledge of the rest of the history of the European world.

He regarded the abiding life of Rome as "the central truth of European history," the bond of its unity, and he undertook his *History of Sicily* (1891-1894) partly because it illustrated this unity. Further, he urges that all historical study is valueless which does not take in a knowledge of original authorities, and he teaches both by example and precept what authorities should be thus described, and how they are to be weighed and used. He did not use manuscript authorities, and for most of his work he had no need to do so. The authorities which he needed were already in print, and his books would not have been better if he had disinterred a few more facts from unprinted sources.

His reputation as a historian will chiefly rest on his *History of the Norman Conquest* (1867-1876), his longest completed book. In common with his works generally, it is distinguished by exhaustiveness of treatment and research, critical ability, a remarkable degree of accuracy, and a certain insight into the past which he gained from his practical experience of men and institutions. He is almost exclusively a political historian. His saying that "history is past politics and politics are present history" is significant of this limitation of his work, which left on one side subjects of the deepest interest in a nation's life. In dealing with constitutional matters he sometimes attaches too much weight to words and formal aspects.

This gives certain of his arguments an air of pedantry, and seems to lead him to find evidences of continuity in institutions which in reality and spirit were different from what they once had been. As a rule his estimates of character are remarkably able. It is true that he is sometimes swayed by prejudice, but this is the common lot of great historians; they cannot altogether avoid sharing in the feelings of the past, for they live in it, and Freeman did so to an extraordinary degree. Yet if he judges too favourably the leaders of the national party in England on the eve of the Norman Conquest, that is a small matter to set against the insight which he exhibits in writing of Aratus, Sulla, Nicias, William the

Conqueror, Thomas of Canterbury, Frederick the Second and many more.

In width of view, thoroughness of investigation and honesty of purpose he is unsurpassed by any historian. He never conceals nor wilfully misrepresents anything, and he reckoned no labour too great which might help him to draw a truthful picture of the past. When a place had any important connexion with his work he invariably visited it. He travelled much, always to gain knowledge, and generally to complete his historical equipment. His collected articles and essays on places of historical interest are perhaps the most pleasing of his writings, but they deal exclusively with historical associations and architectural features.

The quantity of work which he turned out is enormous, for the fifteen large volumes which contain *'his ' Norman Conquest,* his unfinished *History of Sicily,* his *William Rufus* (1882), and his *Essays* (1872-1879), and the crowd of his smaller books, are matched in amount by his uncollected contributions to periodicals. In respect of matter his historical work is uniformly excellent. In respect of form and style the case is different.

Though his sentences themselves are not wordy, he is extremely diffuse in treatment, habitually repeating an idea in successive sentences of much the same import. While this habit was doubtless aggravated by the amount of his journalistic work, it seems originally to have sprung from what may be called a professorial spirit, which occasionally appears in the tone of his remarks. He was anxious to make sure that his readers would understand his exact meaning, and to guard them against all possible misconceptions.

His lengthy explanations are the more grievous because he insists on the same points in several of his books. His prolixity was increased by his unwillingness, when writing without prescribed limits, to leave out any detail, however unimportant. His passion for details not only swelled his volumes to a portentous size, but was fatal to artistic construction. The length of his books has hindered their usefulness. They were written for the public at large, but few save professed students, who can admire and value his exhaustiveness, will read the many hundreds of pages which he devotes to a short period of history. In some of his smaller books, however, he shows great powers of condensation and arrangement, and writes tersely enough.

His style is correct, lucid and virile, but generally nothing more, and his endeavour to use as far as possible only words of Teutonic origin limited his vocabulary and makes his sentences somewhat monotonous. While Froude often strayed away from his authorities, Freeman kept his authorities always before his eyes, and his narrative is here and there little more than a translation of their words. Accordingly, while it has nothing of Froude's carelessness and inaccuracy, it has nothing of his charm of style. Yet now and again he rises to the level of some heroic event, and parts of his chapter on the "Campaign of Hastings" and of his record of the wars of Syracuse and Athens, his reflections on the visit of Basil the Second to the church of the Virgin on the Acropolis, and some other passages in his books, are fine pieces of eloquent writing.

The high quality of Freeman's work was acknowledged by all competent judges. He was made D.C.L. of Oxford and LL.D. of Cambridge *honoris causa,* and when he visited the United States on a lecturing tour was warmly received at various places of learning. He served on the royal commission on ecclesiastical courts appointed in 1881. In 1884 he was appointed regius professor of modern history at Oxford. His lectures were thinly attended, for he did not care to adapt them to the requirements of the university examinations, and he was not perhaps well fitted to teach young men. But he exercised a wholesome influence over the more earnest students of history among the resident graduates. From 1886 he was forced by ill-health to spend much of his time abroad, and he died of smallpox at Alicante on the 16th of March 1892, while on a tour in Spain.

Freeman had a strongly marked personality. Though impatient in temper and occasionally rude, he was tender-hearted and generous. His rudeness to strangers was partly caused by shyness and partly by a childlike inability to conceal his feelings. Eminently truthful, he could not understand that some verbal insincerities are necessary to social life. He had a peculiar faculty for friendship, and his friends always found him sympathetic and affectionate.

In their society he would talk well and showed a keen sense of humour. He considered it his duty to expose careless and ignorant writers, and certainly enjoyed doing so. He worked hard and methodically, often had several pieces of work in hand, and kept a daily record of the time which he devoted to each of them. His tastes were curiously limited. No art interested him except architecture, which he studied throughout his life; and he cared little for literature which was not either historical or political. In later life he ceased to hold the theological opinions of his youth, but remained a devout churchman.

25

Edward Augustus Freeman

ESSAY-RACE AND LANGUAGE

Race and Language, Part I.

[Footnote 1: From "Historical Essays," Third Series, 1879.]

It is no very great time since the readers of the English newspapers were, perhaps a little amused, perhaps a little startled, at the story of a deputation of Hungarian students going to Constantinople to present a sword of honor to an Ottoman general. The address and the answer enlarged on the ancient kindred of Turks and Magyars, on the long alienation of the dissevered kinsfolk, on the return of both in these later times to a remembrance of the ancient kindred and to the friendly feelings to which such kindred gave birth. The discourse has a strange sound when we remember the reigns of Sigismund and Wladislaus, when we think of the dark days of Nikopolis and Varna, when we think of Huniades encamped at the foot of Haemus, and of Belgrade beating back Mahomet the Conqueror from her gates.

The Magyar and the Ottoman embracing with the joy of reunited kinsfolk is a sight which certainly no man would have looked forward to in the fourteenth or fifteenth century. At an earlier time the ceremony might have seemed a degree less wonderful. If a man whose ides are drawn wholly from the modern map should sit down to study the writings of Constantine Porphyrogennetos, he would perhaps be startled at finding Turks and Franks spoken of as neighbor, at finding Turcia and Francia-we must not translate Toupkia and qpayyia by Turkey and France-spoken of as border lands. A little study will perhaps show him that the change lies almost wholly in the names and not in the boundaries. The lands are there still, and the frontier between them has shifted much less than one might have looked for in nine hundred years. Nor has there been any great change in the population of the two countries. The Turks and the Franks of the Imperial geographer are there still, in the lands which he calls Turcia and Francia; only we no longer speak of them as Turks and Franks. The Turks of Constantine are Magyars; the Franks of Constantine are Germans. The Magyar students may not unlikely have turned over the Imperial pages, and they may have seen how their forefathers stand described there. We can hardly fancy that the Ottoman general is likely to have given much time to lore of such a kind. Yet the Ottoman answer was as brimful of ethnological and antiquarian sympathy as the Magyar address.

It is hardly to be believed that a Turk, left to himself, would by his own efforts have found out the primeval kindred between Turk and Magyar. He might remember that Magyar exiles had found a safe shelter on Ottoman territory; he might look deep enough into the politics of the present moment to see that the rule of Turk and Magyar alike is threatened by the growth of Slavonic national life. But the idea that Magyar and Turk owe each other any love or any duty, directly on the ground of primeval kindred, is certainly not likely to have presented itself to the untutored Ottoman mind. In short, it sounds, as some one said at the time, rather like the dream of a professor who has run wild with an ethnological craze, than like the serious thought of a practical man of any nation. Yet the Magyar students seem to have meant their address quite seriously. And the Turkish general, if he did not take it seriously, at least thought it wise to shape his answer as if he did.

As a piece of practical politics, it sounds like Frederick Barbarossa threatening to avenge the defeat of Crassus upon Saladin, or like the French of the revolutionary wars making the Pope Pius of those days answerable for the wrongs of Vercingetorix. The thing sounds like comedy, almost like conscious comedy. But it is a kind of comedy which may become tragedy, if the idea from which it springs get so deeply rooted in men's minds as to lead to any practical consequences. As long as talk of this kind does not get beyond the world of hot-headed students, it may pass for a craze. It would be more than a craze, if it should be so widely taken up on either side that the statesmen on either side find it expedient to profess to take it up also.

To allege the real or supposed primeval kindred between Magyars and Ottomans as a ground for political action, or at least for political sympathy, in the affairs of the present moment, is an extreme case-some may be inclined to call it a reductio ad absurdum-of a whole range of doctrines and sentiments which have in modern days gained a great power over men's minds. They have gained so great a power that those who may regret their influence cannot afford to despise it. To make any practical inference from the primeval kindred of Magyar and Turk is indeed pushing the doctrine of race, and of sympathies arising from race, as far as it well can be pushed. Without plunging into any very deep mysteries, without committing ourselves to any dangerous theories in the darker regions of ethnological inquiry, we may perhaps be allowed at starting to doubt whether there is any real primeval kindred between the Ottoman and the Finnish Magyar.

It is for those who have gone specially deep into the antiquities of the non-Aryan races to say whether there is or is not. At all events, as far as the great facts of history go, the kindred is of the vaguest and most shadowy kind. It comes to little more than the fact that Magyars and Ottomans are alike non-Aryan invaders who have made their way into Europe within recorded times, and that both have, rightly or wrongly, been called by the name of Turks. These do seem rather slender grounds on which to build up a fabric of national sympathy between two nations, when several centuries of living practical history all pull the other way. It is hard to believe that the kindred of Turk and Magyar was thought of when a Turkish pacha ruled at Buda. Doubtless Hungarian Protestants often deemed, and not unreasonably deemed, that the contemptuous toleration of the Moslem sultan was a lighter yoke than the persecution of the Catholic emperor.

But it was hardly on grounds of primeval kindred that they made the choice. The ethnological dialogue held at Constantinople does indeed sound like ethnological theory run mad. But it is the very wildness of the thing which gives it its importance. The doctrine of race, and of symphaties springing from race, must have taken very firm hold indeed of men's minds before it could be carried out in a shape which we are tempted to call so grotesque as this.

The plain fact is that the new lines of scientific and historical inquiry which have been opened in modern times have had a distinct and deep effect upon the politics of the age. The fact may be estimated in many ways, but its existence as a fact cannot be denied. Not in a merely scientific or literary point of view, but in one strictly practical, the world is not the same world as it was when men had not yet dreamed of the kindred between Sanscrit, Greek, and English, when it was looked on as something of a paradox to him that there was a distinction between Celtic and Teutonic tongues and nations. Ethnological and philological researches-I do not forget the distinction between the two, but for the present I must group them together-have opened the way for new national sympathies, new national antipathies, such as would have been unintelligible a hundred years ago.

A hundred years ago a man's political likes and dislikes seldom went beyond the range which was suggested by the place of his birth or immediate descent. Such birth or descent made him a member of this or that political community, a subject of this or that prince, a citizen-perhaps a subject-of this or that commonwealth. The political community of which he was a member had its traditional alliances and traditional enmities, and by those alliances and enmities the likes and dislikes of the members of that community were guided. But those traditional alliances and enmities were seldom determined by theories about language or race.

The people of this or that place might be discontented under a foreign government; but, as a rule, they were discontented only if subjection to that foreign government brought with it personal oppression or at least political degradation. Regard or disregard of some purely local privilege or local feeling went for more than the fact of a government being native or foreign. What we now call the sentiment of nationality did not go for much; what we call the sentiment of race went for nothing at all. Only a few men here and there would have understood the feelings which have led to those two great events of our own time, the political reunion of the German and Italian nations after their long political dissolution. Not a soul would have understood the feelings which have allowed Panslavism to be a great practical agent in the affairs of Europe, and which have made talk about "the Latin race," if not practical, at least possible. Least of all, would it have been possible to give any touch of political importance to what would have then seemed so wild a dream as a primeval kindred between Magyar and Ottoman.

That feelings such as these, and the practical consequences which have flowed from them, are distinctly due to scientific and historical teaching there can, I think, be no doubt. Religious sympathy and purely national sympathy are both feelings of much simpler growth, which need no deep knowledge nor any special teaching. The cry which resounded through Christendom when the Holy City was taken by the Mussulmans, the cry which resounded through Islam when the same city was taken by the Christians, the spirit which armed England to support French Huguenots and which armed Spain to support French Leaguers, all spring from motives which lie on the surface.

Nor need we seek for any explanation but such as lies on the surface for the natural wish for closer union which arose among Germans or Italians who found themselves parted off by purely dynastic arrangements from men who were their countrymen in everything else. Such a feeling has to strive with the counterfeeling which springs from local jealousies and local dislikes; but it is a perfectly simple feeling, which needs no subtle research either to arouse or to understand it. So, if we draw our illustrations from the events of our own time, there is nothing but what is perfectly simple in the feeling which calls Russia, as the most powerful of Orthodox states, to the help of her Orthodox brethren everywhere, and which calls the members of the Orthodox Church everywhere to look to Russia as their protector. The feeling may have to strive against a crowd of purely political considerations, and by those purely political considerations it may be outweighed.

But the feeling is in itself altogether simple and natural. So again, the people of Montenegro and of the neighboring lands in

Herzegovina and by the Bocche of Cattaro feel themselves countrymen in every sense but the political accident which keeps them asunder. They are drawn together by a tie which everyone can understand, by the same tie which would draw together the people of three adjoining English counties, if any strange political action should part them asunder in like manner. The feeling here is that of nationality in the strictest sense, nationality in a purely local or geographical sense. It would exist all the same if Panslavism had never been heard of; it might exist though those who feel it had never heard of the Slavonic race at all. It is altogether another thing when we come to the doctrine of race, and of sympathies founded on race, in the wider sense.

Here we have a feeling which professes to bind together, and which as a matter of fact has had a real effect in binding together, men whose kindred to one another is not so obvious at first sight as the kindred of Germans, Italians, or Serbs who are kept asunder by nothing but a purely artificial political boundary. It is a feeling at whose bidding the call to union goes forth to men whose dwellings are geographically far apart, to men who may have had no direct dealings with one another for years or for ages, to men whose languages, though the scholar may at once for Slaves as Slaves. Russia dealt with Montenegro, not, as far as one can see, out of any Slavonic brotherhood, but because an independent Orthodox State at enmity with the Turk could not fail to be a useful ally.

The earlier dealings of Russia with the subject nations were far more busy among the Greeks than among the Slaves. In fact, till quite lately all the Orthodox subjects of the Turk were in most European eyes looked on as alike Greeks. The Orthodox Church has been commonly known as the Greek Church; and it has often been very hard to make people understand that the vast mass of the members of that so called Greek Church are not Greek in any other sense. In truth we may doubt whether, till comparatively lately, the subject nations themselves were fully alive to the differences of race and speech among them. A man must in all times and places know whether he speaks the same language as another man; but he does not always go on to put his consciousness of difference into the shape of a sharply drawn formula. Still less does he always make the difference the ground of any practical course of action. The Englishman in the first days of the Norman Conquest felt the hardships of foreign rule, and he knew that those hardships were owing to foreign rule. But he had not learned to put his sense of hardship into any formula about an oppressed nationality.

So, when the policy of the Turk found that the subtle intellect of the Greek could be made use of as an instrument of dominion over the other subject nations, the Bulgarian felt the hardship of the state of things in which, as it was proverbially said, his body was in bondage to the Turk and his soul in bondage to the Greek. But we may suspect that this neatly turned proverb dates only from the awakening of a distinctly national Bulgarian feeling in modern times. The Turk was felt to be an intruder and an enemy, because his rule was that of an open oppressor belonging to another creed. The Greek, on the other hand, though his spiritual dominion brought undoubted practical evils with it, was not felt to be an intruder and an enemy in the same sense. His quicker intellect and superior refinement made him a model.

The Bulgarian imitated the Greek tongue and Greek manners; he was willing in other lands to be himself looked on as a Greek. It is only in quite modern times, under the direct influence of the preaching of the doctrine of race, that a hard and fast line has been drawn between Greeks and Bulgarians. That doctrine has cut two ways. It has given both nations, Greek and Bulgarian alike, a renewed national life, national strength, national hopes, such as neither of them had felt for ages. In so doing, it has done one of the best and most hopeful works of the age. But in so doing, it has created one of the most dangerous of immediate political difficulties. In calling two nations into a renewed being, it has arrayed them in enmity against each other, and that in the face of a common enemy in whose presence all lesser differences and jealousies ought to be hushed into silence.

There is then a distinct doctrine of race, and of sympathies founded on race, distinct from the feeling of community of religion, and distinct from the feeling of nationality in the narrower sense. It is not so simple or easy a feeling as either of those two. It does not in the same way lie on the surface; it is not in the same way grounded on obvious facts which are plain to every man's understanding. The doctrine of race is essentially an artificial doctrine, a learned doctrine. It is an inference from facts which the mass of mankind could never have found out for themselves; facts which, without a distinctly learned teaching, could never be brought home to them in any intelligible shape. Now what is the value of such a doctrine?

Does it follow that, because it is confessedly artificial, because it springs, not from a spontaneous impulse, but from a learned teaching, it is therefore necessarily foolish, mischievous, perhaps unnatural? It may perhaps be safer to hold that like many other doctrines, many other sentiments, it is neither universally good nor universally bad, neither inherently wise nor inherently foolish. It may be safer to hold that it may, like other doctrines and sentiments, have a range within which it may work for good, while in some other range it may work for evil. It may in short be a doctrine which is neither to be rashly accepted, nor rashly cast aside, but one which may need to be guided, regulated, modified, according to time, place, and circumstance. I am not now called on so much to estimate the practical good and evil of the doctrine as to work out what the doctrine itself is, and to try to explain some difficulties about it, but I must emphatically say that nothing can be more shallow, nothing more foolish, nothing more purely sentimental, than the talk of those who think that they can simply laugh down or shriek down any doctrine or sentiment which they themselves do not understand.

A belief or a feeling which has a practical effect on the conduct of great masses of men, sometimes on the conduct of whole nations, may be very false and very mischievous; but it is in every case a great and serious fact, to be looked gravely in the face. Men who sit at their ease and think that all wisdom is confined to themselves and their own clique may think themselves vastly superior to the great emotions which stir our times, as they would doubtless have thought themselves vastly superior to the emotions which stirred the first Saracens or the first Crusaders. But the emotions are there all the same, and they do their work all the same. The most highly educated man in the most highly educated society cannot sneer them out of being.

But it is time to pass to the more strictly scientific aspect of the subject. The doctrine of race, in its popular form, is the direct offspring of the study of scientific philology; and yet it is just now, in its popular form at least, somewhat under the ban of scientific philologers. There is nothing very wonderful in this. It is in fact the natural course of things which might almost have been reckoned on beforehand. When the popular mind gets hold of a truth it seldom gets hold of it with strict scientific precision. It commonly gets hold of one side of the truth; it puts forth that side of the truth only. It puts that side forth in a form which may not be in itself distorted or exaggerated, but which practically becomes distorted and exaggerated, because other sides of the same truth are not brought into their due relation with it.

The popular idea thus takes a shape which is naturally offensive to men of strict precision, and which men of strict scientific precision have naturally, and from their own point of view quite rightly, risen up to rebuke. Yet it may often happen that, while the scientific statement is the only true one for scientific purposes, the popular version may also have a kind of practical truth for the somewhat rough and ready purposes of a popular version. In our present case scientific philologers are beginning to complain, with perfect truth and perfect justice from their own point of view, that the popular doctrine of race confounds race and language. They tell us, and they do right to tell us, that language is no certain test of race, that men who speak the same tongue are not therefore necessarily men of the same blood. And they tell us further, that from whatever quarter the alleged popular confusion came, it certainly did not come from any teaching of scientific philologers.

The truth of all this cannot be called in question. We have too many instances in recorded history of nations laying aside the use of one language and taking to the use of another, for anyone who cares for accuracy to set down language as any sure test of race. In fact, the studies of the philologer and those of the ethnologer strictly so called are quite distinct, and they deal with two wholly different sets of phenomena. The science of the ethnologer is strictly a physical science. He has to deal with purely physical phenomena; his business lies with the different varieties of the human body, and specially, to take that branch of his inquiries which most impresses the unlearned, with the various conformations of the human skull.

His researches differ in nothing from those of the zoologist or the paleontologist, except that he has to deal with the physical phenomena of man, while they deal with the physical phenomena of other animals. He groups the different races of men exactly as the others group the genera and species of living or extinct mammals or reptiles. The student of ethnology as a physical science may indeed strengthen his conclusions by evidence of other kinds, evidence from arms, ornaments, pottery, modes of burial. But all these are secondary; the primary ground of classification is the physical conformation of man himself. As to language, the ethnological method, left to itself, can find out nothing whatever. The science of the ethnologer then, is primarily physical; it is historical only in that secondary sense in which paleontology, and geology itself, may fairly be called historical. It arranges the varieties of mankind according to a strictly physical classification; what the language of each variety may have been, it leaves to the professors of another branch of study to find out.

The science of the philologer, on the other hand, is strictly historical. These is doubtless a secondary sense in which purely philological science may be fairly called physical, just as there is a secondary sense in which pure ethnology may be called historical. That is to say, philology has to deal with physical phenomena, so far as it has to deal with the physical aspect of the sounds of which human language is made up. Its primary business, like the primary business of any other historical science, is to deal with phenomena which do not depend on physical laws, but which do depend on the human will. The science of language is, in this respect, like the science of human institutions or of human beliefs. Its subject-matter is not, like that of pure ethnology, what man is, but, like that of any other historical science, what man does. It is plain that no man's will can have any direct influence on the shape of his skull. I say no direct influence, because it is not for me to rule how far habits, places of abode, modes of like, a thousand things which do come under the control of the human will, may indirectly affect the physical conformation of a man himself or of his descendants. Some observers have made the remark that men of civilized nations who live in a degraded social state do actually approach to the physical type of inferior races.

However this may be, it is quite certain, that, as no man can by taking though add a cubit to his stature, so no man can by taking thought make his skull brachycephalic or dolichocephalic. But the language which a man speaks does depend upon his will; he can by taking thought make his speech Romance or Teutonic. No doubt he has in most cases practically no choice in the matter.

The language which he speaks is practically determined for him by fashion, habit, early teaching, a crowd of things over which he has practically no control. But still the control is not physical and inevitable, as it is in the case of the shape of his skull. If we say that he cannot help speaking in a particular way; that is, that he cannot help speaking a particular language, this simply means that his circumstances are such that no other way of speaking presents itself to his mind. And in many cases, he has a real choice between two or more ways of speaking; that is, between two or more languages.

Every word that a man speaks is the result of a real, though doubtless unconscious, act of his free will. We are apt to speak of gradual changes in languages, as in institutions or anything else, as if they were the result of a physical law, acting upon beings who had no choice in the matter. Yet every change of the kind is simply the aggregate of various acts of the will on the part of all concerned. Every change in speech, every introduction of a new sound or a new word, was really the result of an act of the will of some one or other.

The choice may have been unconscious; circumstances may have been such as practically to give him but one choice; still he did choose; he spoke in one way, when there was no physical hinderance to his speaking in another way, when there was no physical compulsion to speak at all. The Gauls need not have changed their own language for Latin; the change was not the result of a physical necessity, but of a number of acts of the will on the part of this and that Gaul. Moral causes directed their choice, and determined that Gaul should become a Latin-speaking land. But whether the skulls of the Gauls should be long or short, whether their hair should be black or yellow, those were points over which the Gauls themselves had no direct control whatever.

The study of men's skulls then is a study which is strictly physical, a study of facts over which the will of man has no direct control. The study of men's languages is strictly an historical study, a study of facts over which the will of man has a direct control. It follows therefore from the very nature of the two studies that language cannot be an absolutely certain test of physical descent. A man cannot, under any circumstances, choose his own skull; he may, under some circumstances, choose his own language. He must keep the skull which has been given him by his parents; he cannot, by any process of taking thought, determine what kind of skull he will hand on to his own children. But he may give up the use of the language which he has learned from his parents, and he may determine what language he will teach to his children.

The physical characteristics of a race are unchangeable, or are changed only by influences over which the race itself has no direct control. The language which the race speaks may be changed, either by a conscious act of the will or by that power of fashion which is in truth the aggregate of countless unconscious acts of the will. And, as the very nature of the case thus shows that language is no sure test of race, so the facts of recorded history equally prove the same truth. Both individuals and whole nations do in fact often exchange the language of their forefathers for some other language. A man settles in a foreign country. He learns the language of that country; sometimes he forgets the use of his own language. His children may perhaps speak both tongues; if they speak one tongue only, it will be the tongue of the country where they live. In a generation or two all trace of foreign origin will have passed away. Here then language is no test of race. If the great-grandchildren speak the language of their great-grandfathers, it will simply be as they may speak any other foreign language. Here are men who by speech belong to one nation, by actual descent to another. If they lose the physical characteristics of the race to which the original settler belonged, it will be due to inter-marriage, to climate, to some cause altogether independent of language.

Every nation will have some adopted children of this kind, more or fewer; men who belong to it by speech, but who do not belong to it by race. And what happens in the case or individuals happens in the case of whole nations. The pages of history are crowded with cases in which nations have cast aside the tongue of their forefathers, and have taken instead the tongue of some other people. Greek in the East, Latin in the West, became the familiar speech of millions who had not a drop of Greek or Italian blood in their veins.

The same has been the case in later times with Arabic, Persian, Spanish, German, English. Each of those tongues has become the familiar speech of vast regions where the mass of the people are not Arabian, Spanish, or English, otherwise than by adoption. The Briton of Cornwall has, slowly but in the end thoroughly, adopted the speech of England. In the American continent full-blooded Indians preside over commonwealths which speak the tongue of Cortes and Pizarro. In the lands to which all eyes are now turned, the Greek, who has been busily assimilating strangers ever since he first planted his colonies in Asia and Sicily, goes on busily assimilating his Albanian neighbors. And between renegades, janizaries, and mothers of all nations, the blood of many a Turk must be physically anything rather than Turkish.

The inherent nature of the case, and the witness of recorded history, join together to prove that language is no certain test of race, and that the scientific philologers are doing good service to accuracy of expression and accuracy of thought by emphatically calling attention to the fact that language is no such test.

But on the other hand, it is quite possible that the truth to which our attention is just now most fittingly called may, if put forth too broadly and without certain qualifications, lead to error quite as great as the error at which it is aimed. I do not suppose that anyone ever thought that language was, necessarily and in all cases, an absolute and certain test. If anybody does think so, he has put himself altogether out of court by shutting his eyes to the most manifest facts of the case. But there can be no doubt that many people have given too much importance to language as a test of race. Though they have not wholly forgotten the facts which tell the other way, they have not brought them out with enough prominence. But I can also believe that many people have written and spoken on the subject in a way which cannot be justified from a strictly scientific point of view, but which may have been fully justified from the point of view of the writers and speakers themselves. It may often happen that a way of speaking may not be scientifically accurate, but may yet be quite near enough to the truth for the purposes of the matter in hand. It may, for some practical or even historical purpose, be really more true than the statement which is scientifically more exact.

Language is no certain test of race; but if a man, struck by this wholesome warning, should run off into the belief that language and race have absolutely nothing to do one another, he had better have gone without the warning. For in such a case the last error would be worse than the first. The natural instinct of mankind connects race and language. It does not assume that language is an infallible test of race; but it does assume that language and race have something to do with one another. It assumes, that though language is not an accurately scientific test of race, yet it is a rough and ready test which does for many practical purposes.

To make something more of an exact definition, one might say, that though language is not a test of race, it is, in the absence of evidence to the contrary, a presumption of race; that though it is not a test of race, yet it is a test of something which, for many practical purposes, is the same as race.

Race and Language, Part II.

Professor Max Müller warned us long ago that we must not speak of a Celtic skull. Mr. Sayce has more lately warned us that we must not infer from community of Aryan speech that there is any kindred in blood between this or that Englishman and this or that Hindoo. And both warnings are scientifically true. Yet anyone who begins his studies on these matters with Professor Müller's famous Oxford Essay will practically come to another way of looking at things. He will fill his mind with a vivid picture of the great Aryan family, as yet one, dwelling in one place, speaking one tongue, having already taken the first steps towards settled society, recognizing the domestic relations, possessing the first rudiments of government and religion, and calling all these first elements of culture by names of which traces still abide here and there among the many nations of the common stock.

He will go on to draw pictures equally vivid of the several branches of the family parting off from the primeval home. One great branch he will see going to the southeast, to become the forefathers of the vast, yet isolated colony in the Asiatic lands of Persia and India. He watches the remaining mass sending off wave after wave, to become the forefathers of the nations of historical Europe. He traces out how each branch starts with its own share of the common stock-how the language, the creed, the institutions, once common to all, grow up into different, yet kindred, shapes, among the many parted branches which grew up, each with an independent life and strength of its own.

This is what our instructors set before us as the true origin of nations and their languages. A may have marched one way, while others marched another way, or stayed behind. We may, if we please, indulge our fancy by conceiving that there may actually be family distinctions older than distinctions of nation and race. It may be that the Gothic Amali and the Roman Aemilii-I throw out the idea as a mere illustration-were branches of a family which had taken a name before the division of Teuton and Italian. Some of the members of that family may have joined the band of which came the Goths, while other members joined the band of which came the Romans. There is no difference but the length of time to distinguish such a supposed case from the case of an English family, one branch of which settled in the seventeenth century at Boston in Massachusetts, while another branch stayed behind at Boston in Holland. Mr. Sayce says truly that the use of a kindred language does not prove that the Englishman and the Hindoo are really akin in race; for, as he adds, many Hindoos are men of non-Aryan race who have simply learned to speak tongues of Sanscrit origin.

He might have gone on to say, with equal truth, that there is no positive certainty that there was any community in blood among the original Aryan group itself, and that if we admit such community of blood in the original Aryan group, it does not follow that there is any further special kindred between Hindoo and Hindoo or between Englishman and Englishman. The original group may not have been a family, but an artificial union. And if it was a family, those of its members who marched together east or west or north or south may have had no tie of kindred beyond the common cousinship of all.

Now the tendency of this kind of argument is to lead to something a good deal more startling than the doctrine that language is no certain test of race. Its tendency is to go on further, and to show that race is no certain test of community of blood. And this comes pretty nearly to saying that there is no such thing as race at all. For our whole conception of race starts from the idea of community of blood. If the word "race" does not mean community of blood, it is hard to see what it does mean. Yet it is certain that there can be no positive proof of real community of blood, even among those groups of mankind which we instinctively speak of as families and races.

It is not merely that the blood has been mingled in aftertimes; there is no positive proof that there was any community of blood in the beginning. No living Englishman can prove with absolute certainty that he comes in the male line of any of the Teutonic settlers in Britain in the fifth or sixth centuries. I say in the male line, because anyone who is descended from any English king can prove such descent, though he can prove it only through a long and complicated web of female successions. But we may be sure that in no other case can such a pedigree be proved by the kind of proof which lawyers would require to make out the title to an estate or a peerage.

The actual forefathers of the modern Englishman may chance to have been, not true-born Angles or Saxons, but Britons, Scots, in later days Frenchmen, Flemings, men of any other nation who learned to speak English and took to themselves English names. But supposing that a man could make out such a pedigree, supposing that he could prove that he came in the male line of some follower of Hengest or Cerdic, he would be no nearer to proving original community of blood either in the particular Teutonic race or in the general Aryan family. If direct evidence is demanded, we must give up the whole doctrine of families and races, as far as we take language, manners, institutions, anything but physical conformation, as the distinguishing marks of races and families.

That is to say, if we wish never to use any word of whose accuracy we cannot be perfectly certain, we must leave off speaking of races and families at all from any but the purely physical side. We must content ourselves with saying that certain groups of mankind have a common history, that they have languages, creeds, and institutions in common, but that we have no evidence whatever to show how they came to have languages, creeds, and institutions in common. We cannot say for certain what was the tie which brought the members of the original group together, any more than we can name the exact time and the exact place when and where they came together.

We may thus seem to be landed in a howling wilderness of scientific uncertainty. The result of pushing our inquiries so far may seem to be show that we really know nothing at all. But in truth the uncertainty is no greater than the uncertainty which attends all inquiries in the historical sciences. Though a historical fact may be recorded in the most trustworthy documents, though it may have happened in our own times, though we may have seen it happen with our own eyes, yet we cannot have the same certainty about it as the mathematician has about the proposition which he proves to absolute demonstration. We cannot have even that lower degree of certainty which the geologist has with regard to the order of succession between this and that stratum. For in all historical inquiries we are dealing with facts with themselves come within the control of human will and human caprice, and the evidence for which depends on the trustworthiness of human informants, who may either purposely deceive or unwittingly mislead. A man may lie; he may err.

The triangles and the rocks can neither lie nor err. I may with my own eyes see a certain man do a certain act; he may tell me himself, or some one else may tell me, that he is the same man who did some other act; but as to his statement I cannot have absolute certainty, and no one but myself can have absolute certainty as to the statement which I make as to the facts which I saw with my own eyes. Historical evidence may range through every degree, from the barest likelihood to that undoubted moral certainty on which every man acts without hesitation in practical affairs. But it cannot get beyond this last standard. If, then, we are ever to use words like race, family, or even nation, to denote groups of mankind marked off by any kind of historical, as distinguished from physical, characteristics, we must be content to use those words, as we use many other words, without being able to prove that our use of them is accurate, as mathematicians judge of accuracy.

I cannot be quite sure that William the Conqueror landed at Pevensey, though I have strong reasons for believing that he did so. And I have strong reasons for believing many facts about race and language about which I am much further from being quite sure than I am about William's landing at Pevensey. In short, in all these matters, we must be satisfied to let presumption very largely take the place of actual proof; and, if we only let presumption in, most of our difficulties at once fly away. Language is no certain test of race; but it is a presumption of race. Community of race, as we commonly understand race, is no certain proof of original community of blood; but it is a presumption of original community of blood. The presumption amounts to moral proof, if only we do not insist on proving such physical community of blood as would satisfy a genealogist. It amounts to moral proof, if all that we seek is to establish a relation in which the community of blood is the leading idea, and in which where natural community of blood does not exist, its place is supplied by something which by a legal fiction is looked upon as its equivalent.

If, then, we do not ask for scientific, for what we may call physical, accuracy, but if we are satisfied with the kind of proof which is all that we can ever get in the historical sciences-if we are satisfied to speak in a way which is true for popular and practical purposes-then we may say that language has a great deal to do with race, as race is commonly understood, and that race has a great deal to do with community of blood. If we once admit the Roman doctrine of adoption, our whole course is clear. The natural family is the starting-point of everything; but we must give the natural family the power of artificially enlarging itself by admitting adoptive members. A group of mankind is thus formed, in which it does not follow that all the members have any natural community of blood, but in which community of blood is the starting-point, in which those who are connected by natural community of blood form the original body within whose circle the artificial members are admitted. A group of mankind thus formed is something quite different from a fortuitous concurrence of atoms. Three or four brothers by blood, with a fourth or fifth man whom they agree to look on as filling in everything the same place as a brother by blood, form a group which is quite unlike a union of four or five men, none of whom is bound by any tie of blood to any of the others. In the latter kind of union the notion of kindred does not come in at all. In the former kind the notion of kindred is the groundwork of everything; it determines the character of every relation and every action, even though the kindred between some members of the society and others may be owing to a legal fiction and not of natural descent. All that we know of the growth of tribes, races, nations, leads us to believe that they grew in this way. Natural kindred was the groundwork, the leading and determining idea; but, by one of those legal fictions which have such an influence on all institutions adoption was in certain cases allowed to count as natural kindred.

The usage of all language shows that community of blood was the leading idea in forming the greater and smaller groups of mankind. Words like puxov, yevos, gens, natio, kin, all point to the natural family as the origin of all society. The family in the narrower sense, the children of one father in one house, grew into a more extended family, the gens. Such were the Alkmaionidai, the Julii, or the Scyldingas, the real or artificial descendants of a real or supposed forefather. The nature of the gens has been set forth often enough. If it is a mistake to fancy that every Julius or Cornelius, was the natural kinsman of every other Julius or Cornelius, it is equally a mistake to think that the gens Julia or Cornelia was in its origin a mere artificial association, into which the idea of natural kindred did not enter.

It is indeed possible that really artificial gentes, groups of men of whom it might chance that none were natural kinsmen, were formed in later times after the model of the original gentes. Still such imitation would bear witness to the original conception of the gens. It would be the doctrine of adoption turned the other way; instead of a father adopting a son, a number of men would agree to adopt a common father. The family then grew into the gens; the union of gentes formed the State, the political community, which in its first form was commonly a tribe. Then came the nation, formed of a union of tribes. Kin dred, real or artificial, is the one basis on which all society and all government have grown up.

Now it is plain, that as soon as we admit the doctrine of artificial kindred-that is, as soon as we allow the exercise of the law of adoption physical purity of race is at an end. Adoption treats a man as if he were the son of a certain father; it cannot really make him the son of that father. If a brachycephalic father adopts a dolichocephalic son, the legal act cannot change the shape of the adopted son's skull. I will not undertake to say whether, not indeed the rite of adoption, but the influences and circumstances which would spring from it, might not, in the course of generations, affect even the skull of the man who entered a certain gens, tribe, or nation by artificial adoption only. If by any chance the adopted son spoke a different language from the adopted father, the rite of adoption itself would not of itself change his language. But it would bring him under influences which would make him adopt the language of his new gens by a conscious act of the will, and which would make his children adopt it by the same unconscious act of the will by which each child adopts the language of his parents.

The adopted son, still more the son of the adopted son, became, in speech, in feelings, in worship, in everything but physical descent, one with the gens into which he was adopted. He became one of that gens for all practical, political, historical purposes. It is only the physiologist who could deny his right to his new position. The nature of the process is well expressed by a phrase of our own law. When the nation-the word itself keeps about it the remembrance of birth as the groundwork of everything-adopts a new citizen, that is, a new child of the State, he is said to be naturalized.

That is, a legal process puts him in the same position, and gives him the same rights, as a man who is a citizen and a son by birth. It is assumed that the rights of citizenship come by nature-that is, by birth. The stranger is admitted to them only by a kind of artificial birth; he is naturalized by law; his children are in a generation or two naturalized in fact. There is now no practical distinction between the Englishman whose forefathers landed with William, or even between the Englishman whose forefathers sought shelter from Alva or from Louis XIV, and the Englishman whose forefathers landed with Hengest. It is for the physiologist to say whether any difference can be traced in their several skulls; for all practical purposes, historical or political, all distinction between these several classes has passed away.

We may, in short, say that the law of adoption runs through everything, and that it may be practised on every scale. What adoption is at the hands of the family, naturalization is at the hands of the State. And the same process extends itself from adopted or naturalized individuals to large classes of men, indeed to whole nations. When the process takes place on this scale, we may best call it assimilation. Thus Rome assimilated the continental nations of western Europe to that degree that, allowing for a few survivals here and there, not only Italy, but Gaul and Spain, became Roman.

The people of those lands, admitted step by step to the Roman franchise, adopted the name and tongue of Romans. It must soon have been hard to distinguish the Roman colonist in Gaul or Spain from the native Gaul or Spaniard who had, as far as in him lay, put on the guise of a Roman. This process of assimilation has gone on everywhere and at all times. When two nations come in this way into close contact with one another, it depends on a crowd of circumstances which shall assimilate the other, or whether they shall remain distinct without assimilation either way. Sometimes the conquerors assimilate their subjects; sometimes they are assimilated by their subjects; sometimes conquerors and subjects remain distinct forever. When assimilation either way does take place, the direction which it takes in each particular case will depend, partly on their respective numbers, partly on their degrees of civilization.

A small number of less civilized conquerors will easily be lost among a greater number of more civilized subjects, and that even though they give their name to the land and people which they conquer. The modern Frenchman represents, not the conquering Frank, but the conquered Gaul, or, as he called himself, the conquered Roman. The modern Bulgarian represents, not the

Finnish conqueror, but the conquered Slave. The modern Russian represents, not the Scandinavian ruler, but the Slave who sent for the Scandinavian to rule over him. And so we might go on with endless other cases.

The point is that the process of adoption, naturalization, assimilation, has gone on everywhere. No nation can boast of absolute purity of blood, though no doubt some nations come much nearer to it than others. When I speak of purity of blood, I leave out of sight the darker questions which I have already raised with regard to the groups of mankind in days before recorded history. I assume great groups like Celtic, Teutonic, Slavonic, as having what we may call a real corporate existence, however we may hold that the corporate existence began. My present point is that no existing nation is, in the physiologist's sense of purity, purely Celtic, Teutonic, Slavonic, or anything else. All races have assimilated a greater or less amount of foreign elements. Taking this standard, one which comes more nearly within the range of our actual knowledge that the possibilities of unrecorded times, we may again say that, from the purely scientific or physiological point of view, not only is language no test of race, but that, at all events among the great nations, of the world, there is no such thing as purity of race at all.

But, while we admit this truth, while we even insist upon it from the strictly scientific point of view, we must be allowed to look at it with different eyes from a more practical standing point. This is the standing point, whether of history which is the politics of the past, or of politics which are the history of the present. From this point of view, we may say unhesitatingly that there are such things as races and nations, and that to the grouping of those races and nations language is the best guide. We cannot undertake to define with any philosophical precision the exact distinction between race and race, between nation and nation. Nor can we undertake to define with the like precision in what way the distinctions between race and race, between nation and nation, began.

But all analogy leads us to believe that tribes, nations, races, were all formed according to the original model of the family, the family which starts from the idea of the community of blood, but which allows artificial adoption to be its legal equivalent. In all cases of adoption, naturalization, assimilation, whether of individuals or of large classes of men, the adopted person or class is adopted into an existing community. Their adoption undoubtedly influences the community into which they are adopted. It at once destroys any claim on the part of that community to purity of blood, and it influences the adopting community in many ways, physical and moral.

A family, a tribe, or a nation, which has largely recruited itself by adopted members, cannot be the same as one which has never practised adoption at all, but all whose members come of the original stock. But the influence which the adopting community exercises upon its adopted members is far greater than any influence which they exercise upon it. It cannot change their blood; it cannot give them new natural forefathers; but it may do everything short of this; it may make them, in speech, in feeling, in thought, and in habit, genuine members of the community which has artificially made them its actual pedigree of this or that Bulgarian, of this or that Russian, we might either find that there was no real kindred between them, or we might find that there was a real kindred, but a kindred which must be traced up to another stock than that of the Slaves.

In point of actual blood, instead of both being Slaves, it may be that one of them comes, it may be that both of them come of a stock which is not Slavonic or even Aryan. The Bulgarian may chance to be a Bulgarian in a truer sense than he thinks for; he may come of the blood of those original Finnish conquerors who gave the Bulgarian name to the Slaves among whom they were merged. And if this or that Bulgarian may chance to come of the stock of Finnish conquerors assimilated by their Slavonic subjects, this or that Russian may chance to come of the stock of Finnish subjects assimilated by their Slavonic conquerors. It may then so happen that the cry for help goes up, and is answered on a ground of kindred which in the eye of the physiologist has no existence.

Or it may happen that the kindred is real in a way which neither the suppliant nor his helper thinks of. But in either case, for the practical purposes of human life, the plea is a good plea; the kindred on which it is founded a real kindred. It is good by the law of adoption. It is good by the law the force of which we all admit whenever we count a man as an Englishman whose forefathers, two generations or twenty generations back, came to our shores as strangers. For all practical purposes, for all the purposes which guide men's actions, public or private, the Russian and the Bulgarian, kinsmen so long parted, perhaps in very truth no natural kinsmen at all, are members of the same race, bound together by the common sentiment of race. They belong to the same race, exactly as an Englishman whose forefathers came into Britain fourteen hundred years back, and an Englishman whose forefathers came only one or two hundred years back, are like members of the same nation, bound together by a tie of common nationality.

And now, having ruled that races and nations, though largely formed by the workings of an artificial law, are still real and living things, groups in which the idea of kindred is the idea around which everything has grown, how are we to define our races and our nations? How are we to mark them off one from the other? Bearing in mind the cautions and qualifications which have been already given, bearing in mind large classes of exceptions which will presently be spoken of, I say unhesitatingly that for practical purposes there is one test, and one only, and that that test is language. It is hardly needful to show that races and nations cannot be defined by the merely political arrangements which group men under various governments. For some purposes of ordinary language, for some purposes of ordinary politics, we are tempted, sometime which does not conform to it we ask for the explanation.

All the larger countries of Europe provide us with exceptions; but we treat them all as exceptions. We do not ask why a native of France speaks French. But when a native of France speaks as his mother-tongue some other tongue than French, when French, or something which popularly passes for French, is spoken as his mother-tongue by someone who is not a native of France, we at once ask the reason. And the reason will be found in each case in some special historical cause which withdraws that case from the operation of the general law. A very good reason can be given why French, or something which popularly passes for French, is spoken in parts of Belgium and Switzerland whose inhabitants are certainly not Frenchmen. But the reason has to be given, and it may fairly be asked.

In the like sort, if we turn to our own country, whenever within the bounds of Great Britain we find any tongue spoken other than English, we at once ask the reason, and we learn the special historic cause. In a part of France and a part of Great Britain we find tongues spoken which differ alike from English and from French, but which are strongly akin to one another. We find that these are the survivals of a group of tongues once common to Gaul and Britain, but which the settlement of other nations, the introduction and the growth of other tongues, have brought down to the level of survivals. So again we find islands which both speech and geographical position seem to mark as French, but which are dependencies, and loyal dependencies, of the English crown. We soon learn the cause of the phenomenon which seems so strange.

Those islands are the remains of a State and a people which adopted the French tongue, but which, while it remained one, did not become a part of the French State. That people brought England by force of arms under the rule of their own sovereigns. The greater part of that people were afterward conquered by France, and gradually became French in feeling as well as in language. But a remnant clave to their connection with the land which their forefathers had conquered, and that remnant, while keeping the French tongue, never became French in feeling. This last case, that of the Norman islands, is a specially instructive one. Normandy and England were politically connected, while language and geography pointed rather to a union between Normandy and France.

In the case of continental Normandy, where the geographical tie was strongest, language and geography together could carry the day, and the continental Norman became a Frenchman. In the islands, where the geographical tie was less strong, political traditions and manifest interest carried the day against language and a weaker geographical tie. The insular Norman did not become a Frenchman. But neither did he become an Englishman. He alone remained Norman, keeping his own tongue and his own laws, but attached to the English crown by a tie at once of tradition and of advantage. Between States of the relative size of England and the Norman islands, the relation naturally becomes a relation of dependence on the part of the smaller members of the union.

But it is well to remember that our forefathers never conquered the forefathers of the men of the Norman islands, but that their forefathers did once conquer ours.

These instances, and countless others, bear out the position that, while community of language is the most obvious sign of common nationality, while it is the main element, or something more than an element, in the formation of nationality, the rule is open to exceptions of all kinds, and that the influence of language is at all times liable to be overruled by other influences. But all the exceptions confirm the rule, because we specially remark those cases which contradict the rule, and we do not specially remark those cases which do not conform to it.

In the cases which we have just spoken of, the growth of the nation as marked out by language, and the growth of the exceptions to the rule of language, have both come through the gradual, unconscious working of historical causes. Union under the same government, or separation under separate governments, has been among the foremost of those historical causes. The French nation consists of the people of all that extent of continuous territory which has been brought under the rule of the French kings. But the working of the cause has been gradual and unconscious.

There was no moment when anyone deliberately proposed to form a French nation by joining together all the separate duchies and countries which spoke the French tongue. Since the French nation has been formed, men have proposed to annex this or that land on the ground that its people spoke the French tongue, or perhaps only some tongue akin to the French tongue. But the formation of the French nation itself was the work of historical causes, the work doubtless of a settled policy acting through many generations, but not the work of any conscious theory about races and languages.

It is a special mark of our time, a special mark of the influence which doctrines about race and language have had on men's minds, that we have seen great nations united by processes in which theories of race and language really have had much to do with bringing about their union. If statesmen have not been themselves moved by such theories, they have at least found that it suited their purpose to make use of such theories as a means of working on the minds of others. In the reunion of the severed German and Italian nations the conscious feeling of nationality, and the acceptance of a common language as the outward badge of nationality, had no small share. Poets sang of language as the badge of national union; statesmen made it the badge, so far as political considerations did not lead them to do anything else.

The revivified kingdom of Italy is very far from taking in all the speakers of the Italian tongue. Lugano, Trent, Aquileia-to take places which are clearly Italian, and not to bring in places of more doubtful nationality, like the cities of Istria and Dalmatia-form no part of the Italian political body, and Corsica is not under the same rule as the other two great neighboring islands. But the fact that all these places do not belong to the Italian body at once suggests the twofold question, why they do not belong to it, and whether they ought not to belong to it. History easily a answers the first question; it may perhaps also answer the second question in a way which will say Yes as regards one place and No as regards another.

Ticino must not lose her higher freedom; Trieste must remain the needful mouth for southern Germany; Dalmatia must not be cut off from the Slavonic mainland; Corsica would seem to have sacrificed national feeling to personal hero worship. But it is certainly hard to see why Trent and Aquileia should be kept apart from the Italian body. On the other hand, the revivified Italian kingdom contains very little which is not Italian in speech. It is perhaps by a somewhat elastic view of language that the dialect of Piedmont and the dialect of Sicily are classed under one head; still, as a matter of fact, they have a single classical standard, and they are universally accepted as varieties of the same tongue. But it is only in a few Alpine valleys that languages are spoken which, whether Romance or Teutonic, are in any case not Italian. The reunion of Italy, in short, took in all that was Italian, save when some political cause hindered the rule of language from being followed.

Of anything not Italian by speech so little has been taken in that the non-Italian parts of Italy, Burgundian Aosta and the Seven German Communes-if these last still keep their Teutonic language-fall under the rule that there are some things too small for laws to pay heed to.

But it must not be forgotten that all this simply means that in the lands of which we have just been speaking the process of adoption has been carried out on the largest scale. Nations, with languages as their rough practical test, have been formed; but they have been formed with very little regard to physical purity of blood. In short, throughout western Europe assimilation has been the rule. That is to say, in any of the great divisions of Western Europe, though the land may have been settled and conquered over and over again, yet the mass of the people of the land have been drawn to some one national type. Either some one among the races inhabiting the land has taught the others to put on its likeness, or else a new national type has arisen which has elements drawn from several of those races.

Thus the modern Frenchman may be defined as produced by the union of blood which is mainly Celtic with a speech which is mainly Latin, and with an historical polity which is mainly Teutonic. That is, he is neither Gaul, Roman, nor Frank, but a fourth type, which has drawn important elements from all three. Within modern France this new national type has so far assimilated all others as to make everything else merely exceptional. The Fleming of one corner, the Basque of another, even the far more important Breton of a third corner, have all in this way become mere exceptions to the general type of the country. If we pass into our own islands we shall find that the same process has been at work. If we look to Great Britain only, we shall find that, though the means have not been the same, yet the end has been gained hardly less thoroughly than in France.

For all real political purposes, for everything which concerns a nation in the face of other nations, Great Britain is as thoroughly united as France is. Englishmen, Scotchmen, Welshmen feel themselves one people in the general affairs of the world. A secession of Scotland or Wales is as unlikely as a secession of Normandy or Languedoc. The part of the island which is not thoroughly assimilated in language, that part which still speaks Welsh or Gaelic, is larger in proportion than the non-French part of modern France. But however much either the northern or the western Briton may, in a fit of antiquarian politics, declaim against the Saxon, for all practical political purposes he and the Saxon are one.

The distinction between the southern and the northern English-for the men of Lothian and Fife must allow me to call them by this last name-is, speaking politically and without ethnological or linguistic precision, much as if France and Aquitaine had been two kingdoms united on equal terms, instead of Aquitaine being merged in France. When we cross into Ireland, we indeed find another state of things, and one which comes nearer to some of the phenomena which we shall come to in other parts of the world. Ireland is, most unhappily, not so firmly united to Great Britain as the different parts of Great Britain are to one another. Still even here the division arises quite as much from geographical and historical causes as from distinctions of race strictly so called. If Ireland had had no wrongs, still two great islands can never be so thoroughly united as a continuous territory can be. On the other hand, in point of language, the discontented part of the United Kingdom is much less strongly marked off than that fraction of the contended part which is not thoroughly assimilated. Irish is certainly not the language of Ireland in at all the same degree in which Welsh is the language of Wales. The Saxon has commonly to be denounced in the Saxon tongue.

Race and Language, Part III.

In some other parts of Western Europe, as in the Spanish and Scandinavian peninsulas, the coincidence of language and nationality is stronger than it is in France, Britain, or even Italy. No one speaks Spanish except in Spain or in the colonies of Spain. And within Spain the proportion of those who do not speak Spanish, namely the Basque remnant, is smaller than the non assimilated element in Britain and France. Here two things are to be marked: First, the modern Spanish nation has been formed, like the French, by a great process of assimilation; secondly, the actual national arrangements of the Spanish peninsula are wholly due to historical causes, we might almost say historical accidents, and those of very recent date. Spain and Portugal are separate kingdoms, and we look on their inhabitants as forming separate nations. But his is simply because a queen of Castile in the fifteenth century married a king of Aragon.

Had Isabella married a king of Portugal we should now talk of Spain and Aragon as we now talk of Spain and Portugal, and we should count Portugal for part of Spain. In language, in history, in everything else, Aragon was really more distinct from Castile than Portugal was. The king of Castile was already spoken of as king of Spain, and Portugal would have merged in the Spanish kingdom at last as easily as Aragon did. In Scandinavia, on the other hand, there must have been less assimilation than anywhere else. In the present kingdoms of Norway and Sweden there must be a nearer approach to actual purity of blood than in any other part of Europe. One cannot fancy that much Finnish blood has been assimilated, and there have been no conquests or settlements later than that of the Northmen themselves.

When we pass into central Europe we shall find a somewhat different state of things. The distinctions of race seem to be more lasting. While the national unity of the German Empire is greater than that of either France or Great Britain, it has not only subjects of other languages, but actually discontented subjects, in three corners, on its French, its Danish, and its Polish frontiers. We ask the reason, and it will be at once answered that the discontent of all three is the result of recent conquest, in two cases of very recent conquest indeed. But this is one of the very points to be marked; the strong national unity of the German Empire has been largely the result of assimilation; and these three parts, where recent conquest has not yet been followed by assimilation, are chiefly important because in all three cases, the discontented territory is geographically continuous with a territory of its own speech outside the Empire.

This does not prove that assimilation can never take place, but it will undoubtedly make the process longer and harder.

So again, wherever German-speaking people dwell outside the bounds of the revived German State, as well as when that revived German State contains other than German-speaking people, we ask the reason and we can find it. Political reasons forbade the immediate annexation of Austria, Tyrol, and Salzburg. Combined political and geographical reasons, and, if we look a little deeper, ethnological reasons too, forbade the annexation of Courland, Livonia, and Esthonia. Some reason or other will, it may be hoped, always be found to hinder the annexation of lands which, like Zurich and Berne, have reached a higher political level. Outlying brethren in Transsilvania or at Saratof again come under the rule "De minimis non curat lex."

In all these cases the rule that nationality and language should go together yields to unavoidable circumstances. But, on the other hand, where French or Danish or Slavonic or Lithuanian is spoken within the bounds of the new empire, the principle that language is the badge of nationality, that without community of language nationality is imperfect, shows itself in another shape. One main object of modern policy is to bring these exceptional districts under the general rule by spreading the German language in them. Everywhere, in short, wherever a power is supposed to be founded on nationality, the common feeling of mankind instinctively takes language as the test of nationality. We assume language as the test of a nation, without going into any minute questions as to the physical purity of blood in that nation. A continuous territory, living under the same government and speaking the same tongue, forms a nation for all practical purposes. If some of its inhabitants do not belong to the original stock of blood, they at least belong to it by adoption.

The question may now fairly be asked, What is the case in those parts of the world where people who are confessedly of different races and languages inhabit a continuous territory and live under the same government? How do we define nationality in such cases as these? The answer will be very different in different cases, according to the means by which the different national elements in such a territory have been brought together. They may form what I have already called an artificial nation, united by an act of its own free will. Or it may be simply a case where distinct nations, distinct in everything which can be looked on as forming a nation, except the possession of an independent government, are brought together, by whatever causes, under a common ruler.

The former case is very distinctly an exception which proves the rule, nation, is something different from those nations which are defined by a universal or at least a predominant language. We mark it as an exception, as something different from other cases. And when we see how nearly this artificial nation comes, in every point but that of language, to the likeness of those nations which are defined by language, we see that it is a nation defined by language which sets the standard, and after the model of which the artificial nation forms itself. The case of the Swiss Confederation and its claim to rank as a nation would be like the case of those gentes, if any such there were, which did not spring even from the expansion of an original family, but which were artificially formed in imitation of those which did, and which, instead of a real or traditional forefather, chose for themselves an adopted one.

In the Swiss Confederation, then, we have a case of a nation formed by an artificial process, but which still is undoubtedly a nation in the face of other nations. We now come to the other class, in which nationality and language keep the connection which they have elsewhere, but in which nations do not even in the roughest way answer to governments. We have only to go into the Eastern lands of Europe to find a state of things in which the notion of nationality, as marked out by language and national feeling, has altogether parted company from the notion of political government. It must be remembered that this state of things is not confined to the nations which are or have lately been under the yoke of the Turk. It extends also to the nations or fragments of nations which make up the Austro-Hungarian monarchy. In all the lands held by these two powers we come across phenomena of geography, race, and language, which stand out in marked contrast with anything to which we are used in western Europe. We may perhaps better understand what these phenomena are if we suppose a state of things which sounds absurd in the West, but which has its exact parallel i race of equal antiquity, the Skipetar or Albanians.

These, as I believe is no longer doubted, represent the ancient Illyrians. The exact degree of their ethnical kindred with the Greeks is a scientific question which need not here be considered; but the facts that they are more largely intermingled with the Greeks than any of the other neighboring nations, that they show a special power of identifying themselves with the Greeks-a power, so to speak, of becoming Greeks and making part of the artificial Greek nation, are matters of practical history. It must never be forgotten that, among the worthies of the Greek War of Independence, some of the noblest were not of Hellenic but Albanian blood. The Orthodox Albanian easily turns into a Greek; and the Mahometan Albanian is something which is broadly distinguished from a Turk. He has, as he well may have, a strong national feeling, and that national feeling has sometimes got the better of religious divisions. If Albania is among the most backward parts of the peninsula, still it is, by all accounts, the part where there is most hope of men of different religions joining together against the common enemy.

Here then are two ancient races, the Greeks and another race, not indeed so advanced, so important, or so widely spread, but a race which equally keeps a real national being. There is also a third ancient race which survives as a distinct people, though they have for ages adopted a foreign language. These are the Vlachs or Roumans, the surviving representatives of the great race, call it Thracian or any other, which at the beginning of history held the great inland mass of the Eastern peninsula, with the Illyrians to the west of them and the Greeks to the south. Every one knows that in the modern principality of Roumania and in the adjoining parts of the Austro-Hungarian monarchy, there is to be seen that phenomenon so unique in the East, a people who not only, as the Greeks did till lately, still keep the Roman name, but who speak neither Greek nor Turkish, neither Slave nor Skipetar, but a dialect of Latin, a tongue akin, not to the tongues of any of their neighbors, but to the tongues of Gaul, Italy, and Spain. And any one who has given any real attention to this matter knows that the same race is to be found, scattered here and there, if in some parts only as wandering shepherds, in the Slavonic, Albanian, and Greek lands south of the Danube. The assumption has commonly been that this outlying Romance people owe their Romance character to the Roman colonization of Dacia under Trajan.

In this view, the modern Roumans would be the descendants of Trajan's colonists and of Dacians who had learned of them to adopt the speech and manners of Rome. But when we remember that Dacia was the first Roman province to be given up-that the modern Roumania was for ages the highway of every barbarian tribe on its way from the East to the West-that the land has been conquered and settled and forsaken over and over again-it would be passing strange if this should be the one land, and its people the one race, to keep the Latin tongue when it has been forgotten in all the neighboring countries. In fact, this idea has been completely dispersed by modern research. The establishment of the Roumans in Dacia is of comparatively recent date, beginning only in the thirteenth century.

The Roumans of Wallachia, Moldavia, and Transsilvania, are isolated from the scattered Rouman remnant on Pindos and elsewhere. They represent that part of the inhabitants of the peninsula which became Latin, while the Greeks remained Greek, and the Illyrians remained barbarian. Their lands, Moesia, Thrace specially so called, and Dacia, were added to the empire at various times from Augustus to Trajan. That they should gradually adopt the Latin language is in no sort wonderful. Their position with regard to Rome was exactly the same as that of Gaul and Spain. Where Greek civilization had been firmly established, Latin could nowhere displace it. Where Greek civilization was unknown, Latin overcame the barbarian tongue. It would naturally do so in this part of the East exactly as it did in the West.

Here then we have in the southeastern peninsula three nations which have all lived on to all appearances from the very beginnings of European history, three distinct nations, speaking three distinct languages. We have nothing answering to this in the West. It needs no proof that the speakers of Celtic and Basque in Gaul and in Spain do not hold the same position in western Europe which the Greeks, Albanians, and Roumans do in eastern Europe. In the East the most ancient inhabitants of the land are still there, not as scraps or survivals, not as fragments of nations lingering on in corners, but as nations in the strictest sense, nations whose national being forms an element in every modern and political question. They all have their memories, their grievances, and their hopes; and their memories, their grievances, and their hopes are all of a practical and political kind. Highlanders, Welshmen, Bretons, French Basques, whatever we say of the Spanish brethren, have doubtless memories, but they have hardly political grievances or hopes. Ireland may have political grievances; it certainly has political hopes; but they are not exactly of the same kind as the grievances or hopes of the Greek, the Albanian, and the Rouman. Let Home Rule succeed to the extent of setting up an independent king and parliament of Ireland, yet the language and civilization of that king and parliament would still be English. Ireland would form an English State, politically hostile, it may be, to Great Britain, but still an English State. No Greek, Albanian or Rouman State would be in the same way either Turkish or Austrian.

On these primitive and abiding races came, as on other parts of Europe, the Roman conquest. That conquest planted Latin colonies on the Dalmatian coast, where the Latin tongue still remains in its Italian variety as the speech of literature and city life; it Romanized one great part of the earlier inhabitants: it had the great political effect of all, that of planting the Roman power in a Greek city, and thereby creating a State, and in the end a nation, which was Roman on one side, and Greek on the other. Then came the wandering of the nations, on which, as regards men of our own race, we need not dwell. The Goths marched at will through the Eastern Empire; but no Teutonic settlement was ever made within its bounds, no lasting Teutonic settlement was ever made even on its border. The part of the Teuton in the West was played, far less perfectly indeed, by the Slave in the East. He is there what the Teuton is here, the great representative of what we may call the modern European races, those whose part in history began after the establishment of the Rouman power. The differences between the position of the two races are chiefly these. The Slave in the East has pre-Roman races standing alongside of him in a way in which the Teuton has not in the West. On the Greeks and Albanians he has had but little influence; on the Rouman and his language his influence has been far greater, but hardly so great as the influence of the Teuton on the Romance nations and languages of western Europe. The Slave too stands alongside of races which have come in since his own coming, in a way in which the Teuton in the West is still further from doing.

That is to say, besides Greeks, Albanians, and Roumans, he stands alongside of Bulgarians, Magyars, and Turks, who have nothing to answer to them in the West. The Slave, in the time of his coming, in the nature of his settlement, answers roughly to the Teuton; his position is what that of the Teuton would be if western Europe had been brought under the power of an alien race at some time later than his own settlement. The Slaves undoubtedly form the greatest element in the population of the Eastern peninsula, and they once reached more widely still. Taking the Slavonic name in its widest meaning, they occupy all the lands from the Danube and its great tributaries southward to the strictly Greek border. The exceptions are where earlier races remain, Greek or Italian on the coast-line, Albanian in the mountains. The Slaves hold the heart of the peninsula, and they hold more than the peninsula itself. The Slave lives equally on both sides of what is or was the frontier of the Austrian and Ottoman empires; indeed, but for another set of causes which have affected eastern Europe, the Slave might have reached uninterruptedly from the Baltic to the Aegaean.

This last set of causes are those which specially distinguish the histories of eastern and of western Europe; a set of causes which, though exactly twelve hundred years old, are still fresh and living, and which are the special causes which have aggravated the special difficulties of the last five hundred years. In Western Europe, though we have had plenty of political conquests, we have had no national migrations since the days of the Teutonic settlements-at least, if we may extend these last so as to take in the Scandinavian settlements in Britain and Gaul. The Teuton has pressed to the East at the expense of the Slave and the Old-Prussian; the borders between the Romance and the Teutonic nations in the West have fluctuated; but no third set of nations has come in, strange alike to the Roman and the Teuton and to the whole Aryan family. As the Huns of Attila showed themselves in western Europe as passing ravagers, so did the Magyars at a later day; so did the Ottoman Turks in a day later still, when they besieged Vienna and laid waste the Venetian mainland. But all these Turanian invaders appeared in western Europe simply as passing invaders; in eastern Europe their part has been widely different.

Besides the temporary dominion of Avars, Patzinaks, Chazars,

Cumans, and a crowd of others, three bodies of more abiding settlers, the Bulgarians, the Magyars, and the Mongol conquerors of Russia, have come in by one path; a fourth, the Ottoman Turks, have come in by another path. Among all these invasions we have one case of thorough assimilation, and only one. The original Finnish Bulgarians have, like Western conquerors, been lost among Slavonic subjects and neighbors. The geographical function of the Magyar has been to keep the two great groups of Slavonic nations apart. To his coming, more than to any other cause, we may attribute the great historical gap which separates the Slave of the Baltic from his southern kinsfolk. The work of the Ottoman Turk we all know. These latter settlers remain alongside of the Slave, just as the Slave remains alongside of the earlier settlers. The Slavonized Bulgarians are the only instance of assimilation such as we are used to in the West. All the other races, old and new, from the Albanian to the Ottoman, are still there, each keeping its national being and its national speech. And in one part of the ancient Dacia we must add quite a distinct element, the element of Teutonic occupation in a form unlike any in which we see it in the West, in the shape of the Saxons of Transsilvania.

We have thus worked out our point in detail. While in each Western country some one of the various races which have settled in it has, speaking roughly, assimilated the others, in the lands which are left under the rule of the Turk, or which have been lately delivered from his rule, all the races that have ever settled in the country still abide side by side. So when we pass into the lands which form the Austro-Hungar national government, another fragment is ruled by civilized strangers, a third is trampled down by barbarians. The existing States of Greece, Roumania, and Servia are far from taking in the whole of the Greek, Rouman, and Servian nations. In all these lands, Austrian, Turkish, and independent, there is no difficulty in marking off the several nations; only in no case do the nations answer to any existing political power.

In all these cases, where nationality and government are altogether divorced, language becomes yet more distinctly the test of nationality than it is in Western lands where nationality and government do to some extent coincide. And when nationality and language do not coincide in the East, it is owing to another cause, of which also we know nothing in the West. In many cases religion takes the place of nationality; or rather the ideas of religion and nationality can hardly be distinguished. In the West a man's nationality is in no way affected by the religion which he professes, or even by his change from one religion to another. In the East it is otherwise. The Christian renegade who embraces Islam becomes for most practical purposes a Turk. Even if, as in Crete and Bosnia, he keeps his Greek or Slavonic language, he remains Greek or Slave only in a secondary sense.

For the first principle of the Mahometan religion, the lordship of the true believer over the infidel, cuts off the possibility of any true national fellowship between the true believer and the infidel. Even the Greek or Armenian who embraces the Latin creed goes far toward parting with his nationality as well as with his religion. For the adoption of the Latin creed implies what is in some sort the adoption of a new allegiance, the accepting of the authority of the Roman bishop. In the Armenian indeed we are come very near to the phenomena of the further East, where names like Parsee and Hindoo, names in themselves as strictly ethnical as Englishman or Frenchman, have come to express distinctions in which religion and nationality are absolutely the same thing. Of this whole class of phenomena the Jew is of course the crowning example. But we speak of these matters here only as bringing in an element in the definition of nationality to which we are unused in the West. But it quite comes within our present subject to give one definition from the southeastern lands. What is the Greek? Clearly he who is at once a Greek in speech and Orthodox in faith. The Hellenic Mussulmans in Crete, even the Hellenic Latins in some of the other islands, are at the most imperfect members of the Hellenic body. The utmost that can be said is that they keep the power of again entering that body, either by their own return to the national faith, or by such a change in the state of things as shall make difference in religion no longer inconsistent with true national fellowship.

Thus, wherever we go, we find language to be the rough practical test of nationality. The exceptions are many; they may perhaps outnumber the instances which conform to the rule. Still they are exceptions. Community of language does not imply community of blood; it might be added that diversity of language does not imply diversity of blood. But community of language is, in the absence of any evidence to the contrary, a presumption of the community of blood, and it is proof of something which for practical purposes is the same as community of blood. To talk of "the Latin race" is in strictness absurb. We know that the so-called race is simply made up of those nations which adopted the Latin language. The Celtic, Teutonic, and Slavonic races may conceivably have been formed by a like artificial process. But the presumption is the other way; and if such a process ever took place, it took place long before history began.

The Celtic, Teutonic, and Salvonic races come before us as groups of mankind marked out by the test of language. Within those races separate nations are again marked out by a stricter application of the test of language. Within the race we may have languages which are clearly akin to each other, but which need not be mutually intelligible. Within the nation we have only dialects which are mutually intelligible, or which, at all events, gather round some one central dialect which is intelligible to all. We take this standard of races and nations, fully aware that it will not stand a physiological test, but holding that for all practical purposes adoption must pass as equivalent to natural descent. And, among the practical purposes which are affected by the facts of race and nationality, we must, as long as a man is what he is, as long as he has not been created afresh according to some new scientific pattern, not shrink from reckoning those generous emotions which, in the present state of European feeling, are beginning to bind together the greater as well as the lesser groups of mankind. The sympathies of men are beginning to reach wider than could have been dreamed of a century ago. The feeling which was once confined to the mere household extended itself to the tribe or city. From the tribe or city it extended itself to the nation; from the nation it is beginning to extend itself to the whole race. In some cases it can extend itself to the whole race far more easily than in others.

In some cases historical causes have made nations of the same race bitter enemies, while they have made nations of different races friendly allies. The same thing happened in earlier days between tribes and cities of the same nation. But, when hindrances of this kind do not exist, the feeling of race, as something beyond the narrower feeling of nationality, is beginning to be a powerful agent in the feelings and actions of men and of nations. A long series of mutual wrongs, conquest, and oppression on one side, avenged by conquest and oppression on the other side, have made the Slave of Poland and the Slave of Russia the bitterest of enemies. No such hindrance exists to stop the flow of natural and generous feeling between the Slave of Russia and the Slave of the southeastern lands.

Those whose statesmanship consists in some hand-to-mouth shift for the moment, whose wisdom consists in refusing to look either back to the past or onward to the future, cannot understand this great fact of our times; and what they cannot understand they mock at. But the fact exists, and does its work in spite of them. And it does its work none the less because in some cases the feeling of sympathy is awakened by a claim of kindred, where, in the sense of the physiologist or the genealogist, there is no kindred at all. The practical view, historical or political, will accept as members of this or that race or nation many members whom the physiologist would shut out, whom the English lawyer would shut out, but whom the Roman lawyer would gladly welcome to every privilege of the stock on which they were grafted. The line of the Scipios, of the Caesars, and of the Antonines was continued by adoption; and for all practical purposes the nations of the earth have agreed to follow the examples set them by their masters.

26

Italian Unification, Cavour, Garibaldi and the Making of Italy

In 1815 at the close of the French Revolutionary and Napoleonic Wars the statesmen representing the great powers, in their efforts to restore stable governance to Europe after twenty-six years of turmoil, came to accept (under the persuasion of Talleyrand-the Foreign Minister of the recently restored French monarchy) that "legitimate sovereigns" should be restored, where possible, to their thrones.

Prior to the first irruption of what developed into French, and European, revolutionary unrest after 1789 the political shape of the Italian peninsula derived in large part from the influence of Papal diplomacy over the previous millenium where the Popes had tended to strongly support the existence of a number of small states in the north of the peninsula such that no strong power might presume to try to overshadow the papacy.

Such political decentralisation may have facilitated the emergence of a number of mercantile city states such as the Florence of the Medicis and the Milan of the Sforzas and to have allowed a scenario where ambitious men such as Cesare Borgia could attempt to establish themselves as rulers of territories won by statecraft and the sword. The burgeoning wealth of these city states, despite much political turmoil, helped to fund that re-birth of classical learning and of artistic expression that is known as the Renaissance.

As time passed some of these mercantile states became reconstituted as Duchies and Grand Duchies. By the mid eighteenth century the north of the Italian peninsula featured a number of such dynastic states together with mercantile republics such as Genoa and Venice. The former Duchy of Savoy meanwhile, originally based on limited territories north of the Alps, had expanded to also include Nice, Piedmont (an extensive territory in the north-east of the Italian peninsula) and the island of Sardinia and was now known now by its senior title as the Kingdom of Sardinia. The Noble House of Savoy maintained its court at Turin in Piedmont.

In the settlements to the Napoleonic Wars statesmen, in their efforts to restore political stability to Europe, reconstituted most of the Duchies and Grand Duchies often under rulers drawn from junior branches of the Habsburg dynasty or otherwise under Habsburg Austrian tutelage. Habsburg Austria was awarded sovereignty over Lombardy and over the former Venetian Republic whilst the Republic of Genoa was similarly entrusted to the House of Savoy. The territories of the chuch that straddled the central portion of the peninsula were again placed under Papal sovereignty whilst to the south the Kingdom of the Two Sicilies (Sicily and Naples) was restored to a junior branch of the Spanish Bourbon dynasty.

Giuseppe Garibaldi, later famous as an Italian patriotic leader, recorded his introduction to the concept of "Italia" as having taken place during a voyage to Constantinople in 1833.

During the course of this voyage he overheard an argument. A young man had been talking about a secret organisation he had joined-*La Giovine Italia*-or Young Italy. One of his companions commented dismissively, "What do you mean Italy? What is Italy?" The young man now spoke enthusiastically of a "new Italy... United Italy. The Italy of all the Italians." Garibaldi recorded that listening to these words he felt "as Columbus must have done when he first caught sight of land". In response to this awakening to the idea of "Italia-Italy" he moved to skake the young man enthusiastically by the hand.

The belief that "Italia" was a desireable possibility can be associated with the change in perspectives that many people, particularly from the more affluent artisan, middle and minor aristocratic classes, underwent after the American and French revolutions away from an acceptance of more purely dynastic patterns of sovereignty and towards aspiration towards "liberal" constitutional, and possibly even overtly republican or national notions of sovereignty.

The central figure in the origin of "Young Italy" was one Giuseppe Mazzini (1805-1872), who in 1821 in Genoa had witnessed the distress of the "refugees of Italy" who were in the process of fleeing into exile after their failure of their revolutionary efforts at winning reform and, moved by their example, had chosen to devote his life to the cause of Italian independence and unity. In 1827 he was initiated into Carbonari movement and was himself forced into exile in 1831 for revolutionary activity. In exile in the French seaport city of Marseilles, then something of a revolutionary hotbed, he advocated subversive activity "even when it ended in defeat" as a method of developing general "political consciousness." He also began to move away from the philosophy of the Carbonari and subsequently founded Giovine Italia (Young Italy) a movement dedicated to securing "for Italy Unity, Independence, and Liberty."

Mazzini's revolutionary vision extended beyond the limited objective of Italian national unity towards the liberation of all oppressed peoples. He hoped for a new democratic and republican Italy that would lead other subject peoples to freedom and liberty and for a new Europe, controlled by the people and not by sovereigns, that would replace the old order.

"The republic, as I at least understand it, means association, of which liberty is only an element, a necessary antecedent. It means association, a new philosophy of life, a divine Ideal that shall move the world, the only means of regeneration vouchsafed to the human race."
Giuseppe Mazzini

After his political conversion of 1833 Garibaldi travelled to Marseilles and enrolled in Young Italy. In February 1834 he was active as a propagandist for Young Italy whilst employed as a sailor in the royal Piedmontese navy, his subversive activitiies were reported to the authorities and, although he evaded capture by the authorities, was sentenced to death in absentia by a Genoese court. He subsequently spent more than twelve years in exile mostly in South America.

From the 1830's a certain sympathy with the idea of a more politically integrated "Italia" was increasingly exhibited by members of the aristocracy and by members of the more affluent artisan, middle and professional classes in the various states of the Italian peninsula.

Camillo Benso Cavour was born at Turin on the 1st of August 1810 into the old Piedmontese feudal aristocracy. Being a younger son of a noble family social tradition steered him into the army such that he entered the military academy at Turin at the age of ten. On leaving the college at the age of sixteen-first of his class-he received a commission in the engineers. He spent the next five years in the army but he spent his leisure hours in study, especially of the English language. During these years he developed strongly marked Liberal tendencies and an uncompromising dislike for absolutism and clericalism. After the accession to the Sardinian throne of Charles Albert, whom he always distrusted, he felt that his position in the army was intolerable and resigned his commission (1831). Cavour's political ideas were greatly influenced by the July revolution of 1830 in France, which seemed to him to prove that an historic monarchy was not incompatible with Liberal principles, and he became more than ever convinced of the benefits of a constitutional monarchy as opposed both to absolutism and to republicanism. His views were strengthened by his studies of the British constitution, of which he was known to be a great admirer such that he was even nicknamed-" Milord Camillo "

During these times the Austrian statesman Metternich was aware of the implicit challenge posed to the settlements of 1815 by those who supported the the formation of "Italy". In letter of April 1847 to the Austrian ambassador to France he wrote:-

"The word 'Italy' is a geographical expression, a description which is useful shorthand, but has none of the political significance the efforts of the revolutionary ideologues try to put on it, and which is full of dangers for the very existence of the states which make up the peninsula."

In 1847 Cavour was involved in the the founding of "Il Risorgimento", a newspaper whose very publication had been facilitated by a recent relaxation of censorship, which became the official voice for the Italian National Movement. He successfully pressed King Charles Albert of Sardinia to grant a constitution to his people [to form a constitutional monarchy]; and in 1848 to battle against Austria as an holder of power in the Italian penisula. The failure of this military action prompted the king to abdicate in favour of his son, Victor Emmanuel.

Cavour became a member of parliament briefly from 1848-1849. Subsequently, he became minister of agriculture, industry and commerce in 1850, finance minister in 1851, and premier or prime minister in 1852.

Contemporaries found it hard to know what to make of Cavour's personality and leave on record impressions of him being both enigmatic and devious. The somewhat brusque and soldierly Victor Emmanuel was prepared to work with Cavour as he seemed to sense that Cavour's talents offered the prospect of extensions of the influence and territory of Sardinia-Piedmont. As Prime Minister Cavour sponsored policies that promoted economic development, allowed some liberalisation in politics, and countenanced reforms that, in ways, compromised the position of the Church. Sardinia-Piedmont had already in 1848 abolished the ecclesiastical courts and introduced civil marriage-policies which had met with the dire protests of Pope Pius IX. Cavour's new measure ordered the closure of some one half of the monastic houses within Sardinian territories.

Cavour hoped to secure the annexation of territories in the north of the Italian peninsula to the Kingdom of Sardinia-Piedmont. He regarded the conservatism and power of Tsarist Russia as being a potent limitation on almost any popularly inspired alteration in frontiers anywhere in Europe. The outbreak of the Crimean War between France and Britain on one side and Russia on the other meant that a Sardinian interest was also at stake as a reverse for the Tsar would leave him less able to limit such popularly inspired changes in frontiers. Cavour also hoped to win friends internationally by sending some forces to co-operate with the French and British in a war against the Russian Empire that was prosecutea in the Black Sea-region in 1854-6. In association with consenting to Sardinia-Piedmont's participation in the

Crimean War Cavour had hoped that the overall situation in the Italian Peninsula would be given a hearing during the post-war international Conference.

For several decades Austria and Russia had been the guarantors of reaction in Europe. Russian intervention in the Hungarian Kingdom in 1849 had been crucial to the recovery of the Austrian Empire. The substantial setback that Russia received in this "Crimean War" and also estrangements that occurred between the Russian Empire and the Austrian Empire, and between the Austrian Empire and the western powers, during the course of the war allowed Cavour much more scope to seek to win gains at the expense of a now somewhat isolated Austrian Empire. This diplomatic isolation was complicated by the Austrian Empire still being distressed by Magyar Hungarian restiveness.

Although a Bourbon monarchy had been restored in France in 1815 at the close of the Napoleonic wars it did not endure. The "legitimist" Bourbon line, disliked for their absolutist tendencies, were replaced in an 1830 revolution by the more junior "Orleanist" branch of the dynasty who consented to rule as "Kings of the French" rather than as "Kings of France". Futher revolution in 1848 saw the Orleanist King abdicate, the French kingdom being replaced by a republic to which one Louis Napoleon, a nephew of Napoleon I (i.e. Napoleon Bonaparte), was elected president. By 1852 Louis Napoleon contrived to overthrew the Republic in the name of order, and styled himself, with the consent of the French electorate, as the Emperor Napoleon III of France.

(Napoleon II being a complimentary titled posthumously imputed to Bonaparte's son from a 'marriage of state' that Napoleon I at the height of his political power had entered into with a daughter of the Austrian Emperor. This son, in his infancy, was the heir presumptive to the extensive empire established by his father and had been styled as the 'King of Rome'. Following on from Napoleon's defeated by a coalition of powers this son, a young man of some promise by all accounts, had been raised as an Austrian princeling under the supervision of Metternich but had died of tuberculosis in his early twenties.

As his life ebbed away this young Duke left the great ceremonial sword of honour he had inherited from his father not to any of his surviving Bonaparte uncles but to his cousin Louis Napoleon.)

Napoleon III had, of his own volition, ideas of intervening in that Italian Peninsula where his uncle Napoleon had been so active in events. Napoleon, in exile on the remote island of St. Helena in the South Atlantic, had left written records that characterised one of the main planks of his policy as Emperor as being that of the championing of states based on nationality. Whilst this is probably a sanitised version of what Napoleon did in what were more truly efforts to extend and preserve the power of his empire Napoleon III considered that European peace would in the long run be promoted by the establishment of states based on the "National Principle". Napoleon III was famously on record as having said that he "would like to do something for Italy." As a Bonaparte with the Boubons restored to the French throne Louis Napoleon had had an interesting earlier life outside France and had actually been active as a member of the Carbonari secret society (which sought to win liberal, constitutional, and national reform) in the Papal States and elsewhere during the turmoils of 1830-1831 during which his own older brother had lost his life from disease and during which his own life was also similarly in grave peril.

After the recovery of Austrian power in the Italian penisula in 1849 Paris became a city of exile for many persons who had been prominent in "Italian" nationalistic and republican agitation in 1848-9. One such person, Daniele Manin, who had been the leader of the Venetian Republic in defiance of Austria during 1848-9, signalled a conditional acceptance of Italian monarchy in the Italian penisula in a statement addressed to Victor Emmanuel II which appeared in the Italian Republican press in September 1855.

"If regenerated Italy must have a king, there must be only one, and that one the king of Piedmont... Convinced that before everything else we must make Italy, as that is the principal question, superior to all others, it (the republican party) says to the House of Savoy: 'Make Italy and I am with you. If not, not."

The sympathies of many in the Italian peninsula who were supportive of a more politically integrated "Italia" found a potent leadership after July 1857 when Manin, a Lombard nobleman named Giorgio Pallavicino, and a Sicilian named Giuseppe La Farina founded the National Society. This society hoped to achieve "the marriage of the Italian insurrection to the army of Piedmont" and took as its slogan "Unity, Independence, and Victor Emmanuel" in the hope that monarchists, federalists, liberals and also those disenchanted with Mazzini's hitherto unavailing leadership of "Italian" republicanism could unite under a common cause.

Manin, Pallavicino and La Farina were offering their support towards the "Making of Italy" rather than the "Aggrandization of Piedmont".

In January 1858, in a dramatic instance of "politically motivated" violence in Europe, an Italian, Count Orsini, and a band of followers were responsible for eight persons being killed and for some one hundred and fifty persons being injured during an explosive attempt on the life of the French Emperor during a visit to the Opera. Orsini, who had earlier been prominent in the Roman Republic that had briefly been established as a result of the turmoils of 1848, now intended to encourage opportunities for reform in the Italian Peninsula by provoking turmoils in France (and more widely in Europe) through the assassination of Napoleon III and expected that subsequent disruptions would probably produce change in the Italian Peninsula that would leave it less under Austrian rule and more liberally governed. Orsini was executed for his crimes in March 1858 but left behind him a testament depicting Napoleon III as an incarnation of the spirit of reaction.

This attempt on the life of Napoleon III was in fact the fourth such attempt by a person "patriotically" committed to forcing change in the Italian Peninsula.

Napoleon III decided to become more deeply involved in developments there-partly in the hope of lessening the likelyhood of yet further attempts on his own life and also partly in the hope of adding lustre to his then failing appeal in France through a domestically impressive foreign policy initiative that could lead to French influence replacing that of the Austrian Empire in the north the Italian penisula.

A pattern of indulgence in complex and devious diplomatic agreements, in the unscrupulous use of force, and of the exploitation of populist sentiment in the interest of the dynastic state, of that type which later came to be called Realpolitik, (tr. practical politics), had an early demonstration after the Crimean War in policies followed by Cavour as the Prime Minister of Sardinia-Piedmont. Cavour sought some form of alliance with the French against Austria in the hope of ensuring that some of those areas of the Italian peninsula ruled directly by Austria, or by Austrian supported rulers, would be more free to join in with a redrawing of the political map of the the Italian Peninsula. Cavour, at this time, seems to have been intent on achieving the integration of several territiories in the north of the peninsula into an extended Sardinian-Piedmontese state rather than upon a political transformation of the entire peninsula.

In May 1858 a Dr. Conneau, a close friend of Napoleon III, visited Turin and made a point of 'advising' Cavour that the French Emperor would soon be spending several weeks at the French resort of Plombieres, this town being located in the Vosges region fairly close to the frontiers of the territories of the House of Savoy!!!

At a subsequent shadowy meeting in July 1858 between Napoleon III and Cavour, (who was supposed to be on route to holiday in Switzerland with some time being spent inspecting railway construction in Savoy!!!), the possibility of France gaining territories on the French side of the Alps from Sardinia-Piedmont in return for assistance in reshaping the map of Italia was mooted. Savoy was a particular object of French desire, it had been annexed to France during the revolution, and was held to be within the "Natural Frontiers" of France.

A principal ambition of Napoleon III as Emperor of France was to achieve the overthrow of some aspects of the settlement made in 1815 at the close of the Napoleonic wars, as these settlements were seen as placing irksome limits on France. The French annexation of Savoy would of itself constitute a breach of the 1815 settlement.

An informal Pact of Plombieres envisaged Piedmont annexing

Lombardy-Venetia and further envisaged the entire Italian Peninsula participating in a Confederation with the Pope as its figurehead. France agreed to support Sardinia-Piedmont militarily against the Austrian Empire. Napoleon III stipulated that any such conflict should be "non-revolutionary", and should be justifiable in the eyes of the world-neither Piedmont-Savoy nor France should seen as instigators.

In Decmber 1858 Odo Russell, a British diplomat usually based in Rome, was informed by Cavour at an interview in Turin, that he, Cavour intended *to force* Austria to declare war. Cavour even went so far as to predict that this would happen "about the first week of May".

On 1 January 1859 Napoleon III, at his New Years Day reception, publicly expressed to the Austrian Ambassador his regret-"I am sorry that our relations are not so good as I wish they were, but I beg you to write to Vienna that my personal sentiments for your Emperor are unchanged". This public notice of dissatisfaction was taken up by wider society-fears of hostilities affected the stock markets.

In these times Cavour prepared a speech which it was intended should be delivered to the Italian parliament by King Victor Emmanuel. Draft copies of this speech were sent to King Victor Emmanuel and to Napoleon III for their approval and, after these were returned to Cavour with some amendments by the King and Napoleon III, Cavour himself had an opportunity to make further deletions and additions during the process of translating the draft into Italian, the result was that on the 10th of January King Victor Emmanuel appeared before his parliament and, as part of his speech declared "While respecting treaties we cannot remain insensitive to the cry of suffering that rises towards us from so many parts of Italy." This sentence could not be expected to go down too well in Austrian circles.

Towards the end of January the understandings agreed between France and Piedmont were formalised through the signing of an "offensive-defensive" alliance. In line with the wishes of Napoleon III Cavour took steps that were designed to ensure that the conflict would seem to have been started by Austria. To this end Cavour arranged for a crisis to be raised where subjects of the Duchy of Modena, where the ruler was known to be supported by Austria, were encouraged by Cavour to express dissatisfaction with the current administration and to invite Victor Emmanuel to come to their aid. On the 23rd of April Cavour was intercepted on the steps of the Chamber of Deputies by two Austrian officers who handed him a note from their Emperor in which Austria demanded the demobilisation of the Piedmontese forces; and if a satisfactory answer was not received within three days the Emperor Francis Joseph would "with great regret, be compelled to have recourse to arms to secure it."

Cavour was well pleased with this development and although he told the Austrians to come back in three days for his answer he had no intention to provide such an answer as would deter the Austrian Empire from military action.

When active hostilities did occur the Piedmontese-French interest prevailed.

During this time of conflict there were revolts, motivated by the "Italian" outlook of the National Society, in several Italian states that featured demands for closer political association with Sardinia-Piedmont. If these closer political associations took place Sardinia-Piedmont potentially stood to gain sway over more territory than was envisioned for the North Italian Kingdom mooted at Plombieres and might become so powerful as to impede French influence in the Italian Peninsula. The unanticipated revolts in several Italian states also had the potential to compromise the position of the Papacy in ways that would be unacceptable to the powerful Roman Catholic interest in France. In more northerly parts of Europe the Prussians seemed to be engaged in military manoeuvres that might threaten the French interest-Prussia as a member of the German Confederation was obliged to assist in the defence of Austria, as a fellow member of the confederation, should her core territories come under threat. The French had suffered much loss of life in two hard fought battles and the Austrian forces had withdrawn into the inherently formidable "Quadrilateral" of fortresses. Napoleon III drew back from his pact with Sardinia-Piedmont and an armistice of Villafranca, concluded in early July between France and Austria without consultation with Sardinia, formally consented only to Lombardy entering upon a close political association with Sardinia-Piedmont stating that several of the states that had experienced revolts should be restored to their former rulers. That is to say that Austria agreed to cede Lombardy not to Piedmont, but to Napoleon III, from whom Victor Emmanuel would then receive it.

Victor Emmanuel felt obliged to accept the situation resulting from the reluctance of Napoleon III to continue as an active ally but Cavour protested in an intemperate fashion and even resigned his post as Prime Minister after explicitly accusing Victor Emmanuel of betrayal.

In the event local plebiscites ensured that Modena, Parma, Tuscany, and the Romagna (i.e. the Papal 'Legations' of Bologna, Ferrara, Ravenna and Forli), where assemblies had voted for close political association with Sardinia-Piedmont, were indeed associated with the Sardinian Kingdom.

Assurances offered during the campaign prior to the holding of these plebiscites that these territories could hope for a degree of regional autonomy were not subsequently honoured.

A particularly keen problem arose from the fact that the Romagna was a longstanding, if restive, part of the territories of the Church-and the Church could only view its alienation from their control as a profoundly intolerable challenge both to itself as such and to its legitimate, indeed divinely ordained, traditions of temporal sovereignty. From the point of view of the Papacy the longstanding territories of the church were "God given" and were as such held in trust by the Popes on behalf of the Catholics of the entire world.

Napoleon III pressed for plebiscites to take place in Savoy and Nice in the hope that these territories would agree to come under French sovereignty, as his price for consenting to Sardinia-Piedmont gaining territory in the Italian peninsula.

Cavour and Victor Emmanuel had shown themselves prepared to exploit Italian Nationalist sentiment in pursuit of annexations of territory to Sardinia-Piedmont. Savoy and Nice were dear to Italian sentiment, indeed Garibaldi, one of Italian Nationalism's populist leaders was actually a Nizzard and was less than pleased by Nice becoming French. Garibaldi actually sent an associate to King Victor Emmanuel peremptorally asking if it was true that Nice had been ceded to France asking for an answer "yes or no".

In reply Victor Emmanuel, whose dynasty had originally held territorial sovereignty as the Dukes of Savoy, insisted that Garibaldi be advised that not only Nice but Savoy also had been ceded. "And if I can reconcile myself to losing the cradle of my family and my race he can do the same."

By the spring of 1860 perhaps a third of what was thought of as "Italian" territory was now under the Kingship of Victor Emmanuel. Similarly about one half of the "Italian" people, some 11,000,000 persons, lived within the Kingdom ruled by Victor Emmanuel. Garibaldi would actually have preferred that there should be an Italian Republic but on balance fell in with the establishment of an Italian Kingdom. This acceptance was based on the practical usefulness of Sardinia-Piedmont as a focus of military power capable of challenging the Austrian Empire.

In late March 1860 elections were held to return an "Italian" parliament which was to convene in early April in King Victor Emmanuel's capital city-Turin.

As part of his first speech to the new parliament King Victor Emmanuel spoke of Italy:-

It is no longer the Italy of the Romans, nor that of the Middle Ages; it must no longer be the battle-field of ambitious foreigners, but it must rather be the Italy of the Italians".

In relation to Savoy and Nice King Victor Emmanmuel spoke of the necessity of some sacrifice "for the good of Italy" even though the relinquishment of these territories "cost my heart dear".

Garibaldi actually planned to intervene in Nice in the hope of disrupting a plebiscite that was intended by the French authorities to endorse the transfer of Nice to France but was prevailed upon to reconcile himself to the alienation of his personal homeland and to involve himself instead in an ongoing Sicilian revolt. To this end Garibaldi applied to Cavour for the supply of large quantities of firearms which he subsequently received, with Cavour "turning a blind eye", from the National Society.

In early May Garibaldi led a seaborne expedition from Genoa, some one thousand strong (and of a wide range of ages), to Sicily. Notwithstanding his effective co-operation in the supply of firearms Cavour publicly opposed this expedition, by Garibaldi, to the south. Units of the Sardinian navy meanwhile, were ordered to provide a discrete "escort" to the expedition.

Cavour was quite prepared to see Sardinia-Piedmont play as full a role as possible in any Confederation of Italian States and would actually have been content with the probably future of Sardinia-Piedmont, with its recent additions of territory, as a free and constitutional state and might not have not sought to risk what had been achieved by looking yet more of Italia to be integrated with Sardinia-Piedmont. A major worry being that too great a growth in the potential power of Sardinia-Piedmont, or too great a challenge to the power or sovereignty of the Papacy being offered, could well lead to foreign intervention in events. Nevertheless Cavour found it politically impossible for a variety of reasons to actually prevent the expedition. Garibaldi for his part, and to the disgust of some avowed republicans amongst the Thousand, announced that the expedition's war-cry would be "Italy and Victor Emmanuel."

The plebiscites held in Savoy and Nice did seem to yield majorities in favour of annexation to France but allegations were widely made that this outcome was engineered to achieve the result required by the agreements between Cavour and Napoleon III.

"Garibaldi and the Thousand" disembarked at Massala in Sicily on 11 May where Sicilians in revolt against King Francis II welcomed this arrival.

In August with Sicily almost completely won from the control of Francis II Garibaldi decided to carry the revolt to the Neapolitan mainland and his forces were joined by many persons variously committed to challenging Bourbon rule or to securing further changes in the overall situation of the Italian Peninsula. The armies of Francis II proved unable to prevent the city of Naples from falling to the effective control of Garibaldi by early September.

Garibaldi hoped to present the territories that he and his

followers had won to the Kingdom of Italy but intended that those territories should include the city of Rome where, incidentally, "Italian" enthusiasm was increasingly evident.

As news of Garibaldi's successes filtered north and word arrived from France assuring him of non-interference, Cavour felt able to call the exploits of Garibaldi and his followers as "the most poetic fact of the century". That being said Cavour feared that an attack on Rome by Garibaldi would lead to French intervention in support of the continued Temporal Power of the Papacy. Cavour also considered that Garibaldi and Mazzini might attempt to set up a Republic in the South of Italy.

Cavour and Piedmont had hitherto "led" and "controlled" the movement towards "Italian" territorial integration-future marked successes by Garibaldi's irregular forces had the potential to somewhat compromise Sardinia-Piedmontese perceived leadership of events.

Cavour arranged for some unrest to take place within Umbria and the Marches (territories of the Church to the south of the Romagna) as a cover for the movement of a Piedmontese army into these Church territories "to restore order." In mid September the Piedmontese army proceeded southwards, through some of the territories of the Church, in order to meet with and dissuade an assault on Rome by Garibaldi. During the course of moving across the territories of the Church the Piedmontese forces clashed with forces recently formed in the service of the Pope but were not thereby prevented from proceeding south. The Piedmontese forces could not have been prevented, but voluntarily refrained, from advancing on Rome at this time.

When the Piedmontese force met up with Garibaldi at Teano in the Kingdom of Naples on 26 October Garibaldi effectively surrendered his gains to Victor Emmanuel with a handshake and called upon his men to salute Victor Emmanuel:-"Hail to the first King of Italy." They responded positively :-"Viva, il Re!" Some local peasants who gathered shortly thereafter were however far more ready to cheer Garibaldi himself as their liberator rather than to enthuse over their unlooked-for new King.

As an outcome of these developments there were annexations

of territory to Sardinia-Piedmont after plebiscites in Sicily, Naples and Umbria and the Marches. Astute observers held that, in the cases of Sicily and Naples, the positive vote in favour of association in the Italian Kingdom was, in part, due to there being no more locally acceptable alternative put on the table for endorsement.

Sicily had long seen itself as being an unwilling colony of Naples and had a tradition of separatist aspiration-the fact that the earlier stages of the most recent uprising against Bourbon rule in Sicily had also featured a strong socio-political challenge by the local peasantry directed against the Sicilian propertied classes caused many influential Sicilians to discount seperatism and to look to Victor Emmanuel and nascent "Italy" as offering some potential support against future socio-political unrest. Cavour's agents (not above stimulating demonstrations against Garibaldi's government) gained support for annexation from middle and upper class groups petrified at the danger of rural and urban insurrection. When a plebiscite took place in October annexation won by an overwhelming margin. A barely imagined Italy became a reality as the outcome of a complex game of class confict, fear, ambition, uncertainty, and military force. What had begun as a homegrown popular insurrection and democrat-led guerrilla warfare ended as an effective royal conquest supported by the island's social elite under the guise of a well-managed plebiscite.

Garibaldi, for his part, voluntarily withdrew from the scene returning to his island home of Caprera ostensibly to resume life as a cultivator of the soil and livestock farmer.

Victor Emmanuel was proclaimed as King of Italy "by the grace of God and the will of the people" by an Italian Parliament in session in Turin in March, 1861. Cavour made speeches in which he asserted that Rome was the only Italian city to which all others could yield precedence and that, as such, Rome must become the capital of Italy. He held however, that this accession to Rome must be by moral means with the assent of the Papacy itself and of France. Cavour further envisaged that with Rome as the Italian capital the Papacy would not exercise temporal power and that there would be a separation of church and state. A "Boncompagni" bill, approved by the chamber of deputies shortly thereafter recognised Rome, still garrisoned as it was by French soldiers in support of the traditional Papal position, as the capital of Italy.

Massimo D'Azeglio, Cavour's predecessor as prime minister of Piedmont suggested, in the first meeting of the parliament of the newly united Italian kingdom, famously suggested that "Italy is made, We still have to make Italians." Many wealthy people had some knowledge of French and of the Florentine-Tuscan "Italian" dialect established through the works of Dante and others as a literary language. Most people spoke regional dialects that were often unintelligible in other parts of the Italian peninsula.

The historic linguistic diversity of the Italian peninsula had come to be seen as being something of an obstacle to the fulfilment of Italian-National aspirations.

"Even in Piedmont, difference of language is our great difficulty: our three native languages are French, Piedmontese and Genoese. Of these, French alone is generally intelligible. A speech in Genoese of Piedmontese would be generally unintelligible to two-thirds of the Assembly. Except the Savoyards, who sometimes use French, the deputies all speak in Italian; but this is to them a dead language, in which they have never been accustomed even to converse. They scarcely ever, therefore, can use it with spirit or fluency. Cavour is naturally a good speaker, but in Italian he is embarassed. You can see that he is translating; so is Azeglio; so are they all...

From a letter by Marchioness Arconati to Nassau William Senior, 6th November 1850

A dynastic "House of Savoy" ruled in Piedmont where it upheld, linguistically, a principally French and Piedmontese court and administration despite having originated north of the Alps in the Duchy of Savoy (where there was a Savoyard dialect!).

This House of Savoy had become a Royal House when in 1713, by a treaty of Utrecht, one of its Dukes, Victor Amadeus II, was recognised as being King of Sicily, (later, i.e. 1720, exchanged for Kingship of Sardinia), as a reward for his co-operation in widespread turmoils over dynastic succession elsewhere in Europe but had continued with its French and Piedmontese court and administration based on Turin in Piedmont.

Thus late-nineteenth century Risorgimento "nation building" in the Italian peninsula, as keenly supported by the rising middle class and artisan would-be "Italian" political nation, occured against a background of the historic existence of many languages and dialects including French, Piedmontese, Genoan, Sicilian, Sardinian and Ligurian. The processes of "making Italians" ultimately included an acceptance of Florentine-Tuscan "Italian" as the desired official language of the newly unified state.

Quite apart from linguistic issues there were also problems of establishing a shared "Italian" civic conciousness and identification against the background where the multiplicity former states had been mainly been administered by reactionary statesmen and clerics and where the majority of the people had lived materially impoverished rural lives.

The population of the Kindom of Italy in 1861 was some 22 million, of whom 8 million lived in the former Kingdom of the Two Sicilies, and of whom 17 million were illiterate. Due to restrictive clauses in the *Statuto* constitution only about one-half million persons were eligible to vote, and of that half million only 300,000 actually voted.

Italian sentiment had its own opinion as to what constituted Italian territory and in 1861 the most notable territories which Italian nationalism could regard as being "Italia Irredente" (i.e. Unredeemed Italy-hence irredentism) were Venice and Rome.

Venice, (where there was a strongly established Venetian dialect), was under the control of the powerful Austrian Empire and unlikely to become easily available to Italian annexation. Cavour warned the Italian parliament that Italy could not make war on Austria single-handed, he still hoped that Venice would be joined into Italy but told the chamber that it was a "secret of providence" whether such a "deliverance" would come "by arms or diplomacy".

The former King Naples and Sicily in these times was living in exile in Rome and followed a policy of somewhat encouraging "brigandage" in Naples and Sicily in the hope that it would facilitate his own return to the throne of the Two Sicilies. The Italian kingdom had to keep tens of thousands of troops in the south in efforts to firmly maintain order and stamp out such "banditism". A French army still defended Rome in the Papal interest. The French forces present in Rome attempted police action against groups, based in the Roman territories, that were actively engaged in such disruptive endeavours to the south in formerly Neapolitan territory. The French were however obliged to hand over any persons so arrested to the Roman authorities-it appeared to the French commanders that there own efforts in this regard were frustrated by the Roman authorities tending to release such prisoners to once again attempt to cause disruption in the south.

France had a long tradition of European power and had long history or regarding itself as being the "Eldest daughter of the Church". Napoleon III in his own day found himself on the horns of a dilemma: if he abandoned the Pope he would incur the enmity of the French Catholics, if he protected the Pope he would thwart Italian patriotism. He himself once famously said that "the occupation of Rome will be the mistake of my reign". In a letter of June 1859 to the French diplomatic representative in Rome Napoleon III had written:-

"There can exist no contradiction between my words and my actions. I wish for the independence of Italy, but I must maintain the authority of the Pope in which one hundred and fifty million of consciences are interested; and I am resolved to maintain order in Rome."

In the case of Rome matters were thus complicated by intangible but telling considerations. Whilst many Italian nationalists might consider that "without Rome for its capital Italy cannot be constituted" it was also the case that sincere Roman Catholics in Italy and beyond regarded the Temporal Sovereignty of the Popes as being beyond question.

It was held that much of the territories over which the Papacy was Temporally Sovereign had been awarded to the church centuries previously by such renowned Emperors as Constantine and Charlemagne and it was also held that it was inherently most undesireable that the head of the Church should be the subject of any Temporal Prince.

In parliamentary speeches of late March, 1861, Cavour had uttered such sentiments as:-

..."the reunion of this great city to the rest of Italy must not be interpreted by the great mass of Catholics in and outside Italy as the sign of the Church's servitude. That is, we must go to Rome, but the true independence of the Pontiff must not be lessened. We must go to Rome, but civil authority must not extend its power over the spiritual order...

...We believe that the system of liberty has to be introduced into all aspects of religious and civil society... we believe it necessary for the harmony of the building we wish to raise that the principle of liberty be applied to relations between Church and State."

Cavour, in these times, through intermediaries, attempted to negotiate the voluntary inclusion of the Roman territories into the Italian state he was attempting to construct. He offered a recognition of a nominal papal sovereignty over all papal territories in a situation where King Victor Emmanuel would, however, have "exercise of the government."

Guarantees over the income of the church, its freedoms from taxation, and of a respected position for the church were also offered.

In the event negotiations were broken off early in 1861 after the pope refused to exchange his temporal power for any guarantee of independence saying:-"This corner of the earth is mine. Christ has given it to me. I will give it up to him alone."

Count Camillo Benso de Cavour died of natural causes in early June 1861.

In 1862 in a manner reminiscent of the way "Garibaldi and the Thousand" had proceeded to Sicily some two years previously a force again led by Garibaldi unsuccessfully attempted to win more territory for Italy by assailing Calabria then part of the remaining territories of the Church.

Alongside the earlier anti-Clerical measures passed by the former Kingdom of Sardinia relations with the Papacy had not been improved by a forced sale in 1859, in the cash strapped Sardinian states interest, of monastic lands.

The Papacy and Cardinal Antonelli contued to hope for the restoration of Romagna, Umbria and the Marches to Papal

Sovereignty. They refused to consider reform of the administration of the remaining territories of the church until such a restoration was brought about.

In the mean time Britain had been the first foreign power to extend recognition to the Italian Kingdom. By mid 1861 France had also offered recognition to the Kingdom of Italy whilst officially deploring that Kingdoms retention of church territories, By mid 1862 those supportive of a restitution of Romagna, Umbria and the Marches to Papal Sovereignty were discomfited by the further recognition of the Italian Kingdom by Russia and Prussia. The King of Portugal, meanwhile, entered into marriage with a daughter of King Victor Emmanuel. This marriage took place despite the fact that, in 1860, King Victor Emmanuel had actually been pronounced to be excommunicated because of his "Italian" policies!!!

Napoleon III did not really relish his role as protector of the traditional Papal sovereignty over Rome and its environs-yet had he not sought to fulfil this role it would lead to serious consequences in terms of relations with the powerful clericalist support his government enjoyed in France. In an attempt to lessen the awkwardness of his position he entered into an agreement, without the consent of the Papacy, with the Italian Kingdom known as the *Convention of September* whereby Italy would herself guarantee the Papal territiories against attack and Napoleon III would withdraw the French garrison within two years. It was accepted that the Pope could recruit an army of ten thousand from the catholic countries of Europe in the interests of the security of the territories of the church. A secret clause endorsed the transfer of the seat of the Italian government away from Turin to Florence within six months.

As French control of Savoy gave them unrestricted access to certain key Alpine passes the recent cession of Nice and Savoy had in any case left Turin somewhat strategically vulnerable from the north-west. There was serious rioting in Turin, involving some fifty fatalities, when the news of the relocation of the seat of government was announced. The population there could, after all, depict itself as having contributed very greatly to the move toward Italian Unification. This move did seem however to let NapoleonIII out of his difficult position as protector of the Papacy and to allow the French an opportunity, from their own point of view, to depict the Italian Kingdom as having decided upon a new and long term capital.

Late in 1864 Pope Pius IX, having become increasingly convinced that modern secular ideas presented a real threat to the Church issued an Encyclical of Papal Letter to which was attached a "Syllabus of Errors" which condemned "the principal Errors of our time." The Syllabus is a series of Articles that condemned some ninety "errors and perverse doctrines" including rationalism, science, democracy, the liberty of the press, secular education, socialism and communism.

The last, eightieth, Article of the Syllabus stigmatized as an error the view that "the Roman Pontiff can and should reconcile himself to and agree with progress, liberalism, and modern civilization."

Many in northern Europe and North America seemed to take the Syllabus to be indicative of obscurantism but most Italians understood many of the Errors to be presented as a none too oblique condemnation of the Italian Kingdom.

During these times the Kingdom of Italy offered to purchase Venetia from the Austrian Empire. This, substantial, offer was refused by Francis Joseph under the advice of the military party at his court who suggested that such a transfer would be contrary to Austria's honour.

Prussia continued to pursue its longstanding rivalry with Austria for predominance in "the Germanies". In April of 1866, against a complex European diplomatic background, the Italian government entered into a Treaty with Prussia by which Italy hoped to gain Venetia from Austria. Although the Austrians themselves subsequently offered Venetia to the Italian Kingdom in return for mere neutrality the Treaty with Prussia was maintained.

The policy makers of the Kingdom of Italy may have hoped to secure other areas of perceived "Italia Irredente-Unredeemed italy") such as Trentino (with Alto Adige or South Tyrol) and Venezia Giulia (a territory that included Trieste-a notably important seaport) in addition to Venetia as a result of direct "Italian" involvement. Both Trentino (with Alto Adige or South Tyrol), partly inhabited by ethnic Germans, and Venezia Giulia, partly inhabited by ethnic Slovenes, were northern borderlands then under fairly direct Austrian Habsburg sovereignty. The policy makers of the Kingdom of Italy may have hoped for a sincere, if reluctant, relinquishment of Venetia, Trentino, and Venezia Giulia, by an Austrian Empire that had been checked in war and considered that Italian opposition would help to ensure that such a check was delivered. The policy makers of the Kingdom of Italy may also have thought that the new Kingdom of Italy should actually fully stand by its treaty obligations such as it had entered into with Prussia.

A "Seven Weeks War" was subsequently contested in the summer of 1866, while "Italian" forces did not make much headway themselves the Italian Kingdom benefited from the way in which Prussian forces overcame those of Austria, and Venetia, which had been formally ceded to Napoleon III by Austria, was given to Victor Emmanuel II, in much the same way as Lombardy had been transferred and was incorporated into the Italian Kingdom. This incorporation was overwhelmingly endorsed by the result of a plebiscite in Venetia.

After hearing this result Victor Emmanuel said...

"This is the finest moment of my life; Italy is made, but it is not completed."

This statement being interpreted as suggesting that the Kingdom of Italy had "unfinished business" in relation to her hoped for capital-Rome!!!

A French army returned to defend Rome early in 1867 after Garibaldi and a large force made a serious armed incursion into these territories from Tuscany. The incursion was opposed by forces, drawn from many Catholic countries, in the employ of the Papacy. This incursion may have had the covert personal support of the King Victor Emmanuel who hoped that the remaining Church territories might fall to the Italian kingdom if Garibaldi prevailed.

As the Franco-Prussian War irrupted in 1870 Napoleon III was obliged to recall those forces garrisoned in protection of Rome in order to defend France herself on 16 August 1870. The Convention of September 1864 with France by which the Italian Kingdom had offered to guarantee the security of the territories of the Church had not in fact been in operation as France had again felt obliged to undertake responsibility for security after Garibaldi's campaign of 1867-given the French withdrawal to meet the Prussian challenge it now came back into operation. The Convention contained a phrase that read "in the case of extraordinary events both of the contracting parties would resume their freedom of action."

Given the absence of the French and more particularly the fact of the Prussian led interest prevailing in the wars after the critical battle of Sedan on 2 September the Kingdom of Italy was largely obliged by the strength of "Italian aspiration" to deem the Prussian victory an "extraordinary event" and to seriously consider a move to annexe Rome and the remaining Papal territories.

On 7 September several Great Powers of Europe were advised by Italian diplomatic channels that Italy intended to take control of Rome but would thereafter support the continued freedom and spiritual independence of the papacy. There was no significant protest from any of the these powers as they seemed to accept that it was now inevitable that the Italian Kingdom would move to annexe Rome.

King Victor Emmanuel appealed to Pope Pius IX for a voluntary acceptance of the protection of the Kingdom of Italy in the "name of religion and peace."

An envoy was sent to the Pope with a personal letter, dated 8 September 1871, from Victor Emmanuel who styled himself as writing "With the affection of a son, the faith of a Catholic, the loyalty of a king and the soul of an Italian" outlining that his soldiers were obliged to cross the papal frontiers to maintain the security of Italy and of the Holy See. Assurances were given in this letter that "the Head of Catholicity, surrounded by the devotion of the Italian people, should preserve on the banks of the Tiber a glorious seat independent of human Sovereignty".

On 11 September the Pope replied saying that he could not admit the demands of Victor Emmanuel's letter nor accept the principles contained therein. Some sixty thousand soldiers in the service of the Kingdom of Italy subsequently moved to seize the Papal territories. The Pope invited the numerous diplomatic representatives that were present in the Vatican to bear witness to this assault and delivered protests to them that were to be conveyed to their authorising governments.

The walls of Rome were compromised after a four hour bombardment on the 20th September, 1870. Some nineteen papal soldiers and forty-nine Italian soldiers lost their lives in the associated battle. This "token" battle was itself brought to an end by the Papacy ordering its defenders to lay down their arms after making a show of resistance consistent with honour. The subsequent annexation of Rome to the Italian Kingdom was resoundingly endorsed by a plebiscite held two weeks later. Rome was now proclaimed as the capital of the Italian kingdom. There was in fact some debate about the wisdom of this move of the Italian capital away from Florence but it seemed that no other designation would be acceptable to the Romans themselves.

Pope Pius IX was offered numerous far-reaching assurances as to the position of the Papacy in a "Law of Guarantees" considered by the Italian Parliament meeting in Florence in January 1871 and passed into law in May 1871. These guarantees would have recognised the Pope as being a Temporal Sovereign with the Vatican and Lateran palaces being deemed to be outside Italian territory and with a large grant equal to previous Papal budgets being made.

Pope Pius and Cardinal Secretary of State Antonelli chose to ignore such a system of guarantees and, when the first installment of monies were offered they were repudiated by Pope Pius :- "Never will I accept it from you by way of reimbursement and you will obtain no signature which might seem to imply an aquiescence in or a resignation to Spoilation."

In June 1871 the Rome became the Italian seat of government and King Victor Emmanuel delivered an address to the parliament of the Kingdom of Italy now convened in Rome. This address begins:-

Senators and Deputies, gentlemen:

The work to which we consecrated our life is accomplished. After long trials, Italy is restored to herself and to Rome. Here, where our people, after centuries of separation, find themselves for the first time solemnly reunited in the person of their representatives; here where we recognise the fatherland of our dreams, everything speaks to us of greatness; but at the same time it all reminds us of our duties. The joy that we experience must not let us forget them...

...We have proclaimed the separation of Church and State. Having recognized the absolute independence of the spiritual authority, we are convinced that Rome, the capital of Italy, will continue to be the peaceful and respected seat of the Pontificate...

A Papal Encyclical that was sent to the higher Roman Catholic clergy in May 1871 had included the following sentiments:-

...it must be clearly evident to all that the Roman Pontiff, if he be subjected to the dominion of another prince and is no longer actually in possession of sovereign power himself, cannot escape (whether in respect to his personal conduct or the acts of his apostolic office) from the will of the ruler to whom he is subordinated, who may prove to be a heretic, a persecutor of the church, or be involved in a war with other princes. Indeed, is not this very concession of guarantees in itself a clear instance of the imposition of laws upon us, upon us on whom God has bestowed authority to make laws relating to the moral and religious order,-on us who have been designated the expounder of natural and divine law throughout the world?...

Pope Pius IX had already depicted Rome as being "in the possession of brigands" after "the triumph of disorder and the victory of the most perfidious revolution" and had styled himself as being the "Prisoner of the Vatican." He insisted on referring to the "usurping" power as a Sub-alpine, rather than an "Italian" government. Decades of deep estrangement between Italy and the Papacy ensued. Pope Pius forbade participation by way of voting or any political involvement in the workings of the "godless" Sub-alpine government.

Quite apart from these tensions between Papacy and Kingdom the new state had other hurdles to face. The census of 1871 showed that only 2.5% of the 26.8 million population actually spoke the

Florentine-Tuscan "Italian" that was to become the language of the state. Also at this time 69% of population were illiterate but this is perhaps largely explicable by the fact that perhaps 60% of the people worked as subsistence farmers on the land and that there had previously been no widespread sponsorship of general education by the church or by the states that had so recently been replaced by the new Italy. The disparity of prosperity between the relatively prosperous north and relatively impoverished south continued as a worrisome factor for many years thereafter.

The Kingdom of Italy that emerged after 1870 was not the dynamic, powerful state that many nationalists had hoped for. The state was mired in debt. The liberal values of the regime suggested that they assume the debts of the states that Piedmont had absorbed in the process of unification. The wars of liberation had been expensive. The loans organized in France had to be repaid. Much infrastructure for a united state had to be created: public buildings in Rome, the new capital, a navy, a unified army, and an educational system, to name a few.

Italy was poor, since its establishment in 1861 the Italian kingdom had experienced great difficulty in balancing its budgets and the liberal, Piedmontese, administrators of the Kingdom of Italy insisted on financial responsibility.

This at a time when the peninsula as a whole lacked economic development and had a poor infrastructure of roads and railways. In the south there was much brigandage and insurrection and in Sicily the Italian government was probably as unpopular as that of the Kingdom of the Two Sicilies had been. In efforts to balance the books taxes were raised on salt and tobacco and more tellingly, as far as the poor were concerned, the tax on milling grain, the Macinato, which had been introduced into Piedmont by Quintino Sella in 1869 was now applied to the entire realm.

Taxes were levied on mules, the omnipresent beast of burden of the peasantry, whilst horses and cows usually owned by landowners were not similarly taxed. There were many instances of serious rioting entered into against the economic policies being followed by the Italian royal administration. In cases the battlecry of the economically distressed rioters was "long live the Pope and

Austria". The birth of the Kingdom of Italy was not proving to be a straightforward affair. Newly united Italy experienced a wave of mass emigration as distressed poor people sought new and better lives in the United States and elsewhere.

It was not just the discontented poor of the south that threatened the stability of the regime. Many adherents of Mazzini and Garibaldi felt betrayed by the state that had emerged. Austria might still hope to restore her position in Italy. And the Church, still headed by Pius IX, condemned the new state and all that it stood for. In these conditions the state had to struggle to survive.

In many areas the masses spoke dialect and not Italian (the formerly "Tuscan" language that had become accepted as a literary language since the middle ages due to the impressive creativity of Dante and others).

When Italy unified in the 1860s the question of languages other than Italian was never considered (several regional dialects continue to survive as 'household' languages) and the administrative model chosen was designed to annex a dispersed and disconnected plethora of pretty states to Piedmont. The national state that emerged was centralized but weak — precisely what might have been expected-other things being equal-to give rise to waves of peripheral resentments and mobilizations.

Liberal doctrine also demanded that the laws and practices be standardized throughout the land. Piedmontese officials, bringing with them new laws and practices that inadvertently undermined the economy of the south. In the event the several states that now newly came under the sovereignty of the House of Savoy in the Kingdom of Italy did so under the existing Piedmontese constitution, under existing Piedmontese laws and existing Piedmontese foreign policy arrangements. King Victor Emmanuel II remained as King Victor Emmanuel II even though "Italy" had never had a King Victor Emmanuel previously. The were cases of resentment, in the south particularly, of the way Piedmontese organisers were deployed in rearranging aspects of the functioning of the territories newly under the House of Savoy.

Mazzini, who had remained committed to his republicanism, died at Pisa on 10 March 1872. At this time he was illegally present, and living under an assumed name, on Italian soil, and was regarded as an outlaw for attempting insurrection against the king.

Cardinal Secretary of State Antonelli informed Odo Russell, a quasi official British representative in Rome, that his demise might allow the relaxation of some of the restraints that Cavour had placed on Italian Republicanism.

Since these times Italians have sometimes tended to characterise Cavour as being the "brain" of Italian Unification-(with Garibaldi being sometimes characterised as its "sword" and Mazzini as its "spirit").

27

The Roman Question

This " Roman Question " where both "Italy" and the Papacy required sovereignty in Rome was resolved some sixty years later through the Lateran Agreements of 1929.

Through these agreements the Papacy was to be regarded as sovereign over a 40 hectare (108 acre) Vatican City State. The Papacy in return recognised the existence and sovereignty of an Italian Kingdom that maintained Rome as its capital city.

Several commentators then and later have made the point that the ministers of the government who entered into these Lateran agreements on behalf of Mussolini's Italy were probably less sincerely religious than the ministers of the Italian Kingdom that had seized control of Rome in 1870.

THE WARS OF GERMAN UNIFICATION BISMARCK-GERMAN HISTORY-1871

During the summer of 1849, and into the summer of 1850, the Prussian Government invited other north German States to enter into a fresh "Erfurt" union on the basis of a new Constitution-to be that accepted by the Frankfurt Parliament of 1848, but altered so far as might be found necessary. The union was to be a voluntary one.

Had this policy succeeded, the Prussia that was most dear to Bismarck's heart would have been no more. Otto von Bismarck was a Prussian aristocrat and was, as such, opposed to this policy of the King of Prussia and his ministers. He took the extreme particularist view; he had no interest in Germany outside Prussia;

Wuertemberg and Bavaria were to him foreign States. In all these proposals for a new Constitution he saw only that Prussia would be required to sacrifice its complete independence; that the King of Prussia would become executor for the decrees of a popular and alien Parliament. They were asked to cease to be Prussians in order that they might become Germans. In a speech to the Prussian Assembly on 6 September Bismarck said:-

" We all wish that the Prussian eagle should spread out his wings as guardian and ruler from the Memel to the Donnersberg, but free will we have him, not bound by a new Regensburg Diet. Prussians we are and Prussians will we remain; I know that in these words I speak the confession of the Prussian army and the majority of my fellow-countrymen, and I hope to God that we will still long remain Prussian when this sheet of paper is forgotten like a withered autumn leaf."

The possibility of Habsburg Austria gaining more influence in the Germanic Confederation, to Prussia's detriment, was very much to the front of Bismarck's mind. He had entered political life almost by accident, having been deputised in the place of another who had been taken ill. Originally prepared to respect Austria, as a champion of conservatism, he had come to view Austria as being a dedicated rival of Prussia with this rivalry only being open to being resolved to Prussia's advantage by the humbling of Austrian claims to predominance in the affairs of the German Confederation.

Throughout his career, subsequent to his coming to resent Austria, Bismarck devoted his considerable efforts to performing several difficult tasks including that of the exclusion of Austria, (as being Prussia's rival), from German affairs and that of the preserving of the Prussian tradition from being eroded by the effects of both Nationalism and Democratisation.

German-nationally minded liberals in northern Germany were inspired by the career of the chief minister to the House of Savoy, Camillo de Cavour (who had, in the summer of 1859, achieved a greater degree of integration of northern "Italian" territory under the leadership of the Victor Emmanuel II), to form, in November 1859, the *Nationalverein* or National Union. This soon grew into being a liberal-national movement actively supported by several thousand parliamentarians, professors, lawyers and journalists who exerted their diverse efforts towards the establishment of a "German" state under sovereignty of the Hohenzollern Kings of Prussia.

In these times Bismarck was serving as a diplomat in the Prussian service and had been accredited to the Court of the Tsar in St Petersburg since the early months of 1859. In March, 1860, whilst on leave in Berlin, Bismarck paid courtesy calls upon the leaders of the Nationalverein in Berlin.

Early in 1861 King Frederick William IV, whose mind had failed, was replaced as King of Prussia by his brother, who had been serving as regent, but who now came to the throne as King Wilhelm I. Bismarck prepared a memorandum on the German question for the consideration of King Wilhelm I, this was delivered to the King at Baden-Baden at the end of July 1861. In this so-called "Baden-Baden Memorial" Bismarck advocated that Prussia should attempt to exploit the growing sentiment of German patriotism by supporting a demand "for a national assembly of the German people".

In March, 1862, Bismarch received a new diplomatic posting that led to his becoming Prussian ambassador to France. From his base in Paris Bismarck took an opportunity to cross the English Channel, in June, 1862. This visit was ostensibly for the purpose of visiting an Industrial Exhibition but Bismarck met several senior British statesmen including Disraeli, leader of the Opposition, to whom he outlined his proposal for bring a form of unity to Germany under Prussian leadership even if this involved a degree of conflict with the Austrian Empire.

That evening Disrali was heard to remark "Take care of that man! He means what he says!"

In September 1862 there was a crisis in Prussia where the Prussian Landtag, or lower parliamentary house, was refusing to approve increased military spending in defiance of the King's wishes. Wilhelm I was advised by his Minister of War, Roon, to send for Bismarck as a formidable personality who might secure the passing of the budget and the associated military reforms in the Landtag.

On the 17 September the crisis had reached such a pitch that

King Wilhelm I seriously considered abdicating his throne. That evening Roon sent by telegraph to Bismarck suggesting that he, Bismarck, should hurry to Berlin and that there was danger in delay. The message in French and Latin read :-*Depechez-vous; Periculum in mora.*

On 22 September Bismarck met King Wilhelm I and assured him that he could form a ministry and carry through the army reforms desired by the king, if necessary against the will of the deputies in the Landtag. Given this assurance the King decided not to abdicate. Bismarck was appointed acting chief minister to the House of Hohenzollern.

Bismarck made an appearance before the Landtag on the 29 September where he spoke expressing his regret at the hostility of the deputies to passing of the military budget and stressed the need for progress to be made on the military proposals favoured by the king. The next day at a meeting of a Budget Committee Bismarck went perhaps further than he his better judgement might have intended in asserting that:-

" The position of Prussia in Germany will not be determined by its liberalism but by its power... Prussia must concentrate its strength and hold it for the favourable moment, which has already come and gone several times. Since the treaties of Vienna, our frontiers have been ill-designed for a healthy body politic. Not through speeches and majority decisions will the great questions of the day be decided-that was the great mistake of 1848 and 1849-but by iron and blood ".

This somewhat agressively phrased speech caused alarm to liberal opinion in the Germanies and beyond. This was in part attributable to subsequent reportage amending its wording to read more pithily as " blood and iron ". This speech has since become known as Bismarck's Blood and Iron Speech.

As Minister-President of Prussia Bismarck arranged things such that the increase in the size of the army took place despite the opposition of the Landtag. The existing practices of the Prussian state allowed Bismarck to continue in office provided the King was willing to remain favourable to his ministry.

In January 1863 the Poles in Russian administered Polish territories again attempted to forcefully win concessions of change from a reluctant Tsar-King. Russia regarded the retention of its Polish lands as a principal aim of policy. Whilst several western states, including France, lost the Tsar's good opinion by offering moral support to the Poles, an offer of assistance to Russia made by Bismarck, that was initially thought presumptuous, left an abiding impression with Russia that Prussia was a state that it should view with favour.

Bismark's support for Russia was practical as well as strategic. Prussia had annexed Polish lands during her own participation in the Partitions of Poland. Bismarck considered that a revived Polish polity might well contest Prussia's continued hold on some of the lands so annexed.

Russia was to take some time to recover from this expense of resources in what proved to be protracted efforts to retain control over Poland.

In 1863 Franz Joseph, Emperor of Austria, proposed that a reform of the Germanic Confederation be discussed by the German Princes in a meeting to be held that autumn in Frankfurt. Franz Joseph urged agreement between the Princes of Germany as the best way of preserving a German Confederation under the leadership of its historic dynasties whilst containing the revolutionary tides of liberalism, democratisation and socialism that were pressing for diverse radical changes.

In the lead up to this proposed conference Franz Joseph met the King of Prussia on 2 August at Bad Gastein and felt encouraged, during a personal interview, that the Prussian king would be agreeable to reforms. Many of the most prominent princes of Germany converned at Frankfurt and authorised one of their number, the King of Saxony-a notably cultured individual who was on terms of personal friendship with the King of Prussia, to personally convey an invitation to attend on behalf of the assembled rulers to the king of Prussia.

The Prussian King was inclined to accept this pressing invitation personally delivered as it was by a King on behalf of more than thirty german rulers. In order to prevent the formulation an agreed approach to the reform of the Confederation Bismarck went to very great lengths, even to the point of reducing the King to tears and himself to nervous exhaustion, in order to persuade the King of Prussia, very much against his own inclination, not to attend. Austria had a preponderance of influence in the Confederation and any agreed reform would probably have been broadly favourable to the Austrian interest. With the abscence of Prussia, which was, after Austria herself, inherently the second most powerful state in the confederation, nothing could be fully decided upon.

Prussian domestic elections of October 1863 saw only thirty-eight deputies being returned who could be relied on to support Bismarck's policies. King Wilhelm I was greatly dispirited by these results and even suggested to Bismarck that he, the King, might possibly expect to be guillotined in the Palace Square. Nevertheless Bismarck continues to follow the military and other policies which had alienated public opinion.

The Emperor of Austria also had domestic troubles to contend with during these times. A so-called February Patent of 1861 had instituted a limited form of parliamentism that was supported mainly by Germanic "liberals" who were comfortable with an autocratic centralism effectively run by the Germans of the Empire largely in the interests of those same Germans. The parliament was largely boycotted by the Magyars, Poles and Czechs who felt themselves to be excluded from real power and representation.

Schleswig and Holstein again loomed to the forefront of European affairs in that the resolution internationally agreed after the difficulties that become critical in 1848 was breaking down. That resolution as enshrined in a Treaty of London of 1852 had envisaged these territories remaining separate from Denmark, but with the Danish King being Duke of Holstein and Duke of Schleswig. Holstein was predominantly peopled by ethnic Germans, whilst Schleswig had an ethnic German majority in its southern areas.

This attempted resolution of 1852 over Schleswig and Holstein featured an early example of the powers proposing that an eventual settlement should be consistent with the nationality of the person's affected rather than on dynastic claims or treaties. Denmark undertook to respect the rights of ethnic Germans in the Duchy of Schleswig. Holstein and the tiny Duchy of Lauenburg were to remain in the German Federation with equal recognition of German and Danish nationality.

In 1863 the Danish King moved to break the traditionally recognised link between the two Duchies and to incorporate Schleswig fully into Denmark. Such a move was supported by the *Eider Dansk* Danish Nationalism of the ethnic Danish majority in the north of Schleswig. In November 1863 the demise of the then King of Denmark allowed a new succession issue to further complicate an issue which Bismarck fully intended to exploit to Prussia's advantage.

Although the Diet of the German Confederation authorised the actual sending of federal forces to intervene in the Duchies Prussia and Austria preferred to act as joint-principals rather than as agents of the Confederation in an extensive intervention that was characterised as being undertaken in support of existing treaties. A so-called Danish War ensued and by February 1864 both Schleswig and Holstein had substantially fallen to Prussian and Austrian forces and a conference of Vienna of October assigned Schleswig, Holstein, and a small territory of Lauenberg to joint Prussian and Austrian control. Bismarck was not alone, in these times, in hoping to take measures, broadly exploitative of populist sentiment, that would enhance the position of a German Kingdom.

In January 1864 Odo Russell, nephew of the British Foreign Secretary and a quasi-official British representative in Rome, in a private audience with the Pope was told that:-

"The example of Italy" (i.e. where the House of Savoy was annexing, with local popular consent, the territories of other Princes) *will be the ruin of the smaller Princes of Germany and I think very ill of the condition of that country. Each of the smaller sovereigns hopes to aggrandise his Kingdom at the expense of his neighbour and all will be swept away like the Grand Dukes of Tuscany, Modena and Parma were in Italy. The King of Bavaria was here and I did what I could to convince him that he was running great risks but he could not see it. His idea is that the House of Wittlesbach should be as powerful as the Houses of Hapsburg and Hohenzollern, and if he had his own way he would begin by annexing Baden and Würtemberg to Bavaria."*

The situation within the lands of the Habsburgs where the parliament, as elected under restricted rules of suffrage, was particularly supported by the Germans of Austria, of Bohemia, and of Moravia, and was largely boycotted by other nationalities was not entirely as Emperor Franz Joseph would wish and after some consideration, and against the advice of most of his his ministers, he responded positively to an article published in the spring of 1865 by the prominent Magyar liberal, Ferenc Deak, that outlined conditions under which the inherently powerful Magyars would find it possible to co-operate more fully with his own exercise of sovereignty. These conditions amounted to a restoration of the Hungarian constitution of 1848 and the virtual establishment of two distict states-one largely German-Austrian and one largely Magyar-that would co-operate fully and that would together function towards the outside world as a single power.

A Convention of Gastein of August 1865 recognised Holstein, (the more southerly Duchy actually bordering Prussian territory),as being under the administrative control of Austria whilst Schleswig was to be administered by Prussia. A small Duchy of Launberg passed absolutely to Prussia after the payment of a steep purchase price.

Prussia, which had previously no major sea-port under its control, was given rights to exploit the potential of the important port of Kiel on the "Baltic" coast of Holstein and was authorised to plan and execute an ambitious "Kiel Canal" from the Baltic coast across Holstein to the North Sea coast. Holstein was also allowed to enter the Prussian led *Zollverein* customs union.

Austria had reason to believe that Prussia was still not satisfied in relation to Holstein and that Italy was not satisfied in relation to Venetia. In September Bismarck secretly sounded out Napoleon III at Biarritz as to his possible reaction to an open conflict between Prussia and Austria. In November Austria received offers of very substantial sums from Italy, if Venetia would be transferred to Italian control, and from Prussia, if Holstein would be transferred to Prussian control. Austria declined both these offers probably deeming it dishonourable for any dynastic state to sell off territories.

In late December 1865 Prussia and Italy entered into a commercial treaty and in January King Victor Emmanuel was invested with the Prussian Order of the Black Eagle. Bismarck continued to work towards securing the Prussian King's permission to enter into a formal military alliance with Italy that would prejudicial to the Austrian interest. It was contrary to the basic principles of the Germanic Confederation that any member would ally with an outside power against any other member of the Confederation. The fact that Prussia intended to secretly ally with Italy shows the seriousness with which Bismarck was pursuing his own version of reform of the Confederation.

In these times Bismarck advised Benedetti, Prussian ambassador to France that:-

"I have succeeded in persuading the King of Prussia to break off the intimate relations of his House with the Imperial House of Austria; to make an alliance with revolutionary Italy; to make arrangements for a possible emergency, with the French Emperor; and to propose at Frankfurt the revision of the Federal Act by a popular parliament. I am proud of my success. I do not know whether I shall be allowed to reap what I have sown; but, even if the King deserts me, I have prepared the way by deepening the rift between Prussia and Austria, and the liberals, if they come to power, will complete my work."

The alliance between Prussia and Italy was finalised in April and promised Venetia to Italy in return for her participation in a war against the Austrian Empire. The alliance was to hold for only three months.

Within days of the Italian alliance having been concluded Bismarck challenged Austria by having the Prussian delegate to the Confederal Diet propose reforms of the Confederation that would be deeply prejudicial to the Austrian interest and also voicing complaints about the way the Austrian administration of Holstein was being conducted. Austrian diplomacy, meanwhile, indulged in some provocations of Prussia including that of requesting that the Federal Diet should adjudicate on the future of the Duchies. A Prussian force was sent into Holstein on Bismarck's orders. A "Six Weeks War" between Austria and Prussia ensued in which the Prussian interest convincingly prevailed despite Austria also being supported by several other German states.

Bismarck had to strenuously and extensively use his powers of persuasion to restrain the forces of Prussia and her allies from making too many claims on an humbled Austria-his arguments were only succesful after the Prussian crown prince interceded with his father to secure the agreement of a relatively lenient peace.

In his personal outlook Bismarck was not a German Nationalist-he was more truly first minister to the House of Hohenzollern. In his view it was necessary to avoid the possibility that a coalition of powers that might otherwise be formed to aid a severely threatened Austria. Should Habsburg Austria be critically damaged it was an open question as to what settlement would spring up in its place-it would be possible that Austria's non-German territories deprived of their admittedly weak bond through the historical sovereignty of the Habsburgs could be re-constituted as a number of unstable, and even radical, small republics.

It would also be likely that if the Habsburgs were more intimately involved with German affairs through the incorporation of German Austria into an extended German state they would routinely rival Prussian influence in political affairs with the support of a coalition of lesser german state interests.

Bismarck considered that a preserved Habsburg Austria, although somewhat humbled in these disputations, could be a possible diplomatic and military ally in the future. Although largely excluded from German affairs in the West it was in Prussia's interest that Austria should nonetheless be allowed an opportunity to re-establish herself as a power to the east.

We had to avoid wounding Austria too severely; we had to avoid leaving behind in her any unnecessary bitterness of feeling or desire for revenge; we ought rather to reserve the possibility of becoming friends again with our adversary of the moment, and in any case to regard the Austrian state as a piece on the European chessboard. If Austria were severely injured, she would become the ally of France and of every other opponent of ours; she would even sacrifice her anti-Russian interests for the sake of revenge on Prussia....The acquisition of provinces like Austria Silesia and portions of Bohemia could not strengthen the Prussian state; it would not lead to an amalgamation of German Austria with Prussia, and Vienna could not be governed from Berlin as a mere dependency...

BISMARCK

Prussia did annexe territories at this time-Schleswig and Holstein, the Kingdom of Hanover, the Electorate of Hesse-Nassau, and the City of Frankfurt together with some smaller territories. Austrian agreement was secured for the formation of a Prussian-led North German Confederation with the inclusion of the independent Kingdom of Saxony. The Austrians secured Prussian agreement that Northern Schleswig could return to Danish sovereignty should the population there so decide in a plebiscite.

MAP OF GERMAN UNIFICATION

Printable version

The conflicts with Denmark over Schleswig-Holstein and between Austria and Prussia are sometimes referred to as "Wars of German Unification" but they were at that time more truly "Wars of Prussian Consolidation". In the wake of these two availing conflicts that had been, in large part, subtly fomented by Bismarck as the champion of "traditional Prussia", and which led to the formation of a North German Confederation in 1867, the Landtag was encouraged to bestow retrospective immunity on Bismarck's unconstitutional acts.

Such retrospective immunity was not the only "reward" that fell to Bismarck at this time as he was raised to the nobility as Count Bismarck and invested with the prestigious Prussian Order of the Black Eagle.

In the wake of the defeat in the "Six Weeks War" the Austrian Emperor, whose position had been weakened thereby, agreed a Compromise (Augsgleich) with the Magyars that re-established the Austrian Empire as Austro-Hungary-an Imperial and Royal "Dual Monarchy" comprised of an Austrian Empire and an Hungarian Kingdom-under a single monarch and with common ministries of Foreign Affairs, War and Finance.

From these times the Austrian aspect of this state developed along lines that showed a preparedness to be somewhat liberal in accomodating its powerful minority peoples whilst within the Hungarian Kingdom the Magyars tended to moreso work towards cultural assimilation of the numerous Slav minorities domiciled in the "lands of the Crown of St. Stephen" but offered many social and civic concessions to those who assimilated themselves to an officially Magyar state. The Magyars thus gained a substantial independence whilst retaining assurance that their King would seek to defend the Hungarian Kingdom with Austrian as well as Hungarian resources.

The North German Confederation operated under a Constitution dictated by Bismarck. The Federal Presidency was vested in the Prussian Crown. The Prussian Minister was to be Federal Chancellor.

A degree of democratisation was allowed in relation to the election of a lower parliamentary house-partly as a means of breaking down the traditional German particularisms in a Confederation that was being formed of historic dynastic states that continued to convene local assemblies. Prussian originated institutions-army, postal service, the Zollverein (Customs Union) etc.,-were effectively extended towards giving the new Confederation a Prussian character.

In order to provide the North German Confederation with an acceptable and distinctive flag Bismarck, in 1867, sponsored the adoption of a Black-White-Red tricolour flag. This flag is widely accepted as being derived from the black and white colours traditional to Prussia in combination with the white and red associated with the Hanseatic League-this being an historic trading bloc with which many states and cities in the Germanies had celebrated traditions of involvement in earlier times.

The adoption of this, unprecedented, emblem tended towards the avoidance of possible ill-will through giving a prominence to the Prussian flag that might prove unwelcome to other German states. It also side-stepped issues associated with the inherent claims of the Black-Red-Gold tricolour emblem of the popular "liberal and constitutional" German tradition. (This Black-Red-

Gold emblem had, moreover, been adopted as the common flag of the alliance of South German states led by Austria during the War of 1866!!!)

Croat nationalism continued to be a powerful centrifugal force such that in 1868 the Magyar dominated Reichstag at Pest agreed to recognise the Croatian Landtag as having competence to consider Croatian domestic matters.

Prussia had long hoped to be dominant in the Germanies north of the river Main, this was now achieved but a groundswell of Germanic sentiment supported the establishment of a more territorially extensive German nation state. Bismarck was keen to preclude threats to Prussian influence in the German lands and was also open to achieving yet more expansions of the territory of Prussia-Germany. In strategic terms the France of Napoleon III was a presumptive opponent of any increased influence being exercised by the Prussian dominated North German Confederation over the states of Southern Germany.

The diplomatic position of France was in one most important respect to the advantage of Bismarck's expansionary policies. There was a tradition of competition and cultural misunderstanding between north and south Germany. That being said there was also a more intense tradition of rivalry between German Europe and French Europe. In the nineteenth century alone Germany had fought a "War of Liberation" against Napoleon in 1813, whilst in 1840 there was a crisis, which blew over, featuring widespread, and popularly supported, German alarm when it appeared that the French intended to seize territories south of the Rhine. Bismarck hoped to exploit German rivalry vis a vis France to precipitate cooperation and solidarity between north and south Germany and also increase acceptance of the Prussian dynasty.

In these times, at the Biarritz meeting and later, Napoleon III of France had more or less hinted to Bismarck that in return for French neutrality at the time of the recent Austro-Prussian War France should expect "Compensations". France had remained neutral, largely out of the belief that the war would be more protracted and expensive of lives and resources than it had been. Napoleon III seemed to anticipate that the position of France would have been relatively enhanced by the exhaustion of Austria and Prussia and had even expected that Prussia would be defeated. France hoped that a third Germany, apart from Austria and Prussia, could be formed based on the South German states. The unexpectedly brief conflict, and decisive outcome in favour of Prussia, with no compensating advantage to France, meant that France, formerly the power of note in Western Europe, had lost much advantage as a result. Napoleon reminded Bismarck that he expected some sort of "Compensation".

In efforts to attain this compensation the French sought part of Belgium but met with British and other opposition, and then the Palatinate on the Upper Rhine but met with Germanic opposition. Bismarck was able to get a written copy of these claims on the Palatinate. Then the French agreed a compact with the King of Holland whereby the French could gain Luxembourg by purchase and Bismarck although initially prepared to accept such a transfer was subsequently made aware of a groundswell of popular "German" opposition to the acquisition of "Germanic" Luxembourg by France and himself decided to encourage such popular opposition. In the Reichstag Bismarck deplored the willingness of a prince "of German descent" to sell to France territory which "had been German at all times".

An international situation resulted from the Spanish being prepared to accept a Hohenzollern-Sigmaringen cousin of the King of Prussia as the successor to their vacant throne. France, which had historical reason to consider itself the foremost power on the western Europe continent, considered that the presence of a cousin of the King of Prussia of the Spanish throne would "disturb... the present equilibrium of forces in Europe" and sought to ensure that this Hohenzollern related candidacy was not merely withdrawn, but was withdrawn in such a way as making it seem that Prussia had climbed down somewhat under French pressure. The disputed candidacy was initially withdrawn without much appearance of a climb-down but French diplomacy persisted in efforts to produce such an appearance. It was in these circumstances in 1870 that Bismarck as Minister-President subtly added Prussian provocations to those of France by editing a so-called Ems Telegram, (that had been sent to Bismarck by the Prussian king outlining an interview that the Prussian king had had with a French diplomat), in order to let it seem that the French diplomat had been disrespectfully treated by the Prussian King. Bismarck ensured that this edited version was published in a special newspaper supplement. France for her part had been seeking a contest of arms in which it hoped to prevail. The "Ems Telegram" provided material which led to a declaration of War. The French Emperor spoke of entering into this war "with a light heart". In the event the Prusso-German interest prevailed in this war and received some support from the states of South Germany.

The outcomes of an ensuing "Franco-Prussian" War, which is also referred to as a War of German Unification, included the formation of a federal German Empire. This "Second German Reich" was proclaimed after the King of Prussia was persuaded to accept the Imperial Crown that had been offered on behalf of all the German Princes by King Ludwig II of Bavaria. The actual announcement taking place in the fabulous Hall of Mirrors in the sumptuous palace of Versailles outside Paris.

The Secong German Empire was a Confederation composed of clearly separate constituent states (4 kingdoms, 5 grand duchies, 13 duchies and principalities, and the free cities of Hamburg, Lübeck and Bremen). Within this Confederation the inherently powerful Kingdom of Bavaria was able to retain its own army, which would fall under Prussian command only in times of war. Bavaria could also retain its own railways, its own postal system, its maintain its own diplomatic contacts. As with the now defunct North German Confederation the Presidency was vested in the Prussian Crown and the Prussian Minister was to be Imperial Chancellor.

Imperial Germany was to operate as a federation with strong central control. Both the short-lived North German Confederation and the subsequent German Empire functioned under constitutional arrangements which, whilst including a Federal Parliament, or Reichstag, elected by universal suffrage, did not concede effective power to that Reichstag. Authority over the duration of administrations, central finances, and the armed forces, residing moreso in a Bundesrat of State delegates dominated by Prussia.

The outcome of the Wars of German Unification considerably altered the European political scene. France deplored the seizure of Alsace-Lorraine by Imperial Germany after the Franco-Prussian War and Bismarck thereafter strove to diplomatically isolate France denying her the opportunity of winning back her lost provinces as an outcome of war. Aside from this limitation on alliances that might threaten Imperial Germany Bismarck hoped that France would progress and be reconciled and was prone to encourage her to direct her energies towards extending sway over parts of North Africa. The German Empire's establishment inherently presented Europe with the reality of a populous and industrialising polity possessing a considerable, and undeniably increasing, economic and diplomatic presence.

28

T. E. Lawrence

LIFE AND WORKS

A young boy read tales of Eastern travel and adventure sitting on a rug in a hut, which hehad built behind an Oxford villa. These stories impressed the boy and he started to dream about the Arabs and the desert. These were no more than the daydreams of a child, whose real destiny seemed to lie in the quiet world of scholarship.

CHILDHOOD

Thomas Lawrence was born at Tremadoc, Wales on August 15, 1888. His parentage can be drawn back to a noble family. He was the second of five illegitimate sons of Sir Thomas Chapman, an Anglo-Irish baronet. His sons were the result of his relationship with Sarah Junner, who was employed as governess to Thomas' four legitimate daughters. Chapman and Sarah decided to leave home and also to adopt the name Lawrence.

The Anglo-Irish Protestant squire had no more than £300 a year. At Tremadoc, this amount was not sufficient and so the family moved to Oxford, where living was cheaper. The young boy got his formal education in Oxford.

Ned, as Thomas was nicknamed, did not like the formal school education. For him it was like an irrelevant and time wasting 'nuisance'. He received basic early education from his elder brothers. The formal education interrupted his personal reading, which he thought more useful than what he studied at school. During those years he was browsing through the books available in all the city libraries. He would lay down with books till late at night, and would go to sleep with books all around him. If something other than the books interested the young man, then it was roaming the country on a bicycle in search of antiquities. His hobby of antiques search grew into a passion after his visits to almost every 12th century castle in England and France during his lifetime.

THE LONELY CHILD

Ned was rather a lonely child. He was more influenced by his mother than his father. Especially the religious and ethical influence of his mother on his character could be seen in his later life too, though he had stopped performing any religious rituals at that time. From his father he inherited gentleness and unobtrusiveness.

His shortness is looked upon as a sign of his singling out himself at school and playground. He was hardly 5 ft. 5 ins., something quite abnormal for a Lawrence boy. His desire to do something unconventional, something strikingly different from others always overpowered him.

His characteristic self-possessed nature was apparent from the childhood. One of his schoolteachers observed, "He was unlike the boys of his age and time, for even in his schooldays he had a strong leaning towards the Stoics, an apparent indifference towards pleasure or pain".

He was different from other boys in more than one way. As the boys of his age, including his brothers, would play various games, Lawrence would slowly sneak out. He did not like any of the organized games like football or cricket. Though physically fit to participate in almost any sports, he avoided them due to a peculiar reason : he hated competition. Robert Graves, his biographer wrote later, "He took no interest in organized games because they were organized, because they had rules, because they had results. He will never compete-in anything".

More importantly, the reason behind his lonely and aloof childhood could be traced to an incident of his childhood. One day he overheard his father talking to his solicitor. The boy could not understand much but somehow he discerned the fact that there was something grossly wrong about his birth. By the age of

10, he almost knew that he was an illegitimate child, and he was the only Lawrence son to know the fact. This incident left a deep impact on his psyche, making him a loner and a brooder.

He used to ponder over the issue of his birth and his inner conflict sometimes became too much to handle. He ran away from home in 1905. He told his friend later that at the age of 17, he 'suddenly found himself'. Through a local recruiting office he joined Royal Garrison Artillery as a boy soldier. The boy saw the raw face of life for the first time here.

The brutish practice of settlement of any quarrel by fight scared him. He wrote later, "Every incident ended in dispute and every dispute either in an ordeal of fists or in a barrack-court-martial whose sentence were too often mass bullying...I can not remember a parade during three months without a discolored eye. Usually five or six men would bore fighting damages". When the things got unbearable, he appealed to his father to take his home.

COLLEGE DAYS

He entered the university at Jesus College, Oxford. He was given scholarship in mathematics but he changed it to history, as had always been dreaming of Arabs and deserts. This subject permitted him to be a free bird and was not obliged to comply with the routine and adhere strictly to the curriculum. He utilized this allowance and read through the nights whatever took his fancy. He rarely attended lectures.

ADVENTURES

Thomas enjoyed very limited social contacts as an undergraduate. He had friends but no acquaintances. He shared the few activities with the friends like roof climbing by night, which he had mastered by scaling the turrets of so many ruinous castles.

Thomas also liked to play pranks with his hostel friends. One of his favorites was leading assaults on a neighbor's room, armed with a soda water siphon and protected by crawling on all fours beneath an inverted bath. He also explored the subterranean tunnels of the Trill Millstream, which flowed beneath the 'little dark shop' in Saint Aldate and returned to lead an expedition in canoes down the dark channel.

PAVING THE PATH

Military history interested him a lot and he took it as a special subject satisfying his hobby. During the study of military history he studied about Napoleon and all his invasions.

His curiosity in history brought him in notice of Dr D G Hogarth, the keeper of Ashmolean Museum. Hogarth offered him to rearrange a neglected collection of medieval pottery. Thomas preformed the mechanical task in an original way and with calculated economy of effort. A job involving routine and, at the same time, skilled knowledge suited him very well. And if there had been no Arabian Desert, he might have lived and died as the curator of a museum.

LANDING IN THE MIDDLE EAST

During his last long vacation at Oxford College, Thomas went to visit and study the Crusader's Castles in Syria. He decided to travel alone and on foot. He set out with a pistol, and an open letter of introduction from Lord Curzon, the Chancellor of Oxford. The next five years he wandered through every part of Syria, Palestine, Mesopotamia, Sinai and Egypt, living as one of the locals.

He learnt to be conversant with all the dialects of spoken Arabic. Though he never disguised as a Mohammedan, he found it convenient to wear an Arab head-cloth for comfort, as the natives were strangely suspicious of a European hat or helmet.

At 21, on his first expedition he photographed at least 50 Crusader's Castles and began to be interested in the remains of the little known Hittite civilization. While he was in some remote spot near the Euphrates, a tribal, out of curiosity dogged him all day, assaulted him and tried to rob his watch. If it were not a shepherd, who accidentally appeared at the spot, the tribal robber would have murdered him for the watch. He returned with a thesis on Medieval Castles for which he was awarded a degree with first-class honors in modern history.

THE SCHOLARSHIP

Thesis on Medieval Castles impressed Hogarth and he persuaded Magdalene College to give Thomas a traveling scholarship for four years. It would help him to study the ruins of the Hittite City, Carchemish. He was granted the scholarship and he soon left to carry out the work of his supreme interest. At Carchemish, several people noted his activities. He was working with a contemporary, C L Woolley, who later described Thomas' extraordinary control over the Arab laborers.

At Carchemish he was seen in shorts and a Khaki shirt and a Jesus College blazer, looking absurdly young. When he was off the work he practiced shooting with a pistol, bathed in the Euphrates, or went boating in a crazy craft with a little outboard engine. In 1913, he met a traveler Hubert Young, a lively subaltern, who wanted to make his way back to India by crossing the Syrian Desert. He also shared Thomas' passion for exploring the Arab world. Late in 1913, Lawrence and Woolley were asked to join a survey of the Sinai Peninsula for the Palestine Exploration Society.

LAWRENCE : THE TOPOGRAPHER

The Sinai Archaeological Survey was undertaken partly with political intentions. Outbreak of war was expected in Europe and clear topography of the area was a must to protect their main channel of communication-the Suez Canal. Lawrence was chiefly responsible for describing the district from about the head of the Gulf of Akaba to as far inland as the rock-hewn ruins of Patra, and Wadi Musa, which, three years later was the main front for the Arab armies.

Lawrence and Woolley returned to England to complete their report. The month of August 1914 gave a new importance to the Sinai survey. The survey got accomplished in book form-The Wilderness of Zin, by C L Woolley and T E Lawrence, which was dedicated to Colonel Newcombe, who helped them in the survey. In September, Hogarth recommended him to assist Colonel Hedley of the Geographical Section of the General Staff in preparing maps of Flanders and Sinai. A few weeks later, Hogarth asked Hedley for his opinion of Lawrence. "He's running my whole department for me," replied Hedley.

THE TURKS AND ARABS

Before the actual outbreak of World War I in 1914 the differences between Turks and Arabs had aggravated beyond a saturation point. Emir, son of Mecca's Sherif had once told that his father Hussein was planning to rule the Arabs. Kitchner was the English Secretary of War and their stand mattered when World War I commenced.

On November 5, 1914, the Sultan of Turkey proclaimed a Jehad, a Holy War to be waged by all Muslims against the enemies. The first step taken by England was to declare Egypt a Protectorate, thus severing its nominal connection with Turkey. Kitchner arranged the troops to defend the Suez Canal. The intelligence service was organized by Colonel Clayton with the help of a brilliant team sent out from England in December-Newcombe, Woolley, Lawrence, Aubrey Herbert and George Lloyd. Lawrence was the expert on Arab affairs in Syria.

His life during 1915-16 was not much known because of the natural reticence of Intelligence Department. His main task at Colonel Clayton's office was to discover and report on the dispositions of the Turkish Army, based on information received from spies. The archaeologist had more information than general staff could believe. He had a flair for detective work, and could usually reduce to candor any disingenuous visitor, by showing his command over his dialect, and acquaintance with his neighbors.

GETTING INVOLVED

Early in 1916, a huge British army withdrew from Gallipoli. Meanwhile, Feisal, the third son of Hussein of Mecca, a European bred, was at Constantinople as one of the members of secret society of Arabs in the Turkish Army. But before he became an officer in the Turkish Army and a Member of the Turkish Parliament, his father had summoned him back to the desert.

Finally began the Arab Revolt at Medina, on June 5, 1916. Hussein's so-called army was formed by the victory of his second son Abdulla near Mecca. Of the 5,000 soldiers, many were Arabs, who joined Hussein in his revolt and thus formed an army. The army initially was not of much military value. There were few arm stores, very little money and no leaders, while every volunteer thought himself to be a commanding officer.

Meanwhile, the army under Feisal surrendered at Medina. At the same time Fakhri Pasha, a Turk was passing through each city like a whirlpool, crushing whatsoever came his way. If the Turk assaults continued then the Arab Revolt was sure to be crushed down and they would have to lose Mecca.

Hussein was clamorous for the promised British aid. It was the time for the Arab Bureau appointed by the British to come in action. Hogarth himself was in Hejaz when these events took place. First help came from navy.

Admiral Sir Rosslyn Wemyss was an independent commander, free of the political entanglements, who had tied the hands of the soldiers in Egypt. With airplane bombing and gunfire from his ships, he forced the Turks to surrender the port of Jeddah to the Arabs. This bounty of the English Navy boosted the Arabs, who had lost the hope after losing Medina to the Turks.

PLAYING HIS CARDS

At this stage Lawrence came into picture. He had applied for a transfer from General Murray's staff to the Arab Bureau. While waiting for the change he accompanied Ronald Storrs, emissaries sent from England to the Arab Bureau on a visit to Jeddah. The two landed at Jeddah on October 16, 1916.

The main purpose of the two was to check whether the revolt could be raised to a national level revolution or not. For the purpose a leader of national level had to be found and they found one of Hussein's sons fit for the job.

Abdulla-the second son was not having the required fire inside him to raise and lead a revolution. Zeid, the fourth son was too young; the eldest, whom he visited at Rabegh, was an invalid. The third, Emir Feisal was facing the Turks far up in the hills of the Holy Province-Mecca, where no Christian could go safely.

Finally with Sherif's help, Lawrence got permission to ride up the Pilgrim's Road to Feisal's camp. The bravery and confidence of Feisal impressed Lawrence.

REVOLT BEGAN

In this early stage of revolt, the British and French military advisers urged Arabs to capture the Turkish stronghold at Medina and the Hejaz Railway, the Turkish line of communication, their 'heart' that pumped fresh blood. If they drove the Turks off Hejaz railway their strength would decline drastically. Lawrence had laid down the plan how to employ the available forces and accomplish the mission.

As per the blueprint, everyone took their positions. Abdulla took up his station astride the Hejaz railway, north of Medina, Feisal moved towards Damascus along with two British officers, Lawrence and Vickery.

Moving towards north meant facing Turks at Wejh and no Arab was ready to face them. Lawrence had a suggestion to clear the obstacle. He proposed to take Navy's help for the purpose. His plan was carried out and as was expected the sailors solved this problem by capturing Wejh. The capture was rightly regarded as a strategic victory if not a glorious victory. It posed a serious threat to Turkish lines of communication. Lawrence's main activity in the campaign was to hamper the railways before the Turk retreat.

This was of great concern as, if they withdrew altogether from Hejaz and reinforced their army in Palestine, the British would be defeated there and would bring down Arab in general rule. His mind in doubts about the part he was playing, his conscience reproached him for making the Arabs the cat's paw of British policy.

Restructuring the Revolt During 10 days in March 1917, when his body was wracked with dysentery, a revelation came to him. While he was pondering on his last six-month experience as an amateur, he thought of guerrilla warfare technique, which was apt for Hejaz campaign. It suddenly struck him that they had almost won the war. They were blind to everything except their concentration on Turkish Army at Medina. This was requisite to the ultimate aim of any combatant nation who had arrayed their army against one another. But for Arabs, their main aim was to drive the Turks out from Arabia. For that it was necessary that they array their trained soldiers against well-equipped Turks.

PLANNING

To fulfil both the purposes Lawrence planned out the pinpricks in which the Turks would occupy themselves and would not be able to fight efficiently.

Lawrence planned out every move. He divided his policy into (1) hecastics, the mathematical element in war, the calculation of numbers and distances-the exact science, (2) bionomics, the wear and tear in material and man-the less manageable factor and (3) diathetics, the psychological understanding of an army. As per the diathotical factor, only Lawrence knew the Arabs among all the British officers. As per the systematic calculation of the policy, Arab's victory was round the corner. The Arab cards at the moment were speed and time, not hitting power.

When Lawrence had come to these conclusions and after shaking off his illness he proposed the idea before Emir Abdulla, but got little encouragement. Abdulla was contended with his easy victories and would put himself to no further troubles.

APPLYING PLANS

Lawrence's plan would not have applied practically if it was not for Sahkir, a chief in Abdulla's camp. The first implementation came on March 28, 1917, with no good result. The mines blew after the train left and caused very little harm. Two days later they tried it again. In those two raids they had cut rails, pulled down telegraph wires and destroyed a culvert, stopping railway traffic for three days. In April, he returned to Feisal's camp eisal, like Lawrence, wanted to extend the revolt northwards to amascus and beyond.

By this time Feisal's army was reinforced with Auda, the fiercest of desert chiefs. He had slain 75 men in fair fight and had married 28 times. The Feisal camp was joined by Nasir, a Sherif from Medina. They rode together and on the 10th day they crossed the railway line and stopped to pull the telegraph wires. They also blew up the railway lines, to the delight of old Auda, who had never seen dynamite before.

ADVANCING NORTH

The next major thing to do was to march towards north. And

any northern operation would have to be based further inland. This proposal faced a crucial problem.

How to supply the essential things to the forces placed in the hinderlands. The nearest supply route to this place was in Turkish hand. Lawrence knew there was an obvious route if it could be secured. Through Akaba, a city at the northern end of the Red Sea, one could reach the inland. Akaba needed to be captured. Before the war, Lawrence had visited Akaba and was familiar with its topography. The scenario had changed after the war. The news from intelligence network reported that the Turks had built heavy defence in the narrow pass leading to Wadi Isthmus.

Akaba could be captured through sea but it was worthless without Wadi Isthmus. Lawrence used local knowledge and tribesman to create a wide circuit inland through the desert and devised a scheme. He took part in his first battle, the Action of Abu el Lissal, on June 2, 1917. The Turks deployed stupidly in the valley below while Auda's men and Nasir snipped them from the hills above. All day long the rifles fired in blazing sunshine till the rifles were too hot to hold.

THE TRIUMPH

This remarkable exploit was accomplished and soon the three small posts down the valley towards Akaba surrendered. On June 6, two months after setting out from Wejh, Arabs held not only Akaba but also the vital mountain passes. Lawrence had brought his Arabs to Akaba and left them there. To keep them organized and boost their moral they needed to be fed and paid. Lawrence had become a good planner and knew the need of the hour.

For the required finance the British in Suez were to be contacted. Without wasting time he started his desert ride covering 150 miles in 50 hours. With eight men and selected camels, he started a journey for two days and nights. Reaching Suez, he was told that officers had shifted to Cairo. He left for Cairo, dressed as an Arab, sun-baked, and reduced by hardship to no more than seven stones in weight. At Cairo, he learnt that some new officer Allenby was the Commander-in-Chief. Lawrence had to explain the situation and importance of the aid to Arabs. He explained his strategy and pleaded his cause before the silent general and eventually convinced him. Allenby put up his chin and said, "Well, I will do for you what I can". That was enough and within time Feisal's army was brought up from Wejh to Akaba with the stores. On July 22, Lawrence again landed at Jeddah. Allenby had sent him back as liaison officer with Feisal.

During this revolt he was so close to the Arabs that he was supposed to have seen 'The Holy Place' of Mecca, which was not open for a non-Islamic person since the days of Prophet Mohammed.

PALESTINE AND GAZA

During the six months when Lawrence had been leading Arabs from Wejh to Akaba, there had been a great change in general course of war. It became more necessary to succeed in the East. Throughout 1917, he supported the Palestine army and by March, Sir Stanley Maude advanced upto Tigris.

Sir Archibald Murray laid a broad-gauge railway across the desert that had brought Nile water to the Palestine frontier. Maude's army entered and conquered Baghdad on March 11, 1917. While they took into confidence some prominent Arabs, they were never considered as independent Allies. Arabs were treated as a subject race saved from oppression and brought under good government. After Maude it was General Murray's turn, who made two attacks on Gaza and killed 1,700 Turks at the cost of 3,000 permanently disabled British soldiers.

THE REVOLT WITHIN

Lawrence camped at Rumm in an eastward valley, until in August he carried out his most celebrated railway raid. Few days after returning from the raid he was off on another raid with Pisani, a Frenchman. He bagged a troop train passing over a culvert. But this time he was bitten by a scorpion and wounded by a bullet. His assertion helped to make the pain lighter. Inward revulsion against the work that he was doing was too subtle.

He had many questions in his mind. The Arabs were fighting for loot and liberty but what was he fighting for ? As his fame grew, so it became distasteful to him. To curb the vanity in his nature he promised himself that he would "Shoot straighter, ride harder, eat and drink less and claim no reward."

AIDING ALLENBY

At Akaba, his English colleagues could not share his scruples and aspirations. He was promoted to a Major at 29, remarkable for his exploits in native costumes. By October 1917, the stage was set for General Allenby's first Palestine campaign. Turks were under the impression that Allenby-the 'Bull' as he was nicknamed, would attack Gaza. Before Allenby disclosed his plan to Lawrence, Lawrence and Feisal were planning to raise tribes in their favor in Syria. To assist Allenby in the assault, Lawrence rode about 400 miles through the desert to Derra junction where he had to cut supplies to the Palestine army by destroying a bridge in the deep Yarmuk gorge. On a dark night their attempt on the Yarmuk bridge failed.

In this mission, Indian fighters aided him. An Indian gave the alarm by dropping his rifle, where upon the Arabs threw their explosives into the ravine and fled; leaving Lawrence and Sherif Ali to make their escape through point-blank rifle fire. In the explosion Lawrence was hurt, and was hit by bullets before Sherif Ali and his men could rescue him.

THE LONELY EXCURSION

Meanwhile the Battle of Beersheba had begun. All through November, Allenby's men pressed on but to no avail. Lawrence spent the greater part of November at Azrak camping with Sherif Ali in a ruined castle.

The soldier in Lawrence could not accept defeat. Dressed as an Arab, he wandered into Turkish garrison town of Derra, to study the lines of approach to the railway junction. But Lawrence got arrested. A`fortnight earlier, he was wounded by five bullets and again he had to suffer humiliation before he was released. 'That night', he wrote, 'The citadel of my integrity had been irrevocably lost.'

Three weeks later on December 11, he was summoned by

Allenby at Palestine, where an honor awaited him-a post at the official entry to Jerusalem. He borrowed a cap and a belt for the purpose and for once he was willing to dress like a British Officer. Recognition for his service by rock-like Allenby was perhaps the one personal tribute acceptable to his tortured spirit, the only man to whom his pride would allow him to bow.

LAWRENCE DISTRUSTED

The early 1918 saw Lawrence busy with battle for Tafileh. He managed to get 30,000 sovereigns from Feisal for the forthcoming campaign and handed it over to Emir Zeid, younger brother of Feisal and leader of the expedition. Lawrence left for a reconnaissance on the east of the Dead Sea. Zeid could not shoulder the responsibility and his advisers persuaded him to pay out all the money to tribals. Lawrence had to pay for Zeid's inexperience and the waste of thousands of pounds was a blot on his honor.

The long campaign, many wounds, torture at Derra, bloodshed at Tafileh, physical exhaustion, mental revulsion, the biting cold, the disgrace, everything was overwhelming. He handed over his authority to his successor, Joyce and made his way to Allenby's headquarters to resign. His resignation was not accepted. For the next few months, in preparation for a major Arab offensive against Derra, he visited Akaba and Cairo carrying the duty of liaison between the British and Arab headquarters.

DAMASCUS ON MAP

Soon Lawrence was out of the phase of distortion. He was back with the ideas that would broaden the British territory. On June 18, Lawrence was back in Palestine asking permission for a flank attack on Damascus. He was late as Allenby had already started working on this thought. During his stay away from Arab fighting over a month, saw noticeable fall in Arab achievement, setbacks in the fighting about Ma'an and no great Bedouin raids, until Allenby took the bold step of sending a camel corps under Major Buxton to hold them tight.

LONER LAWRENCE'S LONGING

Lawrence joined the camel corps at Rumm, where there were

many English in the troop. He did not feel comfortable with Englishmen and with Arabs also he felt alien. At Rumm, a strong feeling was getting on his nerves-outcast from both the worlds, a lonely stranger in either army and yet an inevitable link between the two. At Palestine, in the staff this 'link' was Lieutenant Colonel T E Lawrence.

It was a mere fiction. He never used his rank nor wore his medals. From time to time he was promoted but that made no difference to him whether standing with the Arabs or with Allenby. He could approach him directly without any ceremony. The revolt had passed through a cycle in which he had become the driving force. In the beginning, he was just a British officer sent to Feisal's aid, but by the end he was one of the senior officers.

Approaching his 30th birthday, he remembered a promise he had made to himself : to win knighthood and a general's rank, and that they were now within his grasp. Though he got no satisfaction from the sense of power and neither reminder of any brave deeds gave him sense of pride but ultimately he succumbed to it.

RECONCILIATION WITH SELF

Lawrence hated the two parts he was compelled to play and when he stripped off the two disguises to examine the real self, he hated them but kept them private. It was equally true that without Lawrence, Arab Revolt could have been easily crushed and it was he who helped to fight and strengthen Arabs for a good cause. But the other side of the coin was equally ugly.

The main purpose of British to assist the Arabs was to oblige them and ultimately to get power. Britain had also made Sykes-Picot treaty with France. Lawrence, giving his 100 per cent services, when gazed at these folds he vehemently criticized his self. But amidst all these internal conflicts, he could never reach to a conclusion or could not voice his inner self. He was flowing along the channels, contributing his best to the flow of the channel.

CAPTURING DAMASCUS

To raft the white water of revolt, the major task was to take over Derra before Damascus, which was the main railway junction on which Turkish Army depended, as it was 'their lifeline'.

Lawrence, with Allenby, made the required arrangements-it was to seize the town and to cut its communication with the Turkish troops. As per the plan, on September 16, 1,200 Arab regulars and large number of Bedouin took on Derra. On the very next day the task of the Arab Northern Army was accomplished. De-communicated from all ends made Derra stand in isolation and with no other way out but to surrender to Arabs. This made Damascus an easy target, which was handicapped without the strong shield of Derra.

The 4th and 5th Arab Divisions marched towards Damascus encircling it. The Turks were totally surrounded and were left without any medium of communication.

ORGANIZING DAMASCUS

The dawn of October 1, was the day of frenzied rejoicement for all. Amidst the celebration of the victory it was necessary to lay out the basic infrastructure before the chaos could turn the victory into a mess.

In two days, he set up the framework for the administration, which continued for next two years. The police, railway service, fire brigade, sanitary service, telegraph, streetlights, markets were re-established and paper currency was also introduced. After furnishing the basics, on the third day Lawrence found that Turkish military hospital was abandoned by the staff.

Overwhelmed by the sorry scenario at the hospital, he walked barefoot among the stinking corpses of 56 dead, 200 dying and 700 sick of dysentery, lying there forgotten.

Lawrence's first priority was to find a doctor to prevent the worst situation. A doctor was found and he could relieve the casualties but still the scene was so appalling that the frustrated doctor, taking Arab dress clad Lawrence to be the man who had allowed the hospital to lapse into such a misery, slapped him on his face, calling him a, 'bloody brute'. Lawrence laughed and turned the other cheek. In a way, he was responsible for all this sufferings.

TOWARDS ENGLAND

October 4, the day finally arrived when he could shed off all the burden of Arab revolt. Allenby and Feisal entered the town and Lawrence performed his last ritual of handing over the responsibility to Allenby. Tired of strain and in a sense baleful revolt he asked for leave. As victory became sure the participant groups started dreaming of the fulfillment of their personal interests. Arabs hoped for self-governance.

Lawrence's role as a guerrilla leader was over after Damascus and after unloading the cares on the broad shoulders of Allenby, he left Arabia with the intention of starting a new career as a disciplined soldier on the Western Front.

Meanwhile the 'pie' he had cooked of liberating Arabia had many mouths to devour. The inevitable conflicts for power began. The French, who almost had the leftovers, were furious on the division of the pie, as they were the major contributors.

FRENCH AGONY

Palestine was under the British and Syria under the French rulers. There were many participants of the revolt who believed that Arabs had got more than they deserved.

A Frenchman, who had served the whole campaign and remained as a political officer in the Lebanon, recorded in his diary that English had created a legend that the Arabs conquered Damascus and thus permitted the existence of the inefficient Arab Government.

Evidently, it was a British plot to bring Syria under control of Feisal and his British patrons. In this respect a French High Commissioner was appointed to study the situation. After reconnoitering the situation, he immediately ordered 20,000 troops to assert the French claims to Syria against Arabs and English. The conclusion of the survey made Lawrence obvious victim of the hassle. A case against Lawrence was drafted by Colonel Bremond, a French officer.

If the entire revolt was studied, then it was obvious that French contribution was always there at all crucial points.

PARIS PEACE CONFERENCE

Lawrence left for England and reached there on November 11, 1918, on Armistice Day. The only reward he accepted for all his services in the Gulf was the rank of a Colonel. Leaving the Middle East did not disconnect him totally from that part of world. He became a member of British Delegation at the Paris Peace Conference in 1919. To represent the 'liberal' Arabia, Emir Feisal had arrived to participate in the Peace Conference.

At Versailles Conference, Lawrence played two important roles. He represented the Foreign Office delegation and also acted as an interpreter to Emir Feisal. The French stuck to their stand, they wanted the Sykes-Picot Treaty to be put into action. Lawrence's efforts to present the Arab cause on behalf of Emir Feisal fell on the deaf ears.

PROMOTING ARAB CAUSE

After the failed attempts at the conference, he left for Egypt to fetch his private papers. On the way his flight crashed near Rome. The pilot was killed. Lawrence survived the accident with two broken ribs and damaged lungs. The accident could not hinder this 'English Arab' from working privately for the Arab cause. Paris Conference, though, had not contributed in his favor but had surely changed British stand on Arab cause.

All his achievements were well known to British government but for general public he was a part of the newspaper headlines. During August 1919, an American journalist, Lowell Thomas, arrived in London. Thomas had visited Akaba during the revolt, and Lawrence had encouraged him to write about the Arabs' 'fight for unsung'. Thomas wrote about this forgotten hero of the war. This was the only period in his life when he actively sought publicity, giving interviews in order to advance Arab cause.

SEVEN PILLARS OF WISDOM

Renouncing the public life, he concentrated on writing a book on his Middle East experiences named Seven Pillars of Wisdom. Writing the book was a penance on himself as he alone had seen the revolt from both sides. And it was his responsibility to record all that he had seen and gone thorough. He thought it was his duty to ensure to his countrymen that their efforts have not been forgotten, and to the Arabs to ensure that their views behind the war should be male known in England.

The first draft of the Seven Pillars of Wisdom was lost when Lawrence left it in the refreshment room at Reading railway station. After that Lawrence thought he should wash his hands off it but Hogarth, always his best counselor, persuaded him to try it again. Early in 1920, the second draft of the book was prepared.

"The lost draft', wrote Lawrence to a friend, 'was shorter, snappier and more truthful than the present version which was done from memory." He revised his second draft and also consulted some writers, including Mr and Mrs Bernard Shaw who were responsible 'for all the present semi-colons'.

NEW AVENUE

The British had provoked the rebellion out of the partial policy and to suppress it British government had spent a huge amount. The situation worsened and Winston Churchill, the Prime Minister of England, had to interrupt. He set up a Colonial office to find solution and persuaded Lawrence, to join the office as an adviser.

Lawrence was tired of responsibility and to get away from it he planned to enlist as an aircraftman. Renouncing his old life he gave up his name, and adopted new name John Hume Ross. After four months as J H Ross he was discovered by the press and had to discharge the dress.

PUBLISHING SEVEN PILLARS OF WISDOM

By then he was convinced that life in ranks was his only course. And with the help of highly placed friends he got himself re-enlisted almost immediately in the Tank Corps as Thomas Edward Shaw. He served there until mid 1925 at Bovington Camp in Dorset. After 1923, much of his leisure was spent in revising Seven Pillars of Wisdom.

He supervised each and every stage of printing. He spent lavishly on color portraits and other embellishments. All these expenses raised the crest and a copy cost about £90. This was three times the price of subscription and in order to repay the bank loan he had to sanction general publication of an abridgement of Seven Pillars of Wisdom called Revolt in Desert.

Both the books Seven Pillars of Wisdom and Revolt in Desert were hugely acclaimed and they quickly paid off his bank loan. It even earned him enough to lead a lavish life if he had not dispersed the surplus to a charity.

Encouraged by the literary success he thought writing was a new avenue for him. During 1927 and 1928 he wrote another book, The Mint, based on notes he had made during his first Royal Air Force enlistment. The Mint passed such harsh judgment on the RAF regime that the publication would have damaged the reputation of the service Lawrence had loved. He therefore stipulated that it should not appear before 1950.

TRANSLATING ODYSSEY

He was posted in India in the end of 1926. He was stationed at Karachi for about 18 months. He rarely left the camp and refused many offers for writing. But in 1928, posted in Miranshah, his imagination was put on fire by an invitation to translate Homer's Odyssey. It was mainly because the offer came from Mr Bruce Rogers, the American typographer.

The American edition of his Odyssey was highly appreciated. It earned him enough to enjoy a carefree retired life. He had earned enough to buy a small house at Cloud's Hill with the help of his income from journalism and translation. Odyssey had fetched him handsome revenue and he could furnish the house with the only luxury he required, a hot water system and a plunge-bath.

INNOVATOR LAWRENCE

The last services in the ranks saw Lawrence as an innovator. He was posted at a flying boat unit at Plymouth. At the beginning of 1931, he witnessed a flying boat crash, quite close to the shore. The old-fashioned rescue-launch was so slow that many lives were lost because of the delay. As it happened, he made a faster motor-launch. He and a friend recommended RAF to adopt the launches. Before things could materialize he retired on February 26, 1935.

But during World War II, these launches played a vital role and proved to be a wild card.

A SOLDIER'S DEATH

Lawrence was back home at Dorset. "I find myself wishing', he wrote to one friend, 'that my own curtain would fall. It seems as if I had finished." Perhaps he had the intuition. On the morning of May 13, 1935, he was thrown off his motorcycle while swerving to avoid a boy on a bicycle near Bovington Camp. On May 19, he died in the Military Hospital without returning to consciousness.

Death was like any other adventure that he carried all through his life. He readily delivered himself to the supreme command without any glory or greed. He performed his duty from the depth of his heart, never expecting rewards. He never expected recognition or sought gratitude from others. But diamond can not be buried in the mines for long; its glare attracts the minds with purpose, who can place before the world the legendary wonder.

GAIUS CORNELIUS TACITUS

Publius or Gaius Cornelius Tacitus (born around AD 56-died around AD 120), was a Roman historian. Born into a wealthy family living in Gaul. He was a friend of Pliny the Younger and married the daughter of Cnaeus Julius Agricola, who governed in Roman Britain. Tacitus received the best education available to a Roman from a good wealthy family. Public speaking skills, oratory and debate, which were considered the most important areas of study for a young man destined for a career in imperial service or senatorial office. Tacitus was a senator during the reign of Domitian. In AD 97 he was appointed substitute consul under Nerva, and in AD 112-113 he held the highest civilian governorship, that of the Roman province of Asia in Western Anatolia.

Tacitus objected to great concentration of power in the hands of the early emperors. Though he hated imperial power and in his writings tries to paint every emperor as a corrupt despot, he hated civil war and anarchy even more. He had a particularly heavy bias against the emperor Tiberius, whom he portrayed as a sinister and cruel emperor, purging his opponents from the Senate by having them tried for treason and executed. He showed scorn for Claudius and Nero, and even his writings about Augustus contained some belittling and snide remarks. His writing is full of tales of corruption, government scandal, and innocent people being destroyed or having their good names ruined because of the emperor's lust for power. It was Tacitus' belief that the emperor had so much power in his hands that no man could occupy the throne without being corrupted by that power.

Tacitus wrote at least 16 books, but books 7-10 and parts of books 5, 6, 11 and 16 are missing. Book 6 ends with the death of Tiberius and books 7-12 presumably covered the reigns of Caligula and Claudius. The remaining books cover the reign of Nero, perhaps until his death in June 68 or until the end of that year, to connect with the Histories. The second half of book 16 is missing. We do not know whether Tacitus completed the work or whether he wrote any further associated books. Of the Histories only the first four books and 26 chapters of the fifth book have survived, covering the year 69 and the first part of 70. The work is believed to have continued up to the death of Domitian on September 18, 96. Tacitus also wrote three shorter works: the Agricola, a biography of his father-in-law Gnaeus Julius Agricola; the Germania; and the Dialogus.

The first of his works was the Dialogus [dialogue], a discussion of oratory in the style of Cicero, demonstrating to some degree why Tacitus was celebrated as an eloquent speaker; this work was long disputed, but his authorship is now generally accepted. Tacitus was primarily concerned with the balance of power between the Roman senate and the Roman Emperors. His writings are filled with tales of corruption and tyranny in the governing class of Rome as they failed to adjust to the new imperial régime; they squandered their cherished cultural traditions of free speech and self-respect as they fell over themselves to please the often bemused emperor.

Tacitus then wrote a biography of Agricola, expressing his admiration for his father-in-law as a good and able man. His small treatise De origine et situ Germanorum [concerning the origin and location of the Germans], commonly called the Germania, supplies (along with the earlier account of Julius Caesar) the principal written material on the Germanic tribes. His treatment of the Germanic peoples outside the empire is of mixed value to historians. Tacitus uses what he reports of the German character as a kind of 'noble savage' as a comparison to contemporary Romans and their (in his eyes) 'degeneracy'. Despite this bias, he does supply us with many names for tribes with which Rome had come into contact. Tacitus' information was not, in general, based on first-hand knowledge, and more recent research has shown that many of his assumptions were incorrect. In fact, contemporary historians debate whether all these tribes were really Germanic. He is also to blame for the misnaming of the Battle of the Teutoburg Forest, which did not quite take place in the saltus Teutoburgiensis, as he claimed in the Germania.

The moral purpose and severe criticism of contemporary Rome, fallen from the virtuous vigor of the old republic, also underlies his two long works, commonly called in English the Histories (of which four books and part of a fifth survive) and the Annals (of which twelve books-Books I-VI, XI-XVI-survive). The surviving books of the Histories cover only the reign of Galba (AD 68-69) and the beginning (to AD 70) of the reign of Vespasian but give a thorough view of Roman life-persons, places, and events. The surviving books of the Annals tell of the reign of Tiberius, of the last years of Claudius, and of the first years of Nero. The account contains incisive character sketches, ironic passages, and eloquent moral conclusions. The declamatory writing of the Dialogus is replaced in the historical works by a polished and highly individual style, a wide range of vocabulary, and an intricate and startling syntax. The Annals (ab excessu Divi Augusti) was Tacitus' final work, covering the period from the death of Augustus Caesar in AD 14. One well-known passage from his writings mentions the death of Christ (Annals, xv 44)'.

Bibliography

Althaus, Horst: *Hegel und die heroischen Jahre der Philosophie*, Munich, Carl Hanser Verlag, 1992.

Börm, Henning: *Prokop und die Perser*, Stuttgart, Franz Steiner Verlag, 2007.

Crowther P R: *Humber Perspectives. A Region through the Ages,* Hull University Press, 1990.

Darwish, Adel and Gregory Alexander: *Unholy Babylon: The Secret History of Saddam's War*, London, Diane, 1991.

Franklyn Mansfield: *Gravity is a Mystery*, New York, NY, Crowell., 1986.

Joseph E. : *A Historical Atlas of South Asia,* New York, Oxford University Press, 1992.

Lossing, Benson J.: *The Pictorial Field-Book of the Revolution,* New York, Harper, 1859.

Nash, Roderick: *Wilderness and the American Mind,* Revised ed. Yale University Press, 1962.

Peckham, Howard H.: *The War for Independence, a Military History,* Chicago, Univ. of Chicago Press, 1958.

Richard P.: *Dictionary of Scientific Literacy,* New York, NY, John Wiley & Sons, Inc. 1992.

Russell, Paul: *Freedom and Moral Sentiment: Hume's Way of Naturalizing Responsibility,* New York & Oxford, Oxford University Press, 1995.

Said, Edward: *The Politics of Dispossession,* Random House, 1994.

Stewart, Jon: *The Hegel Myths and Legends,* Northwestern University Press, 1996.

Wilson, W. R.: *Humic Substances, Peats and Sludges*. Royal Society of Chemistry, Cambridge, 1997.

Index